AKIM-

TH

HISTORY OF A FAILURE

By MAJOR W. F. BUTLER, C.B., F.R.G.S

The Naval & Military Press Ltd

published in association with

FIREPOWER
The Royal Artillery Museum
Woolwich

Published by
The Naval & Military Press Ltd
Unit 10 Ridgewood Industrial Park,
Uckfield, East Sussex,
TN22 5QE England
Tel: +44 (0) 1825 749494
Fax: +44 (0) 1825 765701
www.naval-military-press.com

in association with

FIREPOWER
The Royal Artillery Museum, Woolwich
www.firepower.org.uk

The Naval & Military Press

MILITARY HISTORY AT YOUR FINGERTIPS

... a unique and expanding series of reference works

Working in collaboration with the foremost regiments and institutions, as well as acknowledged experts in their field, N&MP have assembled a formidable array of titles including technologically advanced CD-ROMs and facsimile reprints of impossible-to-find rarities.

Printed and bound by Antony Rowe Ltd, Eastbourne

AKIM-FOO:

THE

HISTORY OF A FAILURE.

AKIM-FOO:

THE

HISTORY OF A FAILURE.

By MAJOR W. F. BUTLER, C.B., F.R.G.S.

AUTHOR OF "THE GREAT LONE LAND," ETC.

" 'Tis not in mortals to command success,
But we'll do more, Sempronius."
We'll do without it.

WITH ROUTE MAP, ETC.

SECOND EDITION.

𝕷onbon:
SAMPSON LOW, MARSTON, LOW, & SEARLE,
CROWN BUILDINGS, 188, FLEET STREET.
1875.

AKIMFOO:

THE HISTORY OF A FAILURE.

———◆———

CHAPTER I.

THE last white hill crest of the Wild North Land had sunk beneath a horizon of pine-trees. Prairie, forest, ice-covered lake, frozen river, rushing rapid, mountain-peak, and rock-shadowed canon, had faded into the haze of things that lie far away in the by-gone.

Of all the long wanderings of the snowy winter and slow-coming spring, there remained only these few shreds and patches of recollection which the wanderer picks from his pathway, to carry on with him into a future time. And never is there a moment when these shreds and patches are of such little use to us as at the termination of a long journey. The work is over, we have got back to civilization and the old tracks again; around us men come and go along the well-worn roads to which we are strangers now. Behind us lies the confused mass of our late enterprise, shapeless—for time has not yet come to place its several portions in their true positions;—before us, an unknown realm into which the imagination scarcely dares to penetrate, so vague and vast are its hidden possibilities.

More than a year before the date of which I now speak (the early autumn of 1873) I had set out upon a long journey. Little by little the vast distances of the North had been conquered. Night after night the camp had been made deeper in these remote regions where Nature wraps herself in a wilderness so limitless that the roll of the human tide will beat for centuries in vain against her vast desolation.

And now it was all over—the dim shadowy waste; the long reach of the silent river; the pine-woods, over whose forked tops the low-hung moon looked at endless stretch of frozen lake and ice-piled shore line; the giant mountains, whose peaks slept in an eternity of snow—all had sunk back again into an oblivion as deep as the rest from which the wanderer's footsteps had for the moment roused them.

Wandering down the Pacific slope to California, and crossing the Continent in eight days (it had taken me eight months to cross it 1000 miles farther to the north), I stood once more on the Atlantic shore. I was uncertain where to turn to.

Would I cross the ocean to the old familiar haunts again, or go back to the solitudes, the red man, and the camp fire?

I had left horses in the meadows of the Saskatchewan, and there were scattered dogs that had drawn my sleighs in half the fur forts across the frozen North.

One evening (it was the 30th of August) I entered the melancholy-looking room where, 'neath a gloom, as of some great disaster, Hotel America consumes its dinner. More from habit than from any expectation of finding

news, I took from the boy newsvendor at the door the
evening paper. During the melancholy meal the "Free
something or other" lay unread beside me. At last,
glancing at its Telegraphic Summary, I read as follows:—
"Great Britain.—It has been decided to despatch an
expedition against the Ashantees on the West Coast of
Africa. Sir Garnet Wolseley will command. He will be
accompanied by a select staff of officers, amongst whom
will be several of those who served on the Red River
Expedition. It is expected that the campaign will be
finished in March, and that the troops will return to
England in April. Sir Garnet will sail for Africa on the
8th September."

I read to the end, then read over again, rolled up the
paper, and walked straight to the Telegraph office.

"Will you send that message immediately?"

The clerk read,—

"To Sir Garnet Wolseley.

Ashanti Expedition. Remember ——. Will sail by
first steamer."

" Yes, that's right."

Before I left the office the wire was "clicking" the
message to England.

There used to be an old game played by boys at school,
which bore the name of "Follow the Leader." It did
not call for much thought, or demand the exercise of much
discretion on the part of the following; yet it was a
useful pastime for all that; and, although the tendency
of to-day is somewhat against following a leader in anything, and faithful service to a chief is deemed derogatory
to the well-being of the democratic boy or man, it is
nevertheless a spirit which has done some great things
in its time, which has written its results deeper perhaps

on this old earth of ours than all the individuality that
ever sprung, or will spring, from the masterhood of the
many and the serviceship of none.

Well, if this old game which we played as boys did not
call for much thought or reflection, neither did the resolve
which I had now made.

Three years before I had been one of a small band who
followed Wolseley into the solitudes of North America,
when he led his little army across that wilderness of rock
and water, pine-tree and precipice, which lies between
the head waters of the St. Lawrence and the lake called
Winnipeg.

The leadership of that time made the following a
pleasant task, and among the followers there was not one
who was not ready to do hard work again in the footsteps
of the leader. True, there would be many fresh hands
anxious to cast their fortunes into this new enterprise on
the fever-stricken African coast; for the fame of the
chief had already widened out over a larger area, and the
men who looked to Wolseley as the rising star of the
British army might be counted by hundreds in those
ranks where, despite the chop and change of Par-
liamentary strife, there still burned, fresh and bright, the
true spirit of English chivalry.

But if to the young blood of the army Wolseley was
the rising star, to those who had known him in other
times, and followed his leadership in other lands, he was
already the risen star; and it was enough to say to
any one among them, "Wolseley leads," to insure an
unquestioning following.

In my own case there could be no mistake. True,
there lay the Atlantic between me and the starting-point;
but the Atlantic had been quickly bridged before as the

prelude to another enterprise; and if it intruded itself a
second time, the only thing was to cross it again, and to
cross it quickly too; there was but scant time to lose.
Here was the last day of August, and the start was to be
on the 8th September.

To catch that start seemed impossible if the cable spoke
truly; but there are many delays in such things; and
even if the date still held punctual, that extra 3000 miles
which I had to cross would entitle me to " a few minutes
law," and I could follow to the fight.

Quebec, Boston, and New York send steamers weekly
to England. From the latter port there is a vessel
starting almost daily. A glance at the list informed me
that the " Russia " would sail on the 3rd September from
New York. I was late for the Saturday boat from Quebec.
The " Russia " was the next, and, better still, the best
and fastest ship that sailed the stormy Atlantic.

And now I had little to do, save to part from and
pension off an old friend. He had followed me into
many lands, but the one I was about to seek he could
not enter. For many a month he had shared food and
fortune, drawn my load by day, and slept beside me
at night; rendering a debt of toil and trust, the value
of which it would not be easy to put into words; but
now the service and the fellowship must here alike
end, and the old dog and his master go their different
ways.

For me, the master, the change from Arctic cold to
African heat would be bad enough, but for him—the dog
—it would have been a hundredfold worse. I could
readily cast aside the blanket-coat, the fur cap, the moose-
skin " mittaines;" but the woolly coat, the bushy tail,
the immense neck-muffler of soft fur and long hair, with

which Nature had adorned the burly person of the "Untiring," were as unalterable as the pace and pluck which
she had also given him.

The story of that long fellowship, and the wild scenes
through which it was carried, has been told in another
book; but the record of the "Untiring's" progress
through the territories and civilized States of the great
Union has yet to be unfolded.

For the present it will be sufficient to say that, after
many adventures, the Untiring had arrived at the Atlantic
seaboard, apparently to regard that ocean with the same
almost placid indifference which he had already bestowed
upon the Pacific. His progress through the States of the
Republic by boat and coach, by road and rail, had been
attended with some slight misapprehension on the part of
the citizens regarding his exact species. On the shores of
Puget Sound, in Washington territory, a group of small
boys imagined that they beheld a Cinnamon Bear, and,
regarding me in the light of the chain-and-collar man,
had the temerity to inquire, " What time is the show to
begin, mister ?"

On another occasion, an old lady travelling in a stage-
coach (in which the Untiring, having been rated and
charged as a first-class passenger, was also travelling as
such) ejaculated, "Laux, look at that 'ere Coon !" In
the long railroad journey from San Francisco to Boston,
he afforded ample opportunity to innumerable conductors
and baggage-men to graduate in the degrees of extortion
to its highest limit. I can unhesitatingly say that, with
the exception of a single Mormon baggage-man on the
short line between Ogden and Salt Lake City, I did not
encounter one individual connected with railroad baggage
transport in the West who had not become so contaminated

by contact with the Untiring as to demand double the correct sum as remuneration for his conveyance.

The stern morality and high probity of these railroad officials in the United States is so fully established, that I can only account for their peculiar conduct on this occasion by the supposition that the fault lay on the side of the dog; just as the horse is the cause of turf villainies at Newmarket, and the scenery in Switzerland or at Niagara must be held responsible for all the hotel swindles. Be that as it may, despite overcharging, curious classification, and many mistakes as to genus, the Untiring had reached in safety the Atlantic; and now the time of parting had come. The paths that for 8000 miles had lain together must here separate.

It was a simple business. In these things animals have perhaps the advantage of us; they don't know what is about to take place. They look at us almost to the last as though the life was always to be the same.

Never had the Untiring's tail been more proudly elevated, his ears more erect, than on the evening when I led him to his new home, and introduced him to his future friends. Although he had been born and bred in remotest savagery, his deportment was as polished as the oaken floor on which he stepped.

When the moment of departure arrived, he had nevertheless to be secured with chain and collar. A collar had long been an accustomed burthen to him; but heretofore it had been used to draw me along with him, now it was to keep us asunder.

When he found that he was to be tied, he howled with that peculiar moan which only his breed and the wild wolves of the North can send through the pine-woods. Old dog, good-bye! One doesn't waste much time over these things; but perhaps the Good-byes that are said short and curt, or are not said at all in spoken words, are the ones given to the hardest parting—their echo is within, and their memory lingers long.

He stopped the howl; there was a strain at the chain that would not break, a tug at the collar that would not draw or hawl, and the long fellowship was ended. Then, as we drove away to the port where the steamer lay in the moonlight, the old dog stopped his moan, as dogs in mental pain sometimes do, to listen—to listen in the vain hope that the sound of footstep or of hoof-beat may be returning instead of going away; and then, on the night air, the howl rose louder than before, until the link of sound was lost in distance.

A steamer of colossal size, and rich in all that gilding, paint, and lighting can do, carries golden New York to and from its favourite watering-place.

On this night there was an unusual crowd on board the vessel. There had been a wedding, or a dance, or something of more than ordinary "brilliancy" in the watering-place, and a dense crowd covered the deck and saloon, and filled the gangways and galleries, which, like the tiers in a theatre, ran round the vessel.

This gorgeous steam-ship had a history. She had cost some millions of dollars, had broken the company which constructed her, and finally had become the property of the notorious Mr. Jim Fisk.

An English millionaire becoming proprietor of a large steam-ship or two would probably have rested content with his acquisition. Not so Mr. Fisk. Having gazetted himself Admiral, and dressed himself in the full uniform of his rank, he appeared every evening at the hour of sailing on the quarter-deck of his ship. It would appear, however, that he was content with the rôle of Port Admiral, and did not ambition the more onerous duties of the open sea, as he was in the habit of quitting his vessel at the moment of her departure.

Traces of Mr. Fisk's peculiar ideas of luxury were still visible on board the steamer; there were singing-birds in large cages; there was a German band, and French beds. The band and the birds made much noise; the birds watched the band, and the band Watched the Rhine; and, finally, the passengers preferred good French beds to bad German music.

The boat was crowded to excess, so that "a state-room" and a French bed were things not for me; but a blanket had too often been my bed in the forest to be a hardship here, and, getting possession of one, I rolled myself up on a table, and dreamt of the long nights in the North and the old dog again.

At twelve o'clock next day the "Russia" steamed out of New York, with what is called " the usual complement of passengers." Somewhere off Fort La Fayette a small tug steamed violently towards the colossal Cunarder, whistling, puffing, and splashing as she came. "There," said a bystander, "that's meant as a good-bye to some railway or mining man. I always estimate the amount of financial scheming and commercial villainy there is on board this ship bound for Europe, by the quantity of steam-whistling and ' good-bye' puffing that goes on as we clear yon point. There must be some great rascals on board, this voyage."

In due time the "Russia" touched the shores of England. It was early on the morning of the 13th of

September. Late on the previous evening another steam-ship had sailed out of the Mersey; she was called the " Ambriz," a vessel of the West African trade. She bore a young General and a goodly company of gallant men, bound on a distant enterprise.

The " Russia " coming in, passed the " Ambriz " going out, somewhere off the wild race of Holyhead.

There were many lights from ships at sea, and light-houses on shore; and out of that gallant little band on board the " Ambriz," there was many a one to whom these misty lights were the last glimpse in life of English land.

I had lost little time, and the big ship " Russia " had steamed her best, without stint of coal or stress of storm; but, for all that, I had missed the start, and there was nothing for it but to follow to the fight.

CHAPTER II.

" MAN wants but little here below" for the work of war or travel.

The word "outfit" is a term of great commercial value, but of little practical importance. Given a stout gun, a good pistol, a few pairs of strong boots, two or three suits of tweed, and half a dozen flannel shirts, a wide-awake hat, and a man may be considered "outfitted" for anything that the four quarters of the globe might be likely to bring forth.

A well-filled pocket is of far more consequence than a well-filled trunk, and whether it be for Vancouver or Van Dieman, for Patagonia or Pegu, the real outfit is English gold.

Fully two-thirds of the usual conventional outfit will be found utterly useless before one is a week in the new land. The kettle whose peculiar function was to boil water without fuel, the very acme of kettles in Oxford Street or Cornhill, will be found to do anything and everything in the world, except boil water. That admirable institution by which bed, bath, and board, are combined in one and the same article, owing to some little hitch in its mysterious mechanism, offers to the wearied traveller a board when it should turn up as a bed, and becomes a bath just at the moment when there is not a drop of water to be had.

If it be an African outfit which you have provided yourself with in Piccadilly or Cornhill, you will find some of the most cherished articles put to strange uses by your trusted Krooman from Palmas, or your grinning henchman from Old Calabar.

It is curious to notice how quickly these clever " dodges " collapse in contact with the rough but simple ways of the wilds. With a knife, an awl, an axe, and a bit of line, a wild man will perform most of the " skilled work " of the wilderness. He will build a boat, make a snow-shoe, a bridge, a house, a horse-cart, or a dog-sleigh ; if he can't, he is not worth his salt, and the sooner he turns " tame man " the better. He does not hold the clever dodges in much repute ; he has probably seen their inevitable collapse too often to have much faith left in them ; a gun that will carry and kill farther than his own, and that will go off after it has been submerged in a lake or river, will excite his admiration ; but for the rest—he thinks his own gear of shoe and sleigh, cart and canoe, halter and hobble, best fitted for his work—and he is right.

I remember going to a renowned outfitter in London, preparatory to setting out upon an expedition. I wanted a few flannel shirts, silk handkerchiefs, stockings, &c. ; the purchase was soon effected, but upon mentioning my destination to the worthy man, he evidently regarded me as a humbug. " We have an Explorer's Room, sir," he bluntly remarked. " Would you not like to inspect our stock ? Some of the most celebrated travellers have procured their outfits from us, I can assure you, sir. If you are really going to travel, sir ;—Eh ? "

To attempt the work of travel or exploration without a visit to the " Explorer's Room," was an act which he

deemed irrational and absurd, and indicative of an im-
postor; a man had no right to hunt white bears except in
proper "polar spectacles," or seek for sport in South
Africa without a pair of patent " hippopotamus leggings,"
or a helmet of felt.

War, however, differs from mere travel, inasmuch as it
necessitates a uniform dress and fixed armament. On
the· present occasion it had been determined to subdue
King Coffee in grey Canadian home-spun, an Elcho
sword-bayonet, unblackened leather boots, and a cork
helmet. These articles take at any period some little
time to get ready, but at the period of which we speak, it
had become a matter of no little difficulty to procure some
of them. The sudden demand of some forty or fifty
officers for Canadian home-spun had depleted the big city
of London of that article, and although the cable had
been employed to supply the city with the exhausted
fabric, none had yet come from across the ocean.

At length a substitute was found, and on the last day
of September, exactly one month after I had in America
gleaned tidings of an Ashanti war, I sailed away from
England for Africa.

It was a dark, gusty afternoon, filled with the forecast
of the coming winter; there was the smoke of the huge
city to make murkier the misty autumn evening, and the
Mersey looked its worst as the tender bore away from
wharf to steamer.

The steam-ship " Benin " was a sad contrast to the
magnificent " Russia," whose deck I had quitted but one
fortnight earlier. It was the difference between America
and Africa; they were the opposite poles of comfort,
speed, and cleanliness. Low in the water lay the ill-

shapen craft; dirty with coal and cargo were the low decks, and dirtier still the saloon and close, ill-ventilated cabins. A few passages earlier, eleven men had died out of her small crew, two cabin servants and a steward being of the nnmber; but these little items of information we did not know at the time of sailing, and it was as well that they should have been revealed at later stages, or perhaps the murky autumn evening would have worn a drearier hue.

But if the vessel itself was wanting in everything that makes ship-life pleasant, the man who commanded her seemed sufficient in himself to counterbalance every disadvantage. His was not the suavity of the conventional sea captain. He had seen life and death in many phases on this dismal coast to which his ship was bound again; and in his quiet, handsome face, tinged with thought, and his voice, gentle as a woman's could be, I often thought I read the sad story of West African travel. He was in the prime of manhood; he was the picture of health and strength; yet that night, as we rounded out by the grim shore of Anglesea, he looked his last on English land.

" I hope to be back again by Christmas," he said to me. " I hope to spend Christmas-day at home."

It was the old story. The " Benin " went and came, and ere Christmas had come she was at anchor in the muddy Mersey again; but her brave, kind captain lay out in a hammock shroud somewhere in that " vast and wandering grave " which throbs against the sands of Equatorial Africa.

Pitching and rolling over the Bay of Biscay, the " Benin " held her slow course to the South. African passengers are not, as a rule, a lively race; they seem to suffer under a weight of inertia; if they are novices, about to enter Africa for the first time, they are engaged in firing off revolvers at peaceable porpoises, or molesting unoffending members of Mother Cary's family.

On the present occasion the "Benin" carried some passengers well known in African travel.

He of the Congo devoted himself to skinning an ant-eater; he of Zanzibar practised single-stick with such assiduity that he succeeded one day, off Sierra Leone, in single-sticking the eye of another passenger, and leaving it sightless for life. This feat put an end to the single-sticking of the Tanganika traveller, and left the ant-eater skinner to pursue alone his meaner task.

Early on the morning of the seventh day after leaving England, the outline of an island mountain rose above the sea. It is one well known by name over the earth, but seldom I think is its full beauty realized. Sailing in from the rough northern seas, from the huge billows of the "rolling forties," and with the smoke-darkened landscape of Liverpool still a recent picture on memory's canvas, the traveller looks upon Madeira as on some fairy-land of beauty: and it is perhaps as beautiful a bit of nature as can be found the wide earth over.

Out of blue waves a great mountain mass rears its peaks to the skies. The ocean which laves the rocks of Madeira is well fitted to form the setting to such a gem; it sends its coolest, freshest, softest breezes to fan the rugged brow of the lofty mountain; it gathers up showers so gentle, that they seem like wreaths of feathery gauze around the fair hill-sides of the beautiful island; a thousand varied tints stream through these floating showers from the brilliant sun above, and fall in shafts of many-coloured light on Ruivo's scarped sides and Machico's glistening rivulets. Groves of green nestle in valleys, where once the earthquake rumbled, and the fire torrent ran downwards to the sea; colours, bright and vivid, soft and refreshing to the eye, lie spread along the slope which rises from the ocean; white villas with dark-brown roofs peep out from groves of laurel and palm; and over all, the grim peaks of Ruivo and Machico, and the Arrierro, come and go through the rifts of vapour which float lazily around their stupendous precipices. Across the giant fissures in the upper mountain the rainbow has thrown bridges of light, and at times one sees beneath the brilliant arches, the silvery threads of mountain rivulets as they flash over some lofty precipice, or fall in foam down the steep ravines, as they hurry to the ocean with the message of the sky.

So much for the sight, it has a rich banquet spread before it: but the ear is feasted too; the blue sea falls on the grey rock with the music of a dreamland, and all the evening long, the mellowed chime of bells floats out upon the wave, from the towers of church and convent built high up Torrezha's side.

Nature is fond of antithesis. She has placed her most beautiful islands off the shores of her most hideous continent. Madeira and Teneriffe belong to that continent which has the Sahara and the Soudan as the leading features of its scenery.

We looked at this earthly paradise only from the deck of our vessel; for a senseless quarantine kept us prisoners on board; yet perhaps it was better thus to see it; for the scenes thus looked upon, live in memory as pictures free from the recollection of the discomforts which attend upon actual existence in their midst.

There is an old story in Madeira that the earliest

inhabitants were two lovers, who, fleeing from Brittany, were driven by wild tempests to this island.

Machico still tells from his cloud-wrapt summit the word-worn story of these happy castaways : for surely if Love, since it quitted Paradise, ever found on earth a fitting bower, it was here amidst the wild vines and violet-covered rocks of this sea-girt heaven.

We sailed away from Madeira, and on a wild dusky evening in early October the "Benin" rounded the east cape of Teneriffe, and cast anchor a cable's length from the mole of Vera Cruz. The outline of the mountain isle lay jagged and dark, against an orange and pale saffron coloured sky ; the surf thundered loudly on the shore, and a heavy bank of cloud hung over the glorious Peak. It was a wild and desolate-looking scene, destitute of all softness or brightness of colouring ; yet behind that outline of rugged mountain lay a picture of marvellous beauty. " Oratava is the most beautiful spot I have ever seen on the earth," says the German's greatest traveller.

It was near midnight when we steamed from beneath the shadow of this weird-looking isle, and saw the scattered lights of Santa Cruz grow dim in distance : the colossal Peak had hidden its head in gloomy vapour.

I was destined to see it under other circumstances. Little more than five months later, two men held up a fainting man to a narrow port-hole on the lower deck of another steamer, to behold a glorious prospect. The deadly African fever had for a moment left him, and they raised his worn frame to take one look at the Peak—at the earth which he seemed on the verge of leaving.

Outside the narrow port there lay, touched by the wing of a gentle breeze, a sunset sea; beyond rose a mountain mass, and high up in heaven one glorious peak stood

above all other summits; there was snow upon his crown,
and along his fissured shoulders there were dark seams,
whose shadows lay against the glitter of their rugged
edges in the dying sun. The calm of a vast peace seemed
to rest on sea and heaven. If ever sight of earth looked
fair to the weary eye of man, it was this vision of Teneriffe
seen through the narrow port—this sight of snow to the
feverish eyes of the sick man. In the wild moments of
delirium, visions of the snow-sheeted lakes of North
America, when the Aurora had flickered over their white
bosoms, had come and gone in the phantasies of fever;
and now, as the men raised him to behold the unmatched
glory of this island peak set in the midst of a vast ocean,
the phantasy of long nights seemed to have taken form,
and snow had come to gladden and to cool his fever-
heated eyes.

It was a sight only seen for a moment; for even as he
gazed the weary head sunk down upon his breast, and
they laid him back again upon his narrow bed. Yet,
short as was that vision, it has never been forgotten.

But this is of a future time.

Two days later, on the 11th of October, a long low
coast, rose above a glittering sea; a coast of glaring sand,
on which no blade of grass, no vestige of life was visible;
a slanting, sandy shore, lashed by a furious surf; the grim
desert of Sahara, upon whose sands no raindrop ever
falls, no streamlet ever flows, and a sea upon whose lonely
waters scarce ever a sail is seen.

Here before us lay Africa, in all the blinding glare
of sunshine, surf, and endless sand.

CHAPTER III.

DARKLY, like the gloom of a moonless night, or the image of a colossal cloud upon a landscape, lies the shadow of Africa upon the fair face of the earth.

This continent holds the extreme of all that is revolting in man and in nature; horrible as the images of Indian idols are the people of the land; hideous alike are their customs, their persons, and their worship; eaters of human flesh, full of cowardice, and of cruelty; half tiger, half monkey; without law, art, honour, truth, or justice. From Sahara to Kaffraria, from Palmas to Zanzibar, the African race stands to-day as it stood 3000 years ago; hopeless to man, and cursed by heaven. And the land where dwells this hideous race seems as hopeless as its people. Half rainless desert, half feverish swamp, and tropic forest; its rivers teeming with monstrous reptiles; its forests filled with uncouth beasts; malaria and poisonous vapour ever rising from its myriad marshes; and its coasts and mountains fanned by withering breezes which carry death and destruction on their noxious wings.

Such is the Africa of to-day. As much a land of mystery as when, four hundred years ago, the Caravels of Portugal first coasted along those dreary equatorial shores.

There is no necessity now to go back to the early ages

c 2

of the earth in order to trace down the stream of African discovery from its earliest source to the present time; for us here, the Africa of Greek or Roman is of little moment. Our history begins with the time when the Old World was found too small for the giant Latin race; who, stretching forth their arms west and south, touched Equatorial Africa on one side, and America on the other.

But even with these times, when small men in little ships did giant work in unknown savage seas, we have but little to do. Yet, in scanning some old page of African travel, it is curious to note how similar are the circumstances of to-day with those of 2000 years ago. Hanno abandons his enterprise because of dearth of food, and some earlier Persian explorer is given the choice of death for a political crime, or a voyage of discovery to Equatorial Africa.

To us, African exploration may be said to open with Park and close with Livingstone. Between these men what a host of brave names are links and rivets in a long chain of death. Denham, Clapperton, Landor, Oudeny, Dillon, Laing, Toole; all sleep out somewhere in that pitiless land, where the sands of the Sahara merge into the palm-leaves and giant grasses of the Soudan.

As in America, so has it been in Africa. Spain and Portugal might lead the way; Columbus or Diaz, Ercilla or De Gama might draw from the unknown globe new continents and islands; but to England, destiny gave the empire of this new earth, and decreed that either the echoes of savage law should relapse to pristine barbarism, or give back alone the accents of the English tongue.

In following the steps of France and Spain in the New World, it fell out that England was to people a savage continent from the Bay of Hudson to the Gulf of Florida;

in following the ships of Portugal along the coasts of Africa, it fell out that not even the enterprise of the Briton could prevail over the eternity of the curse which hangs o'er Africa.

To the end of time there will be found believers in the negro; nay more, the man-and-brother theory is one likely to expand rather than contract. There are so many people in the world who wish to do good by their fellow-men, but who must go abroad to do it, and who will give a ten-pound note to a native of Negroland, when they would grudge a tenpenny to a native of Wapping, that the negro is likely to form a prominent object on platform and lecture-table for many a coming year. Then there are also so many persons who, starting with a complete and comprehensive disbelief in Christianity and the Bible, are ever ready to become the champions of some remote race on the Nile, or the Niger, and to prove incontestably that everything between an ape and an apache is a man and a brother. As this last-named class (described a long time since by the great Corsican as people ready to believe everything save the Bible) are annually on the increase, we may reasonably expect the negro to hold his own for many a year against all comers, unless, perhaps, the shores of the open Polar Sea should be found peopled by a lower race of beings, or the missing tail should at length gladden the professorial eye.

Nevertheless, in spite of platform or professor, those who know the negro best, like this man-and-brother theory least. In this case seeing is disbelieving. Nature framed this black man for labour; art would pervert him to idleness. We have stopped slavery on the West Coast, or rather, stopped the exportation of slaves; and with what result? You shall hear. His Majesty of Dahomy,

Ashanti, or Benin, may now execute ten negroes, where before he killed one. In old times Quacco, or Quabina, fetched ten or twenty pounds in the slave-mart, he was an object of value, a thing to be cared, a prisoner whose life should be spared. All at once we put an end to this export; but we do not put an end to slavery, it is as deeply rooted an institution as ever. Houssa, and Dahomy, Benin, and Wassaw, and Ashanti, give and take their slaves as of yore; but now the article has lost its value; has become, in fact, a drug, a cheap plaything, and may be tortured or beheaded at will. It is true we closed the slave-marts of the New World, the markets which were close beneath our eyes, and therefore shocking to our senses; but what about the execution-places of the African capitals, which we could not see, and which therefore did not shock us?

We wept over that story of Mrs. Beecher Stowe's; but, alas! there was not a tear shed, nor a thought given to the thousand wretches whose blood stained the cotton wood stools of African kings, from the Orange river to the Sahara.

We are a curious do-what-you-like-but-don't-let-us-see-it sort of people. That wily Scot in his back parlour on the Sabbath, with his black bottle on one side, and his Bible on the other, is by no means an exceptional type of character with us; outside in the street a decent respectable body, inside in his snuggery a terrible old drunkard.

But to the African. It will be asked, What then do you advocate? Would you go back to slavery again, the middle passage, the mart, the sundering of ties, &c.? We answer, No. Still there was a middle course worth at least the trouble of a trial. Slavery was one pole, total emancipation was another; between them lay serfdom, forced labour, and half-a-dozen other means of making the African fulfil that law of earning his bread by the sweat of his brow.

Of all the earth's inhabitants this negro is the only man who denies this ordinance. He makes his woman work, and he earns his bread by sitting on his heels and hams, staring vacantly at space. He is as strong as a hippopotamus, and quite as ugly; but despite his strength, the summit of his labour is to grease himself until his black hide glistens like coal tar, and his immense mouth grins from ear to ear with the huge animalism of his delight.

Twin-brother of this negro-theory of ours has ever been that other theory best expressed by the phrase " opening up Africa." We have had this idea on the brain during very many years, and very many brave men have we sent forth to perish in the vain mission of unlocking the great dark gateway of Central Africa. One by one they fall by swamp, or sand, or fen, or forest; and behind them closes the dreary pestilence-guarded portal, which opens to let many men enter, but never permits them to return.

From the North we have tried this opening up by the long sandy wastes which spread in endless silence from Mourzouk to Bornou, and Tchad. From the East we have tried it with more show of success as to life; but even with scantier results as to trade, or settlement, than on any other side. From the West we made repeated attempts to pierce this impenetrable land; until every tribe from Senegal to the Gaboon has heard the dreary story of a fevered white man toiling through marsh and thicket, searching for, the fetish only knew what, and laying down his life at last pierced with a score of spears;

or wildly raving in maddening fever of the far-away island
home he was never to see again. And now, what has
been the result of all this "opening up"? I will shortly
tell you. The Nile is to-day nearly as great a mystery as
it was 2000 years ago. The Congo is an unknown river.
No man can tell the parent rill of the Niger. We have
written a few more names ending in boo, and beginning
with uoo, on the big blank of the African map, and to do
so, we have left the bones of a score of gallant men to
form fetishes or demon charms for the beggar kings of
the Soudan.

When De Soto yielded up his life on the shore of the
turbid, rolling Mississippi, he caught a glimpse of a day
not very far distant, when his countrymen would be a
power in the new land of his death; when La Salle fell
from the treachery of his coward followers, there passed
across his glazing eyes a vision of peopled cities, and
meadows glistening with grain, in the glorious land he had
discovered; and when the gentle Marquette laid down his
worn frame on that lonely cape by the far Wisconsin shore
of Michigan, he knew that millions would yet draw from
the sleeping wilderness around him the untold comforts
of home and husbandry.

Yes, these pioneers laid not down their lives in vain!
but how bitter must have been the moment when many a
poor African wanderer felt his strength ebb from him,
conscious to the bitter end that this vast, dark, loathsome
continent was ever useless to his race.

From Park to Livingstone it has ever been the same
story: the palm-leaved landscape, the village of wattles
and sun-baked mud; the negroes swarming forth to gaze
upon the toil-stricken and way-worn stranger; the dreary,
dusty pathway; the brazen, burning sun lying like a globe

of fiery metal over everything. Broad-leaved forest; burning sand; the copper-coloured sky; the poisonous vapour curling above the reptile-simmering swamp. We see it all in brain-pictures that rise before us, through all that long monotony of dreary peril; from the first whose gallant life went out at the rapids of Boussa, to the last who, refusing to leave his task while life was left him, turned off into that vast land amidst whose labyrinth of marshes lies hid the story of the Nile, and toiled on, " a ruckle of bones," until the dauntless spirit left at last its worn-out cage.

But to Guinea again. About the time when Columbus was dreaming his dream of empire towards the setting sun, the hardy adventurers of Portugal were beginning to sail farther into the expanses of the vast Southern Sea, which promised them a highway to the realm of gold, the fabled lands of Ind and Cathay.

Sailing south, they beheld strange sights and wonders. The sun at noon flamed in the mid-zenith of a fiery sky. Strange starry figures rose at night from the southern horizon, and climbing the skies, upreared upon the meridian the image of a colossal cross. At times the ships standing to the east sighted different parts of a low, surf-beat shore, a shore of white glistening sand, backed by a gark-green fringe of palms, and close-set tropical foliage. This seemingly endless coast stretching to the south, making a huge trend to the east, and again running south, was Africa. At times, standing to the west, the mariners saw island summits rising out of the clear blue sea, and as the Caravels drew nearer, lofty crests loomed amid the clouds, and these islands of the ocean beheld the stranger ships ruffle the blue waters of their lonely seas.

At last the southward-seeking shore came to an end.

In an ocean, whose waves ran higher than ever these hardy seamen had seen waves run before, an ocean tossed by what seemed an eternity of tempest—a vast mountain cape looked out upon the south. The starry cross had risen high in the midnight heaven ; the sun now hung far away in a northern sky ; season, stars, and sea had changed ; the world seemed come to end in gloom and tempest ; and, dismayed at the prospect before them, the rovers turned back to Portugal ; and a fame, second only to one as a discoverer, slipped from Diaz, who feared to pass the Cape of Storms, to make De Gama's the proudest name in Lusitania's history.

It was at the close of the fifteenth century that De Gama laid at the feet of the Portugese monarch the keys of Asia, through the gateway of the Southern Sea ; his discovery ended for a time the importance of Guinea.

The riches of Hindostan soon eclipsed the rude nugget wealth of Africa, and the long stretch of sea-board to which we have given the names of Gold Coast, Ivory Coast, and Grain Coast, would, perhaps, have sunk into a forgotten fable, if Europe had not determined to seek in Africa that manual labour which was destined to turn the jungle-covered islands of America into groves of sugar and spice.

About the time when France and Spain were busily engaged in murdering each other in the fens of Florida, a veteran English sailor was bringing the first cargo of African slaves to America.

For more than two hundred years the trade thus inaugurated flourished. England, Spain, France, Denmark, Sweden, and Holland shipped their loads of human freight from the Gold Coast. Bristol grew rich, Liverpool rose from the muddy swamps of the Mersey. Quacco, Cobina, and Coffee were busily engaged in growing tobacco in Virginia, and sugar and coffee in Jamaica and Surinam.

Not unfrequently they found their way to England, brought over as the trusty servants of planter and colonist when they returned to the old country to end their days, until the broad, repulsive features of the Negro became a common sight in the waiting-rooms of persons of quality. But all this changed with the American war. When sin ceases to pay, we have a happy knack of finding out that it is wrong; so after a bit, when Virginia, and Georgia, and the Carolinas had ceased to belong to us, we began to denounce this trade in African flesh, and to denounce it in no stinted terms. Finally, the slave-trade ceased, and Quacco, Cobina, and Co., becoming, as we have said, a drug in their native land, were handed over to the executioner.

While the slave-trade lasted, it was only necessary for European powers to maintain forts or factories along the coast; knowledge of the interior tribes, or of the formation of inland posts of trade, was not requisite; but when it ceased, the energies of Liverpool took a fresh turn. We might not require Africans, but the Africans still wanted gunpowder, rum, and cotton cloth, and these articles we were ever ready to supply to them.

For long, long ages the sea had sent nothing to Africa; no sail had ever darkened these lonely waters, no boat had ever breasted that ceaseless surf.

The people living on the shore were a wretched race; they dwelt in a dense and pestilent forest; they knew nought of even the savage craft of iron or of cloth. Warlike kingdoms existed far in the interior; but on the coast every village had its king, and every king was a miserable mendicant. All at once the great blue lake changed its long known nature. Ships came, bearing with them

wonders untold; guns, gunpowder, and countless other
items. Here was a revolution. The shore so long deemed
worthless, suddenly became of value; the great blue salt
lake gave gunpowder, guns, and rum ; tribes inland heard
with wonder of these ships and their crews of white men,
and their stores of wonderful things; each struggled with
the other to get to this gift-giving sea; kingdoms grew
where village kings had been before, and from far inland,
where the great dripping forest ended in broken clumps
of tree and jungle, three Pagan kingdoms rose out of these
wars, holding in check the Moslem negroes of the open
country on the north, and conquering when they chose the
feeble clans which held the sea-board on the south.

Of these three kingdoms Ashanti was the most powerful. Its rulers understood best the African character, and
ruled in accordance with that knowledge. The African is
by no means an unreasonable or unreasoning being. He
merely takes his reason in a manner different from us. To
argue with an African is simply to waste time; to persuade
him, there is only one method, and that course the rulers
of Ashanti followed to the letter. If a man disobeyed,
they flogged him; if he repeated it a second time, they
cut his ears off; if he disobeyed a third time, they cut his
head off. Not only did this last act prevent his ever dis-
obeying again, but it exercised a powerful impression upon
the minds of the wide circle of his friends and neighbours.

Acting on this principle, Ashanti grew to great power;
the other nations succumbed one by one. It is not im-
probable that had another nation treated its subjects in a
still more persuasive manner, and decapitated in the second
act, instead of in the third, it would have attained to
greater influence than the dreaded Ashanti-foo.

Traders are habitually timid, and the action of England

on the Gold Coast was in keeping with the rule. We framed our forts to hold slaves, rather than soldiers. Whenever a village on the coast became bumptious, the inevitable frigate cast the traditional shell among the everlasting cocoa-nuts; the natives rushed out on the sands, then again rushed back into the forest; the marines landed; four goats and twelve fowls were captured, and the war was over.

But it was a different story whenever the army of the great Ashanti-foo came seawards from Coomassie. For months they rolled slowly along, a living river of jet-black naked men; between the stems of the mighty trees, through the dense thickets of interwoven creeper and matted tendril; over the yellow muddy rivers came the dark stream of lithe-limbed soldiery, and the vast vaults of the tropic forest rang with the clarion horns of the myriad chiefs who moved at the summons of the ruler of Ashanti.

Constant conquest gave to these negro hordes a bravery which is foreign to the African character. A despotism savage, cruel, and insatiable, wrought from the dull mass of negro paganism the highest form of organization and government which Africa has yet produced. To disobey the mandate of a chief, to run away in battle, to fail in the transmission of an order, were crimes punishable with immediate death. "If I go back in fight," sang the soldier of Ashanti as he went to battle, "I die. If I go on I die. It is better to go on, and die." He went on, and he conquered. The timid tribes whose friendship we had fostered were scattered before his resistless march. Denkera, Akim, Assin, Fantee, and Wassaw ran from their wattle villages into the impenetrable forest, or sought in coward crowds the trading forts along the shore.

Nigh seventy years ago, in 1806 a great Ashanti army appeared upon the shore. Pent between the sea and their enemies, the people of Fanti turned to flight; but they fell in thousands, and the victorious Ashantis, following them into the waves, slaughtered myriads in the foaming surf.

"You are Lord of the sea, as well as of the land," was the message sent by the victorious chief to the King of Ashanti. "I have dipped my sword into the blue water, and I send you the salt drops to Coomassie." Not far from this scene of slaughter, a large white castle stood upon a ledge of rock close to the surf. It was the English Fort called Annamaboo, some five miles from Cape Coast Castle. The walls were high and steep, black muzzles of guns looked through narrow embrasures. The victorious army of Ashanti, flushed with triumph, cast itself against these ramparts; the black muzzles vomited flame and death, and the naked soldiery of the forest fell in hundreds beneath the surf-beat walls. Up to this time we had been so intent on trade that our governors on the coast had never thought it worth their while to ascertain the Ashanti character. They took it for granted that they resembled the cowards on the coast who fled before a musket-shot. But now we were to be undeceived. The Ashantis were as cool under fire as the English soldiers, whom they picked off with a fatal aim as they worked the guns.

The governor was wounded, and the close of the first day's fighting saw the garrison reduced to eight or ten men.

Thrice the assault was renewed, for this was the first time that the conquerors had ever met these large black guns, and it was difficult to teach such obstinate savages the stern lesson that a coward at the breech of a big gun is frequently a better soldier than the brave man at the muzzle of it.

Baffled in their onslaught against the white slave castle, the Ashantis fell back into their own domain, the great forest. From east to west, they had ravaged the entire territory, until at length a shameful peace was effected by the surrender by the English Governor of two runaway chiefs who had sought refuge in our castle, and whose delivery the Coomassie King had long demanded.

This act sealed the fate of the English name, through many a long mile of territory lying back from the Gold Coast. The white man had surrendered slaves to the negro King of Coomassie. The power of Ashanti was complete. "I see you are a quiet people," said the King of Ashanti to the English envoy. "You do not want to fight. You only want to trade." About the same year another great despot pronounced his celebrated epigram, "They are a nation of shop-keepers."

Ashanti triumphed, and withdrew. The buying of slaves went on. Flushed with the renown which followed the campaign against the English Protectorate, the armies of Coomassie turned north against other foes. Fifty miles north of Coomassie the dense tropical forest, whose gloom overshadows for 200 miles the sea-board of Africa, comes to an end in patches of grass and tree clumps, which finally merges into the desert of Gofan. In this open country Moslem nations had established themselves. But the wave which began at Mecca 1200 years ago, had ended at this dreary tropic forest. Inside that belt of jungle the Moorish rider could not go, and with Gaman, and Gofan, and Soudan the domain of the negro Mussulman ceased.

Warring with those desert States on the North, the
Ashantis still maintained their conquering character;
Gaman was overrun; the gold of the Barri River offered
rich plunder to the invaders, and many a slave from far-
away Houssa, and the kingdoms around Lake Tchad, was
brought back to Coomassie to be exchanged at Cape
Coast Castle and Accra for the guns and gunpowder of
the trading Englishman.

Time went on. You can never conciliate the African
until you have first beaten him. He became more and
more aggressive. His armies moved again into the Protectorate in 1811 and 1816, and ravaged it from end to
end. When Phairshon swore his celebrated feud against
Mactavish, he did not burst into the land of his enemy
more terribly intent on murder and ravishment than did
the hordes of this Ashanti king; but though the pipers of
the negro monarch were more numerous and quite as
melodious as those of ta Phairshon, they did not, as in
the case of the highland chieftain, altogether outnumber
the fighting-men.

At last, in 1824, it was determined to send a soldier
against this aggressive and restless people. A man whose
character stood high with the nations along the whole
coast-line of West Africa, was deputed to undertake
the management of this enterprise. For years he had
braved the deadly climate of this fearful region with
impunity. His appearance was commanding; tall, white-
haired, yet full of activity and energy, he impressed the
African as much, perhaps, as it is possible to impress
him by the outward semblance of anything, save the rod.
He spoke the usual palaver in the great hall of the
Castle; he received the usual protestations and oaths of
the mendicant kings who flocked to get his presents. The

Ashanti army was moving down along the Prah, threatening Wassaw, Akim, and Assin. Each wretched king asserted that his particular province was the one the enemy was bound to devour. Each miserable tribe would only give its soldiers to defend its own territory. This disastrous war has lately been exhumed from its forgotten tomb, and unfairly criticised. MacCarthy—for that was the name borne by the white-haired Irish chief—erred, it is said, in dividing his forces. In reality his forces divided themselves.

The Assins would only fight in Assin, the Wassaws in Wassaw. He sent a few officers to each tribe, gathered together what men he could, and moved into Wassaw on the right of the Prah.

About fifteen miles inland from the coast he encountered the army of the Ashantis. It was the same story, repeated in our own times, to the writer of these pages, in all save its final tragedy. The native allies fired a few shots and fled; the kings whose oaths had been pledged with all the solemnity of "fetish rite" and "custom," abandoned the man who had toiled and tramped on foot for days, through the dripping, poisonous forest, to fight for them. And the old soldier, worn out and exhausted, was surrounded by hosts of unseen enemies, and fell at last at the foot of one of those colossal trees which rise high over the dense sea of tangled foliage. Fifty years have gone by since that disastrous day; yet still the memory of MacCarthy is fresh amongst the cowards who deserted him, and the conquerors who took his life.

In a Fetish temple of vast repute north of Coomassie the Ashantis keep with religious care the skull of the white-haired Irish chief. And though no oath or sworn promise will ever bind an African negro to the faintest

D

trace of truth; yet, if there be a vow which will carry him one step into the realm of honesty or honour, it is that which he swears when he invokes the name of Sir Charles MacCarthy.

CHAPTER IV.

WE have not many names in our English history which call for more than a dutiful amount of hero-worship. We have always been a practical sort of people, and our heroes have generally partaken somehow or other of that quality, and been desperately prosaic persons. Even our greatest sea captain, brimful of heroism and glory as he was, is yet remembered among us more for his famous death signal of duty than for any other deed or saying of his life.

In olden days we had our heroes ; they figure thickly enough in the old, old pages of England's story ; but ever since we leant upon Dutchland and Germany for support, and ever since the false and fickle Scottish race lost England's crown in that long day's fighting on the Irish river bank, our heroes have been somewhat of the beer and pudding type, and our leaders have either led men by virtue of that disciplined bravery which is inherent to the British soldier, or commanded their following by the stern but cold dictation of a dogmatic duty.

To this rule there have been exceptions, not very many in number, but very brilliant in nature. There was something more than duty in that grave scene on the Corunna coast ; Plassy and Arcot had in them a ring which differed widely from the leadership of fifty fields of more world-wide renown ; and when Wolfe muttered that line which tells so pithily the bourne of all human glory, while his

boat breasted the wild St. Lawrence current under the
rocks of Abraham, he stood perhaps of all men the foremost hero of England's later history.

Wolfe, Clive, Moore, young leaders of young soldiers—
chiefs who drew men along with them by an influence
which was more potent, perhaps, in the past days of the
world than in these ages of our own; men more or less
of that stamp which has found its greatest exponent in
the Corsican. Their beginnings are all alike; they foot
the lofty ladder from the lowest round.

Birth yields them few advantages; Death sometimes
seals the latest laurel upon their brows. They are the
same in all nations, and among all peoples; in savage
lands, where men move in tribes, they are called chiefs,
and they rule by the force of bravery and the right of brain
power. In civilized kingdoms they are called by many
names—Marshals, Dukes, Lords; sometimes Kings and
Emperors; often only by the common titles of conventional
command; but through History and Time the Princedom
or the Peerage, nay, even the Empire or the Kingdom are
of small account, and the simple name given at the
parish church font sends a deeper thrill through the
future than all the high-sounding significations the world
may give its leaders.

And now, having read so far as this, upon those who
lead men in times of strife, people may ask, What does all
this mean ?   To what end does it tend ?

The answer is not far to seek.

About three and twenty years ago there was that
amount of excitement in a certain family in Dublin which
attends upon the launching in life of a new scion. A young
man had got his commission in her Majesty's service, and
was about to enter a field wide enough in the eyes of

ose who looked with fond looks upon his coming career;
t not wider than the expanse which youth sees spread
fore it, as it steps from the threshold of home through
e gateway of the future.

It was a time fit for the advent of a young leader. The
l traditions were about to die, and the new era was
out to dawn.

A great chief had just died. The man who of all men
iresented the stern and sublime stolidity of Britain, had
it passed away. To the end he had been consistent.
e had opposed to the last the percussion arm, because
aterloo had been won by soldiers begrimed by the
uttering discharges of the old flint musket. He had
iisted the wishes of his veteran soldiers that their breasts
ght bear the simple record of those fifty fields on which
eir tireless valour had reaped for him the richest harvest
glory ever won by English leader. There were men
l and grizzled, living in that obscure indigence to which,
ien a time of danger has passed away, a grateful nation
egates her sons as surplus soldiery; there were thou-
ids of such men, we say, who, looking upon boy-soldiers
aring on their breasts the names of battles fought on
dus or Sutlej river shore, thought that they too might
permitted the slight boon of carrying those badges of
avery upon breasts which had been exposed on the
lge of Albuera, or at the death-grasp of Corunna: and
t this request had been denied.

Well this is not to our purpose, further than to mark
e end of such things, and the coming of a new *régime*.
other ways than this was the time auspicious for a new
ief. The long peace was drawing to a close. Over the
de world nations and empires were astir; that curious
mpact known as the settlement of Vienna was about to

be undone; an Empire had arisen in France, which although it was but the feeble burlesque of that real Imperialism of which it claimed to be the natural successor, was still destined, despite its threefold nature of stock-jobber, soldier, and *coulisse,* to work great changes in the world around it. At a moment of profound peace, a great world's fair was inaugurated in England, and great men proclaimed that the reign of violence was o'er, and that henceforth it was to be all a world of sheep-bleating and shuttles.

Twenty years ago, this very winter, there was wild work being done along the shores of the Euxine. The old army of England was dying, and it was after the manner of its history, dying· hard; amidst much bungling, vast incapacity, and wholesale maladministration. Men knew there was one course open to them, and that course was as clear as though it came under the more favourable circumstances of victory and success.

In the dark line of the trenches, in digging which men so often dug their own graves, the young man we have just spoken of played his part. We all remember the long dark story of that winter; we know that after that fierce fight in the bush-clad slopes above Inkerman, the gloom of November deepened around our wasted army; which by turns besieging and besieged, dwindled down to a gaunt and stricken skeleton of what had been the finest army ever sent from English shores. We know too how that gaunt remnant of ill-clad, half-fed men, held these wet, soddened trenches, while the winter wore itself away, and the grave-mounds darkened the old fallen snow on the crest of Cathcart's Hill; but while these broad facts are clear before us, how little do we know of that inner life of the individual—that every-day adventure of the unit, which goes to make up the great picture of war, which we deem so familiar to our fancy!

Here is a single item from the life of a unit.

One day a young officer passed down along the muddy track which led from the British camp to Balaclava. He was dressed in the summer uniform of his regiment, and already the winds blew chill from the brown hills beyond the Tchernaya, and winter was close at hand. The thought uppermost in the young man's mind was this matter of clothing, as, nine times out of ten, the most pressing physical want will be the absorbing thought, even amidst times, the hours of which are precious to history.

As he went briskly along, the figure of a sailor appeared in sight. " Jack " came along with that easy swing of his race which he maintains whether in the presence of rags or of royalty. On the present occasion he was resplendent in warm clothing, he had picked up a winter kit somewhere, and put it all on at once. There was a large rough pea-jacket, double-breasted, and big-buttoned; there were boots which looked as though they had swallowed their owner for breakfast that morning, but just kept a little of him still above ground for dinner in the evening; there was the usual fur cap of the skin of some nondescript animal, between a racoon and a rabbit, and there were some other items of muffler and ear-flap too numerous for mention. The sight of this fully-clothed man riveted the attention of the young officer, and when they met the following conversation took place.

" Well, Jack, that's a good coat you have got on. Do you know where a man could get another like it?"

Jack looked askance at the coat, and delivered himself of the opinion that from Constantinople to

Cronstad there was not another coat like "this ere garment."

"Would he sell it?"

"Yes, he would."

"The price?"

"Six pounds ten shillings."

The coat changed backs, the money pockets. Jack seemed so pleased with the transaction, that it occurred to the officer that the boots might follow the coat. The same sum was demanded for the "seven-leaguers," and Jack hauled himself out of them, handed them to their new morsel, and went his way quite as much at his ease in shirt-sleeves and bare feet, as he had been in pea-jacket and seven-leagued boots.

"I think," said the officer long afterwards to the writer of these pages, "I owe my life to that coat, and those boots; I lived the whole winter in them, and when spring came they were still intact."

On trifles such as this the wheel of fortune turns in the lives of great men.

The young soldier rose rapidly. Lieutenant in two years, captain in three, major in five. In war men rise fast, or sink low; and from 1852 to 1858 England knew few years of peace. Despite the peaceful platitudes of princes or politicians, despite the freest trade and largest exhibitions, it was found that nations held their tenure of existence by the sword, and by the sword they had to keep it, even as in the days of Norman William.

It is curious to take up an old army list, and to look back upon the early days of a chief. Ensign, lieutenant, captain; as we read, there come glimpses of the barrack-room, of soldier's dinners, orderly duty, guards, the nightly round of sentries on the lines of Chatham, or the elm-lined ramparts of Portsmouth. All these are the early routine work, which finds its afterpart in the forethought of a campaign, or the leadership of an army.

In some respects our little army is far behind the armies of the world. Its social life is so well defined, and moves by such fixed causes, that men hesitate ere they permit their glances to stray beyond a narrow horizon. To be a captain, to reach the rank of major, perhaps to command a regiment, is the extent of their ambition, and these limits they reach.

Of old it was said of the French army that every recruit had a spare place in his knapsack for the bâton of a marshal, and the marshals of France who had been private soldiers could be reckoned by scores in these days.

Burmah, Crimea, India, China; through scenes of stockade-strife, toil of trench, the death-struggle around Lucknow, the capture of China's strongest city, the young man passed a graduate in the university of fame. Europe and Asia gave him his earliest fields; America and Africa have yielded him his latest triumphs.

If he had been a leader of Indian tribes in Prairie land, the men who followed him would, from the character of his expeditions, have named him "the long arm, or the man who strikes afar;" even at present he is known to the Ashantis as "the chief who fights, but doesn't sleep." Savages are fond of reducing to epigrammatic form the characters of their chiefs, just as they give to their mountains or their rivers names of practical significance, and Wolseley might have been named "the long arm of the British power."

In America he had carried an expedition across six

hundred miles of savage wilderness, and brought it back
by the same wild route in the limits of a single summer.
Through pine swamp, and o'er ledge of rock; down
roaring torrents, and rushing rapids; across the grim
lakes of that Laurentian wilderness, he had led his hardy
followers, and though no fighting greeted the little column
as it emerged into the open prairies of the Red River,
enough had been done to show that the head which had
devised the work was of that stuff which is scarce among
men, and dear to nations in their hours of peril.

This expedition to the Red River was hard work well
done; but it was easy, compared to the task soon to be
assigned to the young general.

We have seen in the preceding chapter how the
aggressive character of the Ashantis had been fostered
by the timid policy so long in vogue upon the Gold Coast,
and what disastrous results had followed a war waged
by the forces of Fanti-land, and led by a few British
officers.

Some two years after the death of MacCarthy, a check
had indeed been given to the Ashanti power, in a great
battle fought in the open grass country which lies behind
the port of Accra; but this check was not by any means
conclusive, and although a treaty of peace was shortly
after entered into by the king, the impression that an
Ashanti army could always beat any force England
might send against it, remained a leading article of belief
along the coast. Fanti and Ashanti were agreed upon
one common point, and that was the superiority of the
latter over all the world.

Seated under the Fetish tree, in the street of the
Croom in far-away Ashanti, the prowess of the nation was
discussed in much the same terms as one may hear in the

present day, in some ale-house of North Germany, when over beer and pipes the capture of London is debated by some beery and bumptious Brandenburgher. The treaty of 1831 was soon forgotten, Ashanti armies moved again into the Protectorate.

In 1853 it was determined by the British Government that Ashanti should be invaded, and Coomassie taken. Portions of two West India regiments were ordered to achieve the exploit; an unlimited number of Fanti, Assin, Akin, and Wassaw levies were to aid and abet the dusky warriors of the Antilles. The various kings and chiefs of Fanti had taken the " big oath;" greased themselves instead of their guns; drunk the Cape Coast rum, and sold the English powder to the allies of Ashanti.

The farce of this undertaking would have been laughable, if behind it there lay not a stern tragedy. There were white men with these two black battalions; white men who died like sheep in this fearful forest; portions of the two regiments reached the Prah; a camp was formed. The men died in scores; the white officers went down almost to a man. No Ashanti appeared to terminate sooner the suffering of the wretched soldiery. It is needless to say that not one single Fanti, Akim, or Assin soldier appeared out of the 17,000 promised. At length the stores and guns brought up with so much labour were cast into the Prah, and the wretched remnant of troops crawled back to Cape Coast Castle.

The track which this expedition had cut through the forest to the banks of the Prah soon became obliterated by the fast-growing foliage. Not a vestige remained of it twenty years later, when the army of Wolseley passed over the same route; but vestiges of another kind were found

on the road. At one of the posts of supply a small
stockaded fort was erected during the late war ; in cutting
the trench which ran outside the palisades, two graves
were struck, and two skeletons laid bare. The forest had
long covered over the spot ; but the spade of the workman
had struck it at random and turned up the white bones of
some forgotten officers who had perished on the track :
but we are anticipating.

The experience of '53 was soon forgotten. A Colonial
Empire, the largest and greatest the world has ever seen,
managed upon a system which would ruin in a twelve-
month the machinery of the most ordinary railway or
banking corporation in England, is not likely to afford
aught to those who study it, save oft-repeated instances
of disastrous bungling.

Again the game of conciliation was tried with the
Ashantis. Our faithful allies, Fanti Guacco, Assin Coffee,
and Wassaw Quabina were informed that henceforth in
time of danger they were to help themselves (the only idea
they had ever entertained on that point was to help themselves whenever they could to our rum and powder).

Diplomacy was deemed the true gateway to the heart
of the negro, and, at any rate, palavering was much
cheaper than any other method of government. At first
the palavering method of administrating Africa gave
tokens of success. Everybody promised everything. It
is the custom to bestow presents during, and at the conclusion of, a palaver, in much the same way that champagne
is distributed among the bidders at an auction, or soup
was given at a Church of England exhortation to Irishmen
dying of starvation in the great famine winter. It is a
curious study to read the history of West Africa in the
Blue Books of the past ten years. Blue Books, however,

are not generally read until the vessel of State is fast aground upon some sand-bank, when everybody connected with the sailing of the ship runs in frantic haste to his Blue Book, and placing his finger on the particular shoal, in the diplomatic or colonial chart, on which we are all aground, triumphantly exclaims, "There it is !"

Yes—there it is, and for years back there it was ; but neither the Right Hon. Secretary This, or the Right Hon. Under-Secretary That, or the countless Heads or Block-heads of Departments, or their Assistants or Deputy-Assistants, ever noticed it before, or gave it a passing thought, until the big ship " Great Britain " ran full and fast upon it. But then is there not a hubbub ? Questions are asked. The member for Great Bungle (an able sea-man) gives notice of motion. The captain of the Ship forgets for a moment his mingled study of Homer, Old China, contagious diseases, and the Syllabus. The minis-terial organs, ever in tune with whatever card destiny turns up, assert that this particular shoal had no right what-ever to get beneath the big ship's bottom ; another set of organs (always out of tune when out of office) assert that it was all owing to the negligence of the men at the look-out. The Great Organ of all blows all its stops at once, high and low, treble and bass, and clearly shows that this particular shoal might have occurred in the best-regulated ocean. But all the same, the big ship sticks fast, and then, after much fruitless endeavour to get her afloat, there is heard a cry of " Stand aside, gentlemen, please ; now is our turn !" and up on deck at last, from the hold where they have been so long hidden away, come the real toilers of England's stormy sea. Still to our story.

It may be asked what is the origin of this present war ?

This question of the origin of a war has ever been a
favourite study of ours. We are always intent on knowing why we fight, and nine times out of ten we have not
the faintest conception of what it is all about until the
whole thing is over. In all these reasons for war a senti-
ment we are pleased to term Duty, figures largely in the
programme. Whenever the interests of trade requires a
town shelled or sacked, " Duty " comes into the perform-
ance with the same pertinacious regularity with which the
burning town appears in the public prints. I presume
that it was a consoling thought for the British tax-payer,
that it was a matter of duty to introduce opium into
China, and force cottons upon Japan. These main issues
of Asiatic wars were, however, tolerably clear to us; but
this matter of Ashanti lay in that terrible muddle which
overhangs all things African.

If you ask now, What was the cause of this Ashanti
war, you will be given a dozen different reasons. Transfer
of Dutch fort of Elmina to England ; interference of
Fantis with Ashanti traders coming to the coast; closing
of the roads to the sea; disputes between the people of
Cape Coast and those of Elmina—these, and many other
reasons, will be given ; but the question is really not
important.

The King of Ashanti, with the true instincts of a
savage, found that we preferred trade to war; and when
we acted fairly by him, he deemed it weakness. Kings
of his class generally do. After all, it is of little moment
to trace back a savage war to its turning-point. The
particular road or gate at which a horse may kick or jib
is but a small item in the long list of the ill training
which has produced the final struggle. Cession of fort,
or closing of road, were the straws : but the load was to

be looked for far back in Blue Book bungling and the trader's greed.

In the early spring of 1873, an army larger than Ashanti had ever sent into the British territory, began to cross the Prah. It moved with that slow, easy rate of movement which had always characterized the marches of this conquering African nation. It had many chiefs. Its soldiers were gathered not only from the populous districts lying immediately around Coomassie, but from the distant provinces of Yomoho, Quahou, and Akeyan. Immense trains of carriers, slaves from the interior desert states, accompanied it, bearing gunpowder and iron-stones for ammunition, and gold-dust for the purchase of additional arms and fresh supplies when the coast would be reached. Its destination was unknown; but the port of Elmina, lately transferred from Dutch to English rule, was the point aimed at; for Elmina had for ages been regarded as an Ashanti sea-port, and the tribute " pay note " of the place had been rendered at Coomassie. It is needless to follow the advance of this slow-moving river of men in its course through the great forest of Assin; the story of one Ashanti conquest is the story of another.

In about two months' time the invaders, having meanwhile utterly defeated all the efforts of confederate Fantiland in two pitched battles, and having ruined and laid waste all towns and villages along their track, appeared in the neighbourhood of Elmina, and opened communication with the tribes on the coast at the mouth of the Prah who were formerly in alliance with the Dutch. Affairs were critical. It was the bad season on the coast. The heat of April had given place to the fierce tropical rains of midsummer, and the giant foliage of the forest exhaled disease and death from its myriad nostrils.

Our first attempt to rescue the coast from the grasp of
the Ashantis was enough to daunt us from renewed exertions.   One hundred and twenty marines were hurriedly
sent out.   In three months twenty-seven had died of
disease, ninety-three were invalided, pale and haggard,
skeletons of men.

Elmina had been saved; but the brave man whose brilliant charge had rolled back the dark tide of Ashantis, ere
they swept up to the confines of old Dutch Castle, was
doomed to perish, as so many were destined to go after.[1]

The news of the complete collapse of the Fanti Con-
federation, and of the critical state of affairs along the
coast (for after its check at Elmina the army of Ashanti
had only fallen back upon its forest camp at Mampon, ten
miles inland, and its chiefs still ruled the land) put an end
to the question at home, of whether the whole business
meant peace or war.

• Many very weighty reasons could be urged against an
English expedition.   Of all the regions of the tropic
earth, where nature is so hostile to life that man holds
his tenure of existence upon the shortest and the frailest
leasehold, this West Coast of Africa is by many degrees
the most deadly.   Even at sea, the poisonous breath
sent out from that gloomy forest carried off whole crews
of hardy sailors in the short limits of two or three months'
stay upon the coast; and it might well be asked, if such
were the results of experience under the most favourable
circumstances, what might not be expected when the
conditions of service and exposure were changed to
the depths of that malarious forest, and added to the
privations and exhausting labours of a campaign ?

The ruling powers of the day in England decided upon

[1] Lieutenant Wells, R.N.

sending an Expedition to the coast, but shrank from making it a British one. There happened to be in England at the time an officer whose experience of the coast of Africa along the delta of the Niger had been long and extensive. In early days he had followed the navy as a profession, his middle life had been passed as Governor of the trading settlement of Lagos, in which place he had brought under discipline a body of slaves called Houssas, a race of Moslem negroes whose kingdom lies along the shores of the great Lake Tchad, almost in the centre of Africa.

In the course of his explorations he had visited the mouth of the Volta, and, ascending some miles up the river, had come in contact with a tribe in alliance with the Ashantis. It was known that the Ashantis traded along this river Volta, and drew a portion of their supplies from it. Rumour affirmed that a large city existed on its banks, some 150 or 200 miles from the sea: nothing else was known about it.

It occurred to the officer in question, that two objects might be effected by means of this river Volta. First, Africa might be opened to trade. Secondly, the Ashanti capital might be reached from the upper river. Hostile tribes infested the banks of the lower portions of the stream; a fact which must of necessity have sorely interfered with any movement against Ashanti; but it is said that the officer in question had declared that, given un-limited supplies of rum and rifles, the conquest of Africa was but a question of time.

Now, unfortunately, of all the precious items of this war, Time was by far the most precious. Everything hinged upon time. It was possible for a hardy English constitution to brave this climate of the forest for a few months;

E

many, doubtless, would fall even in these few months, but it was anticipated that enough would still remain to carry a body of men to the Ashanti capital.

To have carried out the schemes of conquest which Captain Glover planned, to have cleared the Volta of the many tribes lying between Salga and the sea, for this was his original programme, and then to have moved into Ashanti, would have involved at the shortest calculation a two years' campaign, and the white men on such a length of service would have had to be renewed six times over.

To set it fairly before English readers, we will bring the matter nearer home.

I will suppose that an English army has to march on Paris through a climate in which the average duration of life is eight months. What would be thought of a plan which involved another movement on the same place by the lines of Holland, Belgium, the Rhine, and Strasburg; through lands as unhealthy as the main road from Dieppe or Havre, and with the Dutch and portions of the Germans hostile to the expedition? Yet to have struck Coomassie *viâ* Salga would have been such another.

Such, in brief, was the original outline of the scheme of Ashanti conquest known as the Glover Expedition— the first which the British Government, thoroughly alarmed by the news of the advance of the Ashanti army on the sea-coast, had determined upon sending out.

CHAPTER V.

WE did not know much about the West Coast of Africa, save that it was unhealthy. Its many subdivisions were puzzling, and by no means interesting. Senegal or Senegambia, Sierra Leone, Liberia, the Gold Coast, the Gaboon, Jella Coffee, Benin, or Calabar, were names that flitted hazily through an Englishman's mind as pertaining to Africa—a knowledge for which he was more beholden to "The Cruise of the Midge," or "Tom Cringle's Log," than to any recollection of early school-day geography.

Most of us knew something about guinea-pigs and guinea-fowls—guineas were things to keep in lively remembrance—but the place that had given its name to them all was strangely unfamiliar to us, nor did the passing papers of the day tend to throw much light upon the matter. Occasionally we were told that trade was brisk; that palm oil was unchanged; that the coast was healthy. This last item of news was meant to be taken relatively, and the words "for the Coast" should have been added to it; for it simply meant that the death rate, at the moment when the steamer left, was not more than in the average ratio of three or four hundred per 1000 head among the white population.

Ashanti we knew to be a country somewhere in the interior of Africa; but the interior of Africa was a large place, and considerable doubt existed as to its geographi-

cal divisions, notwithstanding the labours of many enter-
prising travellers.

" Ashanti—let me see," said a young Englishman to
me one day on board the " Russia," coming from New
York. " What part of India is Ashanti in ?" The man
who put the question was what is called a Rugby man, in
addition to which he had taken his degree at Cambridge,
and, at the period we speak of, had just completed his
educational course by a visit to the United States. It is
possible he was writing a book on America too.

The slow steam-ship " Benin " had passed the Carpenter's Rock in safety, as rounding out from the Sierra
Leone river she turned southward along that palm-
fringed, white-sanded coast, o'er which the Lion Mount
lifts its steel-blue summits.

There was no light-house on the Carpenter's Rock ;
but for the present it wanted not a beacon to warn a
passing ship of its dangers ; for half raised out of the
waves, and half sunken beneath them, lay the hull of a
large steam-ship fast upon the dangerous reef, her funnel
slanting backward, as though she had vainly tried to jump
clear over the narrow ledge. The " Benin " gave her
poor wrecked sister-ship a wide berth (it is a way the sex
have to their sisterhood in misfortune), and held her course
along the southward sea.

Sierra Leone is by no means a lively place ; and two
days' delay had been more than sufficient to make a visitor
satisfied with his length of stay. Its principal feature is
its graveyard. Whatever may be said of its want of
accommodation for the living, and as there are no hotels
or lodging-houses of any description, that may be questioned, no exception can possibly be taken to the space

allotted to the dead. "God's acre" seemed here multiplied by ten, though the wretched white men did not
number one hundred in the whole place.

The scenery of Sierra Leone is beautiful; one finds it
difficult to associate these swelling hills, and lofty mountains, filled with clumps of broad-leaved palms, with
perpetual malaria; but scenery soon palls upon the
glazing eyes of fever, and the horrors of sleepless nights
would turn to an Inferno the loveliest spot on earth.

There are few places on the broad face of the world, of
which something pleasant may not be said, save this West
Coast of Africa. I remember once riding down the main
street of James' Town, in the island of St. Helena, and
being accosted by a soldier whom I had known years
before in other lands. "What sort of a place is this?"
I asked him, as he walked beside my horse down the
rugged street. "Well, sir, the place isn't unhealthy, and
the water's good," was the reply. Good water and fair
health; after all, they are something in the catalogue of
comforts. Again, I found myself a denizen of a desert
station in the territory of Idaho, where the sage-bush plain
spread around for hundreds of miles, broken occasionally
by the dull brown ridges of barren mountains. A new
comer inquired of an older resident as to the merits of the
station. "Wall, ye see, it's not a bad location this," was
the answer; "it only wants society and good water to
make quite a place of it."

But alas! for the West Coast. Society, water, food,
health, strength, horse, game, atmosphere, and exercise—
everything that can give zest to life— all are wanting.

Some short time ago a young man came to me. He
was about to leave England for this West Coast, and he
desired to obtain information of the new land to which he

was bound. "But is there nothing good about it?" he finally asked. "Surely it must have some redeeming feature. Tell me now, what was the best thing you saw on the Coast?"

"The best thing I saw on the Coast of Africa was a line of weekly steamers to take you away from it," I unhesitatingly answered; and so it was.

Down along the dreary coast sailed the "Benin;" by Palmas, Liberia, and Jack-Jack; catching, or trying to catch, the hardy Krumen of the shore, and anchoring for that purpose off the boiling surf, where the sight of the bee-hive houses, with the palm-tree backing, gave token of a Kru village. Curious work was the catching of Krumen.

When the ship had anchored, a score of mahogany canoes would put out through the surf, capsizing now and again in the heavy seas; but little cared the naked occupants for the upset; to right the craft, and bale half the water out with one hand, as they held with the other to the gunwale, swimming all the while through the boisterous waves, seemed easy work. Then, when the boat would be half empty of water, Kru would lightly vault from the waves into his craft, and, paddling furiously through the seas, kick out with the flat of his foot the rest of the water from the bottom, until the canoe had not a cupful left in it.

I have seen many men play with water; dive, swim, float, and walk through it; but never, on all the shores round' which a wandering life has led me, have I seen aught that approached the perfect mastership of the Kru over the element most hostile to the power of man.

The success of the "Benin" in catching Krus was not

great. The slippery sons of the sea had heard rumours of war farther down the coast; and however well a Kru may fight the elements, he cares not to contend against men in any shape.

When some 150 or 200 naked savages had swarmed up the ship's side from their canoes, a muster of hands ready to go with the vessel would be taken by the captain. The following dialogue would ensue :—

Captain.—" Flat-nosed Bill, you savey me. How many boys you bring me by six o'clock this evening? You savey."

Head Kruman.—" Me savey. Me bring two Kru boys if master dash me two bottles rum and one plum-pudding."

Captain.—" Very well, Bill. I dash you one bottle of rum and one plum-pudding now; and one bottle of rum when you bring me 100 Kru boy. You savey."

Dinner was soon announced, and we descended to the saloon, leaving the deck thronged with Krumen. The time of the sweets drew nigh. A noise sounded at the skylight. We looked up; there was the hideous head of Bill, his great face grinning from ear to ear; his lips opening and closing as he watched the smoking plum-pudding opposite the captain's seat.

" Come down, Bill, and get your pudding! "

Naked almost as when he entered life, save for a small cap on his big skull, Bill entered the cabin, made a duck at the door, and stalked up to where the captain sat. The precious pudding was hot and smoking, and the eyes of the negro actually ate it with prospective delight.

"Take your pudding! "

It was easier to say it than to do it, inasmuch as the dish was not to form a portion of the present.

Bill's hands were large; but the huge ball of the alluring lollipop was larger still; his mouth was huge, but it could not contain that pudding; how could he all at once carry it from the table ?

. Pockets are things as unknown in the toilettes of the tropics as they were in the garden of Eden; nevertheless, Bill was fully equal to the occasion. He took off his skull-cap—the pudding fitted it quite as closely as his head had done—and, cap in hand and pudding in cap, he departed from the cabin as radiantly happy a black man as ever lived between Liberia and Siberia.

Despite the rum and the pudding, the muster fell far short of Bill's promise. When the moment of weighing anchor came, the Kru boys began to jabber incessantly, and as the ship moved away from the anchorage, fully 100 negroes vaulted over the rails, and pitched themselves headlong into the sea.

It was a curious sight to see them splash down into the water by scores from the deck of the steamer; and then, rising like corks to the surface, strike out for the shore.

· The might of Ashanti had even reached this far Liberian Coast, and the Kru boys, who cared not for shark or surf, dreaded being used in some way against the soldiers of the forest.

On the morning of the 22nd of October, the " Benin " hauled in for the shore as soon as daylight broke.

In an open roadstead, many ships of war and transport vessels lay rolling in a heavy swell. Beyond the hulls and masts of these ships, white buildings rose on hills of red brick-coloured clay, and palm-trees backed a shore of glistening sand, on which a white surf ceaselessly broke.

Between the red conical hills a dark green forest showed
grateful glimpses; and far off, to the east and the west,
the same endless shore grew dim in distance, and was
lost in a haze which the foam of the surf cast up into the
hot leaden air of Africa.

Soon there was a boat alongside from the shore.

"What news?"

"The general attacked the Ashantis last week in
the bush, and burned their villages of Essiaman and
Ampenee."

"What loss?"

"Not much on our side. But they are lying about
ike dead cats!" was the English-speaking negro's reply.

Late for the start—late for the first fight. There was
a boat alongside. I jumped into it, and we headed for
the shore. As the Krumen plied their paddles I tried to
draw some items of news from my companion, a control
officer. He was a mournful sort of man, and seemed to
cherish gloomy forebodings of the destiny of the expedition. "See," he said, "yonder boat!"

I looked and saw a boat pulling in the direction of a
large awning-covered steamship, which lay at anchor
farther out than any of the other vessels.

"Well?"

"Well, that's the boat going off with the sick to the
hospital ship, the 'Simoon;' and there's Baker Russell
and two others in her this morning. Very few of the
men now here, I can tell you, will ever reach Coomassie."

Anxious to know who my mournful companion was, I
inquired his name. ——, he answered. The name was an
unusual one. Once before in life I had met it in a mining
camp on the head waters of the Peace river, in the far
north of British Columbia, the most remote mining camp

in remote America. The man and the name had made an impression on me. He had once carried her Majesty's commission, had left the service, and had tried in the New World to recover that fortune which he had spent in the Old one; but it was not to be done, and I found him in this far camp, " a spectre of himself, brooding in the ruins of a life."

I had pitched my tent alongside his shanty, for the companionship of a man was pleasant, and we could talk with mutual interest of old bye-gone times.

Four months had not passed since I had seen him, and now, here in this African surf-boat, was another man bearing the same uncommon name.

" Any relative in America ?" I asked.

"Yes, a brother, somewhere in the west, who used to be in the —th regiment," was the reply.

Life is full of such strange coincidences. When I packed my worn kit on the back of a Hydah Indian, and strapped the ten days' rations of Cerf Vola the Untiring on his broad back, to cross the snow-crowned Bald mountains of New Caledonia; beginning a tramp of 350 miles to the Frazer river, just four months earlier, the last man almost, I had seen in that Wild North Land was the once dashing officer of the " old Slashers ;" and now here, as I stepped into a surf-boat on the African shore, after 15,000 miles of varied travel, the first man I met was the brother of that broken miner !

The boat was cast upon the beach by the high-running surf, and I stood at length upon the Gold Coast. Climbing the worn steps which led to the castle, and going up the wretched street to the quarters of the general, I found the staff assembling for breakfast. There were present some companions in former expeditions; some now met

for the first time; and there was one, whose buoyant air
and fresh sparkling eyes looked as lively and as free from
care, as though the task he was engaged in was one of
common moment, and this deadly African shore land had
been as healthy as a Highland hill-top; nor could the
most cunning observer have caught in the glance of the
bright blue eye, or the light ringing laugh, the shadow or
the echo of pretended gaiety; and yet, only ten miles
distant lay an immense army of Ashantis, camped in all
the insolence of victory. Before this young light-hearted
man there lay a giant's task. Already the dream of
native assistance had vanished, and the skirmish at
Essiaman had proved the Fanti allies to be utterly
worthless. He stood almost alone, face to face with an
immense difficulty.

Fully one half of all that he had been told in England,
respecting matters on this Gold Coast, had already proved
utterly false. All his efforts to raise from the coward
tribes the semblance of soldiers had hitherto met with a
most equivocal success. The country lying behind Cape
Coast Castle, which had been represented as flat, low,
and level, suitable in all respects for railroad construction,
proved, upon inspection, to be rugged, filled with valleys,
and most difficult to work in. Scarce fifty disciplined
soldiers could be got together at any one point. The only
reliable native force, the Houssas, had been taken from
Cape Coast Castle, to the number of 380, and carried to
Accra, seventy miles distant, to form the nucleus of an
army, destined to act far away upon the Volta river; and
this extraordinary act was done at a moment when 40,000
Ashantis lay ten miles away from Cape Coast Castle,
and might have moved upon it, or upon Elmina, at any
moment of the night or day.

True, he had the sailors and marines of the fleet; but to use them on shore at this season of the year was to insure sickness and loss of life from disease, and they were the sheet-anchor of the expedition. He was literally a general sent to war without an army; a skeleton West India regiment, about 100 Houssas, and as many raw Fanti recruits, were all he could oppose to the army of Amonquartier.

He had early written, urging the despatch of English troops to the Coast; for here lay this Ashanti army close to the shore, within easy striking distance of Elmina or Cape Coast Castle, and yet there was nothing to strike the blow with : never was there such a chance thrown away.

Months must elapse before English troops could reach the Coast; months must go by ere a blow could be struck at this Ashanti power lying so temptingly within reach. Hopeless, indeed, seemed then the outlook in that land where delay meant death ; and yet, though keenly the general felt the helplessness of his position, his manner and his bearing were radiant of success.

Three years earlier, in recounting the story of the Expedition to the Red River, I had used the following words of Wolseley, then a colonel :—" For with such men as leaders, the following, if it be British, will be all right— nay, if it be of any nationality on the earth, it will be all right too."

Well, times had changed since then ; he had run many steps up the high ladder of Fame.

After long wanderings in distant lands I had come back again to follow where he led, and when that morning he ran his finger over the wide map of Ashanti, and showed the line by which an Akim or a Wassaw force

might strike the flank and rear of the Ashanti army, as it
would be pressed back across the Prah by the advance
of the main column from Cape Coast Castle, I thought
" Perhaps the words written years ago will come true,
and the march under this sun will be made, even though
all known experience has declared it the most deadly
on the earth."

It was already the end of October. What an ocean of
toil had to be gone through ere the Spring had come in
England—I say in England, for here there was no spring
—no season. This big army of Ashanti, now lying secure
in the confidence of continued victory, was to be defeated
and driven back behind the Prah, and followed as far
again beyond the sacred river to the capital of Coomassie ;
all in four short months, and already the fever ship had
its denizens, and faces began to look wan and pale.

Four days passed. The great yellow ball rose hot and
glaring out of the foamy sand along the eastern shore,
climbed up the copper-coloured sky, and sank at evening into the sea haze again. Men went daily down with
fever, and got up after a three days' illness as worn
and haggard as though a month of sickness had rolled
over them.

The ocean sent its breezes during the day to roll back
for a few hours the poison of the forest ; but with evening the message of the sea was recalled, and the sickly
breath of plant and marsh swept shorewards over the
fetid town, and men awoke at day-dawn to hear the
heavy roll of surf mocking with sound of coolness the dry
hot touch of fever, or the parched throat which drink
could not moisten.

From the Ashanti camp at Mampon no news came ; no

dash of gold or cloth or rum could tempt a Fanti scout to approach the bush-wrapt stronghold; and Amon-quartier burned his powder for "custom," or beheaded his prisoners for "fetish," as though he had determined to live his life within sound of the morning gun from the castle of Elmina.

Four miles nearly north of Cape Coast Castle stood a small redoubt called "Napoleon." Four miles north of Elmina stood another redoubt called "Abbaye." They guarded the main paths which led from the Ashanti camp at Mampon to the two English towns. They held small garrisons of West Indian troops, with two English officers in command; they were the eyes of the English position.

Farther away to the right hand, as one looked towards Coomassie, stood the post of Dunquah, twenty miles from Cape Coast Castle, on the distant road to Ashanti. Here lay a mixed force—a few West Indian soldiers, many native levies, Assins, Anamabous, Winnebahs, Mumfords, Abras, some half-dozen English officers, and two small guns.

This heterogeneous force was commanded by a soldier whose reputation was already high. For six months Festing had braved the climate. His men had all gone down; the stricken remnant of marines had gone back to England, but their chief remained; and when, in another six months from the date of which we now speak, rewards were showered upon the survivors of this campaign in the fever-stricken forest, no honour came with fitter justice than that which made the captain of marines an English knight.

I use the term "knight" in a sense long since but rarely applicable to it. Knighthood to him who stands on some sea-lapped pier, parchment in hand, the incarnation of transcendent British Bumbledom—knighthood to the portly being in whose brief term of civic sway a statue is uncovered or a highway opened—Sir Bore, Sir Beadle, or Sir Bumble—such things have made sad havoc with the glory of the name!

But when the Sovereign lays on the shoulders of such men as Festing the sword of knighthood, one could almost fancy that the vaults and monumental shrines of many an old English cathedral gave forth an approving murmur, as the sleeping heroes of Agincourt or Ascalon welcomed to their desecrated roll a kindred spirit.

Twenty miles further from the coast, and nearer to the Prah, lay another out-fort on the road to Coomassie. At Mansu, the engineer Hume was busy building his stockade and his trench, as though Amonquartier and his army lay before instead of behind him.

It was a curious picture this English position. A few officers, a few black soldiers, some hundreds of worthless Coast levies, on the one hand; on the other, a vast Ashanti army nigh the sea, lying in that mystery which surrounds a crafty, concealed foe; and yet already the outlook was towards Coomassie, and an English fort was being built half way between the ocean and the Prah.

But the men who followed Wolseley to Africa were what might be termed young men. I do not use the term in any sense derogatory to age; but when work such as this Ashanti forest war has to be gone through, youth is perhaps the chiefest condition of success.

In England there is a prejudice against youth. A long-continued series of silver-haired chiefs has made us place too much reliance upon the veteran. We have almost forgotten the true meaning of the word. Applied to soldiers, " veteran" means a man in the very prime of life; applied to generals, it means a man as old as the century. Now and again a Radetsky or a Clyde may make the sunset of a life more brilliant than its noon; but for such as these there will be twenty like Hoche, Saxe, Frederick, Kleber, or Buonaparte.

CHAPTER VI.

On the morning of the 25th October, the sentry on the north rampart of the redoubt Napoleon saw a figure emerging from the forest track which led to Mampon. It was a woman escaping from the Ashanti camp.

She was brought to Cape Coast Castle, where her story gave the first insight into the mystery which hung around the huge camp at Mampon. She had been a slave, and a favoured one, she said, of one Essaloo, the eighth general in rank from Amonquatier. She was often close by when the Ashanti generals debated the prospects of the war.

It was the old story. Essaloo, evidently in love in his own African way, was blind to the fact that his slave was neither deaf nor faithful. And when she ran from his palm-leaved lean-to at Mampon, she carried off with her the secrets of many doughty chiefs from Aquapon to Quasidoomfoo.

The army had broken up its camp at Mampon, and was moving east on Abracrampa. The sick had been sent on to Dunquah under a large escort. Amonquatier had sworn to destroy Abracrampa, and he would keep his oath. He was on his way to Coomassie, but he would strike Abracrampa first.

With no little difficulty I had extracted this amount of information from the faithless one. Domestic details,

F

rival claimants to the heart of Essaloo, and continued ill-treatment on the part of Essaloo's "real wife" (how like we are all the world over !), filled up too much of the narrative. Still the introduction of these domestic woes into the woman's story did much to give credence to the more important items of Ashanti designs which were set at random through them; and when the runaway finished her narrative, it was evident that the army of invasion had relinquished all thought of gaining Cape Coast Castle or Elmina, and had determined to retreat upon the Prah; and to retreat, not as a beaten host, but as one still confident in its prowess to meet and beat anything that would oppose its purpose in the bush.

Abracrampa, Dunquah, and Mansu, all lay on the route it meant to follow : all three places had garrisons.

That night, as we sat at the dinner table at Government House, in the town of Cape Coast, news came from the advanced posts; Dunquah and Abracrampa had begun to feel the approach of the Ashanti army from the west.

Here was a golden opportunity! While the main portion of the Ashantis still lay near Mampon, a large detachment had advanced almost to Dunquah, and there halted. The army was separated; nay, that portion of it which lay near Dunquah was between two English garrisons; but, alas! the garrisons were only such in name. Plenty of officers, fresh and fit for service; plenty of ammunition and arms; but of soldiers only the few West Indian troops who at no point numbered fifty fighting men. Reinforcing Dunquah as best he could, the general tried to strike a blow against the separated enemy placed so temptingly near him.

He ordered Wood to move, with the scant garrison of Elmina, upon Abbaye and Mampon. Fowler was to push a reconnaissance from Napoleon towards the Ashanti position. The main body of sailors, marines, and Russell's native levies would move at daybreak from Cape Coast Castle to Abracrampa.

It was on the night of Sunday, the 25th, that these dispositions were made. A courier started for Elmina to carry the orders to Wood; notice was sent to the fleet to prepare for disembarkation; and to my lot fell the duty of carrying to the redoubt Napoleon the orders for the reconnaissance which was to be made from that place at daybreak towards Mampon. From Napoleon I was to proceed across country to Abbaye, and there, joining Wood's column from Elmina, push on with it towards Mampon. It was left to myself at what time I should rejoin head-quarters. I put a few things together, and set out at midnight for Napoleon.

On the day previous the whole male population of Cape Coast Castle had "taken the field." This operation had been performed with so much noise, powder explosion, women dancing, tom-tom beating, and general buffoonery, that great things were expected on the part of the male population whenever they should come in contact with the enemy. They had been ordered to proceed to Napoleon, there to move under the banners of Fowler and his thirty West Indian braves.

Confident that I should find the "army" of the male population already ranged at Napoleon, I pushed on from the town along the bush-track leading north.

Scarcely two miles from the last hut I began to fall in with the male population; they lay along the path, sometimes across it, wrapped in their white cloths, fast asleep. We threaded our way with difficulty through their prostrate forms. It was in vain I shouted and kicked the entire male population. It would not budge from its resting-place, three miles in rear of Napoleon. "If the Ashantis were going away, why not let them go," thought the entire male population, and the night was a time to sleep, and not to march.

So I vollied at them language which might have been blessings for all they knew, and pushed on to Napoleon.

It was two o'clock in the morning when I gained the top of the hill, and roused the officer in charge. Another hour had passed ere his orders were written out and explained, and then we sat before the camp fire, waiting for the first streak of dawn.

The chances in favour of a successful reconnaissance being made from Napoleon were not many. The garrison numbered twenty-eight West Indians, and thirty of the entire male population; the remaining male population, variously estimated at anything between fifty and five thousand men, occupied strong positions along the Cape Coast road, from which no power on earth, save a few Ashantis, could possibly dislodge them. Repeated messages sent back to the sleeping warriors met with various responses ; first, the soldiers were waiting for their chiefs ; then the chiefs were waiting for the soldiers ; finally, the dawn would wait for no one : through the darkness over the low, rolling hills and forest tops came the boom of the heavy signal-gun from Elmina. It was time for my start.

Descending the hill towards the west, I set out for Abbaye. At the foot of the ridge upon which the redoubt was built some half-dozen men, with sticks and a lantern, passed me, winding up towards the fort. They were the chiefs of the entire male population going to hold palaver with the officer at the fort. Their soldiers would come, they said, some time during the following day.

I crossed the Sweet river, waded through a deep swamp for half a mile, and after three hours' hard marching reached Abbaye.

The advance-guard of General Wood's column from Elmina approached at the same moment. After a few minutes' halt, the column continued its march towards the north.

Four miles from Abbaye we reached a group of palm-leaved huts on a knoll amid the forest. It was Simco, an advanced post of the Ashantis. It was quite deserted, and foul beyond description.

A young officer led the advance. He was keen and eager, and constantly shouted to his mixed force of West Indians and Ahantas to " close up " and " move faster." He spoke very hopefully of the war. Fever had not yet touched him, he said,—almost the only one in Elmina who had escaped it. Just four months later this same eager, gallant boy, still pushing to the front, met his death by the banks of the flooded Ordah, one short march from Coomassie; and to-day, far out in the great forest— England's most advanced sentinel towards the dreary desert of Gofan—sleeps that brave boy-soldier, Eyre.

The column halted at Simco, and awaited the return of a scouting party sent on to Mampon; a few prisoners and an old umbrella was all that could be found in Mampon. The prisoners were too sick to move with the Ashantis; the umbrella was too tattered to take away. The slave of Essaloo had spoken truly—the army of Amonquatier had gone from Mampon, but whither no man could say.

We lay in the sun and stench at Simco for some hours,

the native levies said they had had enough of it, and
refused to go on. The sight of the old Ashanti umbrella,
and the five sickly Ashanti slaves, seemed to arouse in
the breasts of these brave fellows a longing for home.
As far as Wood's column was concerned, it was evident
that the game was up—we were at the wrong side of the
work.

I ran over the distance in my mind. To Elmina ten
miles, to Cape Coast seven, to Dunquah twenty : total,
thirty-seven miles. A long distance—nearly forty miles
before we could reach the right side again—the side to
which the Ashantis had flown.

I got my few bearers together, and set out on a forced
march. By sundown I reached Elmina, and thence,
turning along the shore, reached Cape Coast Castle by
nine o'clock. The town was deserted. Government
House was shut up. Twenty-two hours earlier I had
started from its doors, and had travelled without inter-
mission ; I was hungry, thirsty, tired ; a rigid search in
the lower regions of the house discovered a piece of a
ham, about a wine-glass of brandy, and a bottle of soda
water. With these, hunger and thirst were partially
satisfied, and then, having despatched messengers to
Dunquah announcing the result of the movements on left
of position, I lay down on a sofa at the drawing-room
window to sleep, but not to sleep long—for at midnight
there came the running of many footsteps into the court-
yard, and the noise of many tongues speaking together.

The Ashanti-foo were coming on the town. The chief
of Muree, followed by the chief of some other place hard
by, had come running as fast as his old legs would carry
him to alarm the population. The "entire male population," as we have already seen, being "away at the war"

(they had never budged beyond Napoleon), the entire female population, feeling themselves doomed to instant death, resolved that the ruling passion of their sex should at least be strong at the supreme moment. Seeing the white-robed chief of Muree surrounded by crowds of Fanti ladies, clad only in the covering of night, I collared the old miscreant, and, taking him into the house, endeavoured to extract from him the truth of the matter. For a time it was perfectly useless. Thompson, the interpreter (a hoary-headed old negro, who, since the arrival of the runaway slave, had devoted himself to that faithless Ashanti), was reduced to a perfectly unintelligible state by what he believed to be the imminent peril of the situation. It doubtless appeared to him that the story of the faithless one was nothing but a purposely-designed falsehood, to draw away from the town the general and his soldiers; and now the Ashantis were coming, and she would hand him over to her own people as the earliest victim. At length, some definite idea resolved itself from the universal chaos.

Bodies of Ashantis had appeared on the main road opposite Yamolanza, six miles from Cape Coast Castle, the women of that district had fled to Muree, and hence the alarm. I got rid of the lot, sent a messenger to headquarters with the news, and lay down to sleep again.

Next morning I set out for Abracrampa. At the outskirts of the town of Cape Coast I was met by a band of twenty natives of Jounquah and Mampon, who called themselves "scouts." Three of these I had despatched four days earlier to spy the Ashanti camp, and I had promised large "dashes" if they brought reliable information. They had now returned, bringing seventeen other scouts, and with information confirmatory of the intelligence which I had already received. Attached to this party was a clerical-looking negro, who proffered his services as interpreter. He had been the Wesleyan preacher at Mampon, he said; the Ashanti occupation of his parish had sadly interfered with his ministrations, he had dwelt in the bush for many days, and he was now prepared to fight, interpret, or die, as the case might be, for the trifling remuneration of two shillings per diem.

These twenty men had once been his parishioners. It was true they were not all Christians, but they were excellent scouts; at one and sixpence a day they would do good work. Samuel, their chief, was entitled to an extra sixpence on account of his extra bravery, and there were two other chiefs of lesser renown, whose courage would be adequately recompensed by an additional threepence.

The bargain was quickly struck, and I quitted the dingy outskirts of Cape Coast Castle with my twenty scouts lustily yelling forth the mighty deeds of their new master.

After more than four hours' marching we reached Abracrampa. The general and head-quarters had but just arrived. Some 200 sailors and marines, and four times that number of natives, filled the little town.

I walked straight to the house occupied by the general; the room was filled with officers. "Where were the Ashantis?"—that was the question. "Gone by Jounquah far away to the north!" "Gone by by-roads and distant paths to the Prah!" said many voices together. "Well, what news from the other side? Where are the Ashantis?" This to the new-comer—myself.

"Coming here, sir; on their way to attack this place, and now at Effootoo and Essecroom." Coming to attack Abracrampa! The idea seemed absurd to many who stood by, and who stoutly averred that the retreat would be made by Jounquah and a distant northern line; but it did not seem absurd to the chief, who, seated on a low trestle-bed in one corner of the dingy room, listened much and said little.

"I am not sure that he is not right," I heard him say, as he scanned the map lying before him ; after that, the others might deem the movement on Abracrampa absurd if they pleased.

At daybreak next morning there was much excitement in the little town. The whole force was to move towards Dunquah for a simultaneous attack upon the wing of the Ashanti army camped near that place. The king of Abra's warriors were to lead the column. A lieutenant in the Royal Navy was attached as special service officer to this tribe. By dint of great exertions he got his crowd into something like order, and took them out of the village two hours after the appointed time. This force was frequently alluded to as "Pollard's Army," and was supposed to number about 500 men; on the present occasion, I stood on one side of the pathway as the "army" defiled from the village, and counted them as they passed; they numbered about 140 men. The procession moved in something like this order: first, six scouts, the king, two men with blunderbusses, a man carrying a very old horse-pistol (this was the nearest approach to cavalry I ever saw on the Coast), about fifty men armed with long flint guns, two drummers, two men with powder-barrels, a standard-bearer with an old flag, Pollard himself, some sixty or seventy more men, a flat-nosed negro, with a small smoking-cap on his head, brought up the rear. He was known throughout the force as the "Field Marshal," and the term was not applied to him in a derisive sense.

As this army defiled before me, I watched it with considerable interest; the spectacle was novel at the time. A few weeks later it had become but too common to me, and I was the leader of a host more incongruous, more high-sounding, and as warlike as this "army" of Pollard's.

We reached the ruined village of Assanchi by noon; the day was fearfully hot, the sun streamed down upon the forest until the darkest recess of tangled creeper and massive trunk steamed forth a dense and fainting atmosphere. As we emerged into the overgrown plantain gardens around the ruined village of Assanchi, a couple of shots rang sharply out on the left, and an Abra scout had his leg cut with slugs. A wild scene of confusion now ensued; it was impossible to make the Abras understand the wishes of their chief, and it was only by actually laying hands on them, and placing them in the required position, that they could be got to conform to any plan.

While we were engaged in the work of making a front to the left, from whence the shots had come, another volley announced another foe in the bush. It was close on my left, and, hearing loud shouts, I sprang through the plantains to the spot.

Amidst the leaves and brushwood six or eight men were struggling, some on the ground and some on their legs; in their midst was a short, stout savage, with his hair twisted into spiral spikes, which stood straight up from his head. He struggled with a kind of superhuman

strength, and moved the three or four men, who held him
down, with the fierce twistings of his body. A couple of
the men standing round kept striking him with the butts
of their guns on the back of his head; still they could
not quiet him.

A Houssa was standing close by, with a long knife in
his hand, waiting for an opening to draw it across the
Ashanti's throat. He was so intent on watching his
opportunity that he did not see me.

For a moment the struggling wretch rose off the
ground and gave the Houssa his desired chance; he leant
forward to draw his knife across the neck, but as he did
so I caught him a smashing blow on the ear, and rolled
himself and his knife into the bushes.

At the same instant the Ashanti rose, and, seeing
a white man, threw himself to me, and caught my
hand in his: he was safe. But, at that moment, captor
and captive were alike saved by a fortunate arrival, from
the same fate. Russell's Houssas were close at hand,
coming up from the pathway in breathless haste. A
body of them rushed into the thicket where the struggle
was going on. The Houssa is ever ready with his rifle.
On the present occasion, it was sufficient for these fiery
gentlemen to observe that there was a row going on in
the bushes; it mattered little who were the combatants,
so half a dozen Sniders were levelled through the plantain-
leaves full upon us, by that natural instinct of the African
which prompts him to fire first, and see who he has fired
at afterwards. Fortunately, Russell himself was by, and
the muzzles were thrown up at the loud summons from
his stentorian voice.

Taking the Ashanti in tow, I got back to the ruined
huts again; the column was arriving fast. The sailors

had come up, while I was hastily trying to extract from the Ashanti some information as to the movements of his people—a proceeding which the minister of Mampon looked upon as perfectly useless, urging that there might not occur such an opportunity for killing an Ashanti for a long time—a line of argument which I believe he was prompted to follow, from the belief that the instant decapitation of the prisoner would have successfully concealed his (the minister's) utter ignorance of the art of interpretation. While this parley was going on, there arrived an order from the rear to stop the advance of the sailors at the village of Assanchi.

Meantime, the army of Abras and Russell's natives had turned north-east along the Dunquah path. Judging that too wide a space would intervene between the advance and the main column, if the former were allowed to proceed onwards in ignorance of the halt of the sailors, I pushed on as rapidly as I could to the front. It was a long run to reach the head of the advance, the day was swelteringly hot, the path was deep in mud and water, and the track was so narrow that to pass men on it was laborious work.

I reached the front after a hard run, having passed the Houssas on the track. We sat down to await orders; by a mistake, the halt of the sailors at Assanchi was misconstrued into a countermand of the Abra advance, and a pencil note was sent up from the rear ordering our return.

When we got back to Assanchi the general was there, and the Abras were again ordered forward; but the sailors and marines were exhausted by the march and the intense heat, and, after an hour's halt, the column moved slowly back to Abracrampa.

The Abras pushed slowly on towards Dunquah, and at

evening fell in with the Ashanti camp at Escabio. An immediate panic ensued; the Abras ran in every direction. Pollard fired his revolver at his vanishing army, and found himself left alone. Six or eight of his soldiers joined him after a time, and carried him on their shoulders along a by-path to Accroful.

Thus ended a day of much laborious toil. From Abra-crampa to Assanchi and back was only a twelve-mile march; but the excessive heat and sultry atmosphere, the mud and entanglement of the forest path, made weary and footsore many a strong man.

That day's toil sealed the fate of some gallant men! As I stood at the cross-path of Assanchi, endeavouring to extract information from the Ashanti prisoner through the medium of the minister of Mampon, a young officer came up with orders from the general. To reach the spot he had to run nearly a mile, passing, as he ran, the long string of men along the forest path. His face showed the effects of the run in that burning heat. The eyes were encircled with dark rings; he looked thoroughly exhausted.

Four days after he took ill, and within a fortnight the great ocean, which laves the prison rock of St. Helena, received into its bosom the canvas-shrouded body of Alfred Charteris.

On the following day, the 29th October, the head-quarters moved back to Cape Coast Castle, leaving a garrison to hold Abracrampa. I lingered at the latter place, expecting that the long-threatened attack would take place; but on the 31st there came an order re-quiring my presence at Cape Coast Castle, and I repaired thither.

The "scouts" made much noise as they entered the town; the minister of Mampon received the congratulations of his friends, and in the exuberance of his feelings forgot for the moment the poignant grief he had sustained in not seeing the Ashanti prisoner deprived of his head.

As for the prisoner himself, a moment of great triumph awaited him. It had become absolutely necessary that a letter should be despatched to the King of Ashanti at Coomassie, conveying notification of the intentions of the British Government regarding the war. Now, it was no easy matter to convey a letter to the Ashanti capital. To send a European would only be to add another to the captives already detained at Coomassie; no Fanti would venture upon the mission; of the Ashanti prisoners at Cape Coast Castle, all save this one taken at Assanchi were feeble and worn with sickness. Would he (of Assanchi) go to Coomassie?

I went to the cell in the castle where he was confined, and found him finishing a substantial repast of rice. He had been well washed. His spiral war-spike curls had been closely cut; he looked fat and strong. He recognized me instantly.

"Well, my friend," I said, "how would you like to go to Coomassie?"

He looked at me for a moment with his big intelligent-looking eyes. "I would sooner stay here."

"Why?"

"Because here I will get plenty to eat; at Coomassie my head would be cut off."

The reasoning was sound.

"But if you took a letter to the king at Coomassie from the Queen's general here, your head would not be cut off."

" No."

" Well, we will give you a letter to take to the king at Coomassie. You will have a new cloth and some money; you will be put beyond the last fort on the main road, and then you will have to go as fast as you can to Coomassie. What do you say to that?"

" I will go."

" How long will you take to reach Coomassie?"

" Ten days."

" Very good; you will start this evening before sunset."

It was a change in the prisoner's fortunes, but he took it as coolly as though it was an every-day occurrence. In order to duly impress him with the fetish of the white man, a steam traction-engine was ordered to be held in readiness to convey the prisoner from the town. Shortly before sunset the engine drew up at the castle gate. I brought my friend the prisoner, now transformed into an envoy, from his cell, and mounted him on the locomotive; but, alas! he seemed to regard it as a most ordinary adjunct of the African bush, and neither its puffing nor its screaming caused him the least astonishment.

Upon being told that it was a very great fetish, he nodded his head in complacent recognition of the fact. Perhaps he was glad to have his head to nod, for doubtless the whole thing, from his being put on one, seemed more or less a prelude to his execution.

A vast concourse of Fantis had surrounded and followed the engine, and seemed to think that they could not do better than make a Juggernaut of this novel machine, by getting under its wheels. In mounting the hill from the castle, the locomotive came heavily to grief outside the town; in trying to force its way up a short steep incline, it blew some few bolts and rivets out with loud explosions, and finally came to a dead stop; so the envoy was lowered from his lofty perch, and sent on his way under a small escort, who had orders to enlarge him at Mansu.

This was the last I saw of my friend, but we heard long after that he reached Coomassie safely, and delivered the packet to the king.

And now a new phase of life opened before me.

On the 1st of November the general sent for me. He had a large map before him. " There is the kingdom of Akim, seven or eight days' march from the coast at Accra," he said. " I want you to start in two days for that country. There is a king there named Cobina Fuah, and another king or chief named Coffee Ahencora; they are said to be better than these cowardly fellows here. Their people are said to be old foes of the Ashantis. Go to them; try and get them to move on the Prah, and do something to molest the Ashantis as they recross that river. A steamer will take you to Accra; from thence you will travel inland to Akim. Take with you what you require; bring these twenty scouts with you as an escort. You know what I want done."[1]

This was on the 1st. On the 3rd I had got together a few things—eight stands of Sniders, two Union Jacks, a few servants, a small boy of precocious powers who spoke English and Fanti with ease and correctness, a bag of one hundred gold pieces, a goodly supply of ammunition, some cases of Australian tinned meats, a lot of proclamations and addresses to the inhabitants of Fanti land, and an amount of great expectations, which, if put

[1] See Appendix No. 1.

into cases, would have been bulkier and far more difficult to digest than even the tinned meats of Australia.

But in sober truth, the faith and the hope with which I undertook this mission were not by any means as sanguine as their spoken semblance seemed to indicate. The experience of the last few days had sadly shaken my faith in the native. I had seen so many instances of abject cowardice, childlike cunning, and apish cleverness, that it was too much to expect that a hundred miles or so could make any material difference in the character of the people; but if a thing has to be done, it is as well to do it with a confidence that failure is not a possible contingency, even though that confidence be sometimes but a poor assumption. No; this was but a dreary undertaking, this mission to Akim; like so many other things, it looked well enough on paper, and out of Africa might have had much to recommend it.

I well remember now the feeling with which I watched the scene in the quadrangle of Cape Coast Castle the night before my departure for Accra. The night was gloriously bright with Africa's only beautiful light—moonlight. The white fort seemed built of marble, in the glow that hid the stains of damp and mildew, and the crack of time, and showed only the massive walls and glistening bastions of the wave-washed castle.

The surf was a rolling mass of snow and silver, and its boom filled the air with a music that for once seemed in unison with the calm and cool of night. The large quadrangle was filled with stores and munitions of war; and men were still at work, although night had fallen; for the news of Ashantis gathering round Abracrampa was pressing, and further supplies were being forwarded to the threatened village.

G

I sat on the low sea-wall watching this scene, and thinking no pleasant thoughts on the fortune which compelled me to leave the place at the moment when the excitement of service was about to begin. Outside, beyond the surf, the man-of-war which was to bear me away to Accra on the morrow lay at her moorings, amid the larger spars of frigate and troop-ship.

Almost at my feet the moonlight glinted on three dark letters paved in the ground amid an oblong of lighter-coloured bricks. Letters they were, once well known to English eyes—letters which carried with them an image of a more perfect union between youth, genius, and loveliness than this century of ours has since given to us—L. E. L. The generation that knew her will soon be of the past. Her story is well-nigh forgotten, and it is only from Maclise's painting that we can catch an echo of her beauty. Here in this desolate wave-beat castle, by this dreary equatorial sea, was the end of all her genius and loveliness. She had pictured it herself:—

> " A lonely grave,
> Just where a broken heart might be,
> With not a mourner by its sod."

And now the clank of guns and tumbrils sounded through the courtyard, and the echo of the surf was blended with wilder sounds than the dying girl had ever pictured round her lonely grave.

Next day I embarked at the castle steps, and pulled to the " Decoy." With the exception of my three servants, I was alone—my " army " had deserted. The minister of Mampon, the chief Samuel and his nineteen scouts, had vanished into the bush, afraid to trust their persons into the new country to which I was bound.

Of the loss of their escort I thought little; but even twenty armed ragamuffins are sufficient in Africa to impress the native mind with a sense of military power, provided that they be given permission to help themselves freely to whatever the country affords.

How often in after-times has my worthy servant Dawson (than whom no better judge of his race existed on the Coast) begged that I would permit the armed rascals who followed me to "harry" the crooms and loot the villages of chickens and sheep! So far as personal safety was concerned, the desertion of the scouts mattered little; for more than two months I traversed the bush alone in every direction, from the Coast to the Prah, midst Accras, Assins, and Akims, marching more than three hundred miles through large districts where no white man had ever set foot, yet the shadow of molestation I never saw. Plenty of desertion, falsehood, and treachery of a cowardly, sneaking kind; but of that bolder sort which waylays, robs, or threatens, not the slightest trace could I find.

The "Decoy" had her steam up, waiting my arrival. About four o'clock in the afternoon she rounded her head to leeward, and steamed down along the coast towards the west.

I know not if any of my readers have ever had a man-of-war placed at their disposal. It is an honour usually conferred on princes who have abdicated, or are about to do so; or it is considered a mode of paying respect to the memory of a distinguished man when his remains have to be carried across the ocean for interment in his native land. In either case the honour is one which has no drawback to it. The prince meditating the abdication of his crown, or the defunct *savant* or statesman who has already abdicated his tenure of existence, may be considered equally safe from the unpleasant consequences of sea travel.

But, to the ordinary wayfarer on the journey of life, the fact of having a ship-of-war specially ordered to carry him to his destination is a very questionable honour. It is disagreeable enough to go through that ordeal, which a man politely alludes to, by telling his friends "that he is a bad sailor," on board an ocean steamer in which one is a private passenger; but to be reduced to that worst and weakest ill that flesh is heir to, when one has, as it were, a ship-of-war all to one's self, is something so very lowering to one's personal dignity, that it unquestionably more closely typifies the uncertainty of human greatness than any other misfortune that man can meet with.

With some such feelings as the "First Lord" must sometimes experience, as the Admiralty yacht steams out of the Solent in a heavy sou'-wester gale, bound for the Channel Isles, did I pass the long night on the deck of the "Decoy." Nothing could exceed the attention shown by every one; but so long as the "Decoy" seemed to think that rolling was the great aim and object of a gun-boat, kindness and attention seemed only to bring more fully into light the painful absurdity of my position.

On the whole, I would say to those who may ever have a choice offered to them of being carried to their destination by a ship-of-war, be very careful what you do. If you are what is called a bad sailor, reach it by walking along the shore; go in a row-boat with savages; in an ouniak with Esquimaux, or a sampan with Chinamen; go as a private and unnoticed passenger in steam or sailing ship—swim to it if you can—but don't go in a ship-of-war.

CHAPTER VII.

Accra lay white and foul under a blazing sun.

Probably, in the whole course of its existence, it had never been so drunk as on this 4th of November.

Men lay on their backs in the streets, and, placing their guns on their chests, fired wildly into the air; then other men turned cart-wheels along the roads, firing their flint-muskets as they did so.

The consumption of rum was enormous. The negro is never handsome; but when the negro is drunk, he is hideous. On the present occasion he was very drunk, and very horrible.

The reason of all this was soon explained.

Accra was about to move to Glover's camp at Addah. Dashes of money, rum, and powder were plentiful; and although Accra had not the smallest idea of fighting at Addah, or at any other place, still that part of going to war which consists in stripping naked, firing off guns and getting drunk, is a highly religious African ceremony which cannot with propriety be dispensed with.

It would have mattered little to me whether Accra had been drunk or sober, had I not wanted baggage-carriers for my inland journey; but all the efforts of the Chief Commissioner and his head interpreter were futile to evolve from the dire confusion a score of sober Accras willing to undertake the trip.

From early morning on the 4th to late evening I waited anxiously for my promised men, and often I walked the sun-baked street in the hope of " stirring up " to greater exertion Mr. Addoo; but evening came, and morning came again, and still Accra was drunk and disorderly.

While I am waiting here at Accra, let me say a word about one whose name will ever be associated with the Ashanti war.

It matters not what opinions may be held on the subject of the Volta Expedition, or of the effect upon the ultimate issue of the war of the march of the 800 Houssas and Yourabas from Pong to Coomassie ; there can be but one opinion of the man who organized that Expedition, and led the Houssa column to Coomassie. When Captain Glover was said to have uttered the sentence, that with rum and rifles he would conquer Africa, he spoke a truism in all save time. ' Rum and rifles mean much in Africa, but they do not mean expedition ; and as we have before stated in another chapter, expedition was the one indispensable requisite of this campaign in Ashanti.

Glover had spent his life, or the best portion of it, on this coast, and the ideas formed during twelve years' residence could not easily be changed. West Africa was to him a whole. He looked beyond Ashanti or Dahomey, and saw in the dim interior tribes and people panting for the sea.

The dream of opening up Africa, that fatal vision, had taken strong hold of his imagination.

The Niger had been tried in vain, but there was another large river flowing into the ocean—a river of which men knew little or nothing. It was called the Volta by geographers ; the Adirri by the natives.

A large and populous city was said to stand upon its

banks, 150 miles from the sea. Many independent, savage tribes dwelt upon the lower waters, laying imposts upon the canoe cargoes which sought this city.

Akims, Krepees, Aquapims, Croboes, Aquamoos, and Awoonahs warred and struggled with each other on the shores; and every now and again some bandit chief established himself upon an island in the river, and made war, fleecing all comers on his own account. Such was the Volta!

Much might be done through it to open up the countries lying behind Ashanti—and so thought many men who had made Africa their home. Few amongst such men had suffered their mental vision to range over a wider scope than Glover, or allowed a belief to overspread their better judgment—a belief engendered by the immunity from disease which a few enjoyed—that it was possible to upraise an African Empire as an appendage to the British Crown.

Glover had, as I have said, long looked beyond Ashanti; and when this war broke out, he looked beyond it still: nay, Ashanti was but a secondary part of his programme; the Volta was the first part. All through, he clung to the Volta with a persistency which had its birth and its explanation in the conceptions of earlier years. When ordered finally to quit the Volta, and hasten to the Prah, he did so with reluctance.

The camp at Addah, the camp at Blappah, the camp at Gravie Point, were so many bases on the Volta doubling the work of shipment and trans-shipment. Accra was the real base from which to attack Coomassie. The Volta, the Aquamoos, the Awoonahs, had no more to say to the issue of a campaign in Ashanti than had the people of Zanzibar or Tripoli.

At one period, and I believe for a long time during the war, Glover had sanguine expectations of reaching the upper waters of the Volta before he turned his arms against the Ashantis at all. I have before me a letter to the Secretary of State, in which the tariff of English goods at Salga is given at some length, in order to show the economy which would result from making this city of Salga, or Salaga, the base against Coomassie, and Salga is fully 200 miles from the sea—200 miles of unknown navigation, filled with rock, rapid, and sand-bar.

To have carried out Glover's original plan of a campaign would have necessitated at the shortest estimate a period of three years, and a loss of life through disease, so great that it would be impossible to over-rate it.

It has been asserted that the operations carried out by Captain Glover were detrimental to the success of the main attack. This is simply absurd.

Glover's operations drew to the Volta a portion of the native aid, which might have been utilized on the right flank of the main column, and he depleted Cape Coast of Houssas at a moment when the Ashantis were close to that town, but the main attack would have been fought to precisely the same conclusion. Coomassie would have been taken and burned in the same time, had the Volta Expedition never existed.

What did not influence could not injure. I speak only of the final issues of the war.

This is a long digression—necessary, however, to a just conception of how matters stood.

In a few chapters further on we will see where the real path of the right attack lay. We will see how a force of three or four hundred Houssas, backed by the East and West Akims alone, could have struck a death-blow at the flank of the retreating Ashanti army as it stood pent in by the red tide of the flooded Prah, unable to cross the swollen river. There was a country rich in cattle and fruits to supply the wants of such a force to within two days' march of the Ashanti flank; and when we look upon the land, and on the scene of wild confusion which attended even the unmolested crossing of that Ashanti host, the question will naturally arise, Where, then, was the right attack?

The answer is a simple one.

The right attack was then at the camp of Addah, by the mouth of the river Volta, 200 miles from its true position.

It was late in the evening when I got away from Accra. My motley retainers, to the number of twenty-seven, formed a long straggling line some miles in length. The amount of rum they had imbibed in the day appeared to regulate their several positions in the line of march; thus, those who had fired their brains with liquor seemed bent upon moving as fast as their loads would possibly permit, while those whose legs had shown symptoms of collapse formed a wavering line far away in rear. The more sober few formed a centre, in the midst of which my empty hammock formed the most prominent object.

When one had been kept all day waiting, ready to make a start, but delayed hour after hour until evening had come, the sense of movement was so delightful that nothing short of actual exercise of the body could satisfy the impatient mind. And if ever man had been goaded by the conduct of rascal retainers, I had been that day at Accra. Every hour was precious to me. I had left the army of the Ashantis retreating on the Prah. I came down as fast as steam could carry me to this port of Accra, from thence to strike north to that same Prah, gathering or trying to gather the tribes on my way. To strike the point on the Prah where the Ashantis would cross was to march two miles to every one mile of theirs; nothing, therefore, but speed could bring me on their flank in time. 150 miles of dense forest lay between me and Prahsn—150 miles of broken bush, through the swamps and mud of which no white man had ever marked a footstep. It is not difficult, then, to understand the sense of impatience with which I saw the hours of my first precious day go by in idleness, and found myself baffled and delayed by the innumerable and frivolous pretexts of my drunken negroes. And now, at last, after that weary day of waiting, I found myself treading the sandy shore and plains of sun-dried grass which stretches around Accra; while behind, the native houses, white-walled fort, and the masts of the ships grew indistinct in the haze which gathered eastward as the sun went down.

I forced the pace through the sultry atmosphere, determined that the halt would only be made when the Seccoom river, ten miles distant, laid its broad current across our pathway.

Older Africans would have taken the matter more easily; they would have gone to sleep during the day; and when, in the evening, the final signal for departure would have been given by the drunken carriers, they would have lazily thrown themselves into their hammocks, and been fast asleep again ere the last wretched mud-hut of Accra had lain behind them; but to one fresh from the rapid movement, the early hours, and the ceaseless energy of dog-travel in the great pine-forests of North America, this African proceeding was hard to bear—hard when it

merely meant the irksomeness of useless delay, but *how*
hard when every minute was precious as gold to me, and
each hour lost seemed to double the already too long odds
against success!

The night came quickly on the heels of sunset—a feat
which it performs nowhere with greater celerity than on
this coast of Equatorial Africa. The sickly sunset gave
place to a dull lemon light which overspread the misty
line of the shore. The far horizon, where the sea and
shore met in a dim haze of surf-foam, looked weirdly
distant in the yellow light. A single tall palm, lofty and
leafless to its summit, rose in the nearer distance, its
slender trunk lost in the coming gloom of night, its dark
head of drooping leaves lying broadly out against the
lighter sky. There was scarce a breath of air to stir the
leaves, but the ceaseless surf broke against the shore with
the roll of storm in forest-trees, and the white foam
hissed on the sand as the receding waves died back in
the ocean again.

It was the last sunset I was destined to see for many
months. The forest I was about to enter knew no horizon
in its gloomy depths. Could I have foreseen that for four
months I was to grope my way, as it were, at the bottom
of an ocean, I might now have stayed the rapid pace to
take a longer look at the desolate sea and sky; for, whatever may be the work in which he is engaged, man loses
but little time if he pauses a moment to study the great
picture which nature unfolds before him when the sun
goes down.

Of all the many scenes which rise at times to my
memory of distant lands, those landscapes seen at sunset
come clearer and more frequently than any other.

There is a great ocean in the South o'er which the sun

goes down in times of storm in such a blaze of light, and amid such wild wind-rifted clouds, that the spars of the lonely ship which carries the wanderer are coloured crimson in the midst of a darkening sea. And there is a boundless meadow far out beyond the last white man's fence in America, where, in a solitude of grass almost as vast as the ocean, the sun sinks behind the earth in untold glory.

Often in that now far-away land I have drawn rein or stayed a paddle to look at the evening scene, and often after, these pictures came back again; but now, as I tramped the long line of beach, the wild sunset o'er the surf was of little moment, and in haste to reach the forest I held on without a halt.

It was full two hours after dark when we reached the low banks of the Seccoom. Close by, along the beach, stood the red huts of a fishing village; the river looked wide from the edge of mangrove bushes where the path ended. Some of the carriers had arrived, but many were still far away behind; I determined to camp on the nearer shore, and leave the crossing until the daylight.

The mangroves on the river's edge hummed with mosquitos. The higher ridge of sand, where the fishing village stood, might give us chance of a sea breeze, so we moved up the bank and made a camp in the sand; but the camp was a poor one, the night was close and sultry, the hum of insects filled the heavy air, the thunder of the surf broke on the ear in hollow mockery, for no breeze came from the glassy ocean which lay beyond the outmost line of breakers, and not even the noise of the waves could carry a sense of coolness in such a stifling atmosphere. The negroes swarmed out to look at the strange white man, and women and boys on all-fours jumped from the low arches of reeds which formed the entrances to the nearer huts. I lay in the hammock trying to sleep; but not even the ceaseless millwheel of the sea could lull me into oblivion.

All night long the mosquitos plied their trade, and when the shore-line to the east reddened with the coming day, it was time to quit the now dew-laden sand-bank and strike northwards towards the great forest.

We crossed the river, and found ourselves in a vast marsh : mangrove and broad-leaved lotus, reed, and sedge flourished above the mud and water, and fogs laden with reeking odours rose from stagnant pool and quagmire, as the sun drew off the night-dews from the earth.

Crossing this hot-bed of fever, I emerged on higher and drier land; the forest yet lay some miles distant, and only a few broken evergreen clumps clothed the rough, dry, grassy plain through which the pathway led. The sun poured down his fiercest heat; one would gladly have welcomed even the feverish forest, for shade there was none. At last, after mid-day, we reached a small croom. From a ridge between hills, the last glimpse of sea was visible to the south; around the bush was growing denser, and farther off the tall forest-trees rose against the north.

The weaker ones amongst my baggage-carriers lagged far behind. Again I forced the pace, walking all day in front; once or twice I tried the hammock, but the bearers went so slowly, the staggering gait was so irksome, that I preferred to move on foot along the burning pathway.

The small boy foraging ahead came running back with the news, " King Coffee Ahencora's messenger in village Sa." I reached the centre of the little street; the messenger approached. " King Coffee Ahencora, son of Queen Amaquon, was four villages distant on his road to

Accra to eat fetish (African name for rum-drinking), and
to concoct large schemes of war with the English chief."
That was the purport of the message. "Would I not
await him here, and not move further up the country?"
the messenger asked.

"No, I would not. Return to King Coffee Ahencora,
and tell him he is turning his back upon the enemy. His
place is on the Prah, and not at Accra. Fetish or no
fetish, let him await me at Eni-a-Croom, where he now
lies—go!"

The messengers departed, and I toiled on again.
Evening found us in the forest. Clouds were gathering
overhead; but the village of Accroman was near. At its
entrance another embassy from another king was awaiting
me. Quabina Fuah, of West Akim, was only two villages
distant on the road I was pursuing; he was also bound
on a highly religious rum-consuming expedition to Accra.
He begged I would "await him where I was, and not
toil deeper into the forest."

"Return to King Quabina Fuah; say to him that men
will call him a coward. The Ashantis are not within
100 miles of Accra; there are only women there.
Tell him that if he were only 100 yards off in the
forest instead of two villages distant, I would still go on,
because my face is on the right path, and his is on the
wrong one."

It was long before I could get rid of King Quabina's
messengers; they begged and begged that I would stop,
and finally they made show of going; but a fetish
drumming late in the night, in the forest outside the
croom, told me they were still in the vicinity.

It rained heavily that night; the rain came through
the reed thatch in many places, and the mud floor was

soon a puddle; but a nuisance greater than the rain came
in also. Millions of black ants came from goodness
knows where, and turned my provision-box into an ant-
hill; they revelled in sugar; they formed knobs on the
top of a Worcester sauce bottle; but a large tin of Australian preserved meat became their most formidable
fortress. They issued from its opened lid in countless
myriads. Grand ants and great grand ants might be
seen hurrying away with portions of this stringy Tas-
manian nutriment, as intent on the work of plunder as
though they had been a German *corps d'armée* engaged
on the highly-disciplined and scientifically-conducted loot
of some defenceless French city.

I was up at daybreak, and got away as soon as I could
collect my Accra rascals, whose rum, as evinced by the
fetish, still held out. We had not gone more than a
couple of miles before signs of the approach of King
Quabina Fuah became apparent:—A chief, followed by
some half a dozen "soldiers," preceded by two or three
fellows bearing war-clubs of elephant tusks strung round
with human jaw-bones; a leopard-skin basket for carrying a man at full length; more straggling soldiers; more
elephant-horns, blowing the war-note of the Akim king;
drummers, bearing large earthen and wooden drums,
adorned with many grinning skulls, the heads of which
they rasped with sticks; more men carrying two-handed
swords, provisions, and guns.

We were now in the forest; the path was very narrow.
King Quabina's men had been warned that the white man
was coming, and each chief advanced to shake hands;
but my invariable greeting was "Forward! you are on
the wrong path. Your faces should be turned to Ashanti,
not towards the sea." This proceeding not a little dis-

concerted them as I continued my rapid pace, and left them standing on the path-side.

A louder blowing of elephant-horns, and beating of skull-drums in the forest ahead, announced the near approach of the king.

There was a small village opening on the left. I ordered the Union Jack to be unfolded beneath a lofty palm-tree, supported on long poles it formed a temporary tent, its red, blue, and white crosses keeping off the now nearly zenith glare of the sun. Underneath this tent—for the flag was a full-sized ship's ensign, and covered a considerable area—I awaited the approach of my black king, whose army I hoped to lead to the Prah.

Piping, blowing, and beating, the rascals now appeared—a confused mass of chiefs, soldiers, umbrella-men, horn-blowers, mace-bearers, litter-carriers ; then three women, wives (his Majesty had left seventy-four at home), and, finally, the king himself. He was a sober-looking savage, fat and well greased ; neither the cares of his small kingdom nor of his large household appeared to cost him much anxiety. He spoke with a low and not unmusical voice ; his only garment was a silken robe worn round the body and across the shoulder. On his head he carried a small skull-cap of leopard-skin, the edges of which were cut mitre-like to represent a crown. On one side stood a pipe-bearer ; on the other, a negro carried a large two-handed sword with golden hilt. The drums rasped their loudest tattoo ; the horn-blowers blew their most elaborate flourish ; umbrella-men, skull mace-bearers, wives and interpreters filed off, and squatted on the right and left, and Quabina advanced to the foot of the tree beneath which I was seated. As he approached I rose, shook him by the hand, and motioned him to be seated. His stool, or throne of white wood, was now brought forward from the crowd behind, and on it the fat and somewhat frightened monarch seated his bulky form.

I lost but little time in the preliminary forms of African etiquette. I told Quabina of Akim that we had come to drive the Ashantis from his country; that they were now retreating from the coast, and that the English general had sent me to his trusty and well-beloved Fuah, to aid and sustain him in the coming war. The general's letter was duly read and explained to him. The proclamation issued after the skirmish at Essiaman was also interpreted; and, finally, I sketched the position which he of Akim might attain if he now seized this precious opportunity, and moved his soldiers on the Prah. This over, my black listener, whose big face wore a strangely puzzled expression during the palaver, asked leave to adjourn, and deliberate with his chiefs and counsellors as to what he should do.

They withdrew to a short distance, and remained in close conference for some time. After a little while they again approached my station, and announced that a decision had been arrived at. Quabina seated himself on his stool, and began his story.

It was a long one. It began with a grievance. What African tale does not? It touched on his services during the late war; the number of men he lost at Dunquah and at Jonquah; how ill-requited these services had been. (The rascal seemed to forget altogether that this fighting was for his own land.) It then came to the question of the present journey to Accra; the summons originally sent by Glover to bring him to Accra; the necessity that existed for his visiting that place in order to consult the chiefs of the Coast, and, above all, to do "fetish."

H

Was it not hard upon him, he asked, that Amon
Attah of East Akim, and —— of Crobo, and —— of
Addah, should have received so many good things from
the commissioners—got so much rum and rifles—and that
he, Quabina of West Akim, should be left out in the cold?
Then how was it that there were two English chiefs—one
at Accra, and one at Cape Coast Castle? I told him that
the chief at Accra was second to the chief at Cape Coast;
that it was true much rum, and powder, and guns had
been distributed at Accra; but that the great general at
Cape Coast could, if we wished, give ten times anything
that had been given at Accra; that he was the Queen's
general over all the Coast, and that his word should be
obeyed, and no other man's.

But while I spoke, plain as though it was written
before me, I read in the broad face of the negro king the
utter disbelief of what I asserted. True, at Cape Coast
there was a general; but here at Accra there was a captain, the fame of whose " dashes " of all the good things
of this life had already spread far and wide, and made the
outside negro mouths on the Birrum and the Upper Prah
rivers, water as they heard of them.

It was equally vain for me to point out to the un-
believing Fuah that the dash of 500 guns, boxes of
powder, and bars of lead which he had already received,
had come from the general at Cape Coast, and not from
the captain at Accra; for had not that dash been sent
through Accra, and therefore was it not evident that it
was given by the chief whose head-quarters were fixed at
that port? In fine, he most humbly begged my pardon,
and the pardon of the general at Cape Coast Castle, but
to Accra he must now go.

Stung by his obstinate refusal to obey the general's

order, stung still more by the frustration of all my hopes
of bringing this wretched king's savages to the Prah, and
doing aught to impede the retreat of the enemy across
that river, I tried to arouse some feeling of shame in the
cowardly nature of the man.

"You will find in Accra no soldiers, no chiefs. Yesterday the English captain quitted the place for Addah.
All men have left it; there are only the lame, and the
blind, and the women now dwelling there.

"What will be said of you? It will be told of you, that
at a time when all men were at war; when Fanti, and
Assin, and Denkera were fighting, that Quabina Fuah of
West Akim turned his back to the Ashantis, and went to
dwell with the women of Accra.

"Tell him," I said to the interpreter, "that I can never
go back; that I must go on. If he returns with me now, I
will make him the richest and most powerful king that
ever ruled in Akim. If he goes on to Accra, it will be to
cover himself with disgrace. Here I have only this bag
of gold, and these few rifles for personal use; but I have
as many at Cape Coast as I wish to send for. Let him
return now with me, and gold and rifles shall be his on
the Prah, and not on the coast.

"Here, I will give him these ten pieces of gold now
and these half a dozen Snider rifles, as an earnest of what
will be dashed to him if he comes now to his kingdom."

As I spoke, I took the American fourteen-shooter, and
discharged it fourteen times in rapid succession into the
palm leaves above us. The bullets cut slanting over
Fuah's head, and in a paroxysm of terror he ducked low
at every shot.

A roar of astonishment followed the exhibition of the
American rifle, and I went on. "Yes, I am going now

to Akim. Tell Quabina Fuah that if he comes with me, as the English general has told him, he will be a great king. His name will be told to the Queen of England as that of a brave man. He will be rich and powerful; but if he does not come, I will call him a coward to the English general, and his name will be the name of a woman."

Alas for the eloquence which anger had given me! All was of no use. Again the brute begged my pardon, and the Queen's pardon, and the pardon of the general at Cape Coast; but he must go to Accra to eat "fetish"— yes, he must go, if there was only one old woman in the whole town.

It would be useless now to try to put into words the sensations with which I listened to the miserable negro's final reply. As he kept ducking his head and begging pardon of all persons, I felt inclined to rush at him, and kick him from his stool of State; but not even then did I abandon the attempt to show him the foolish course he was pursuing, and to make him return to his kingdom.

I had brought with me a few bottles of champagne for use on any State occasion. A bottle for the Prah, when we would reach it; a bottle for fever when it would reach me; a bottle for Coomassie, or a comrade, if I should chance to fall in with one in this dreary forest. And now I broached the precious case, and I said to the wretch, "This wine comes from a far-off country; it is very precious. It is a thousand times better than the fetish rum of Accra. Drink it—" Liquor! At last I had touched his feelings. He drained a brimming pewter full, and rolled his eyes and smacked his lips.

Country, name, courage, all seemed no avail; but the

pulse of his honour did seem to respond, however little, to drink—no, not even to that. The light wine of France was but poor stuff, after the fiery poison of Holland or Demerara, and go to Accra he should and would.

I saw the matter was now hopeless. "Then I go north. I will tell all men that I met Quabina Fuah running away from the enemy." I left the palaver. The sun still blazed high in the heavens. Tired with the tiredness that came from toil given in vain, from a sense of a glorious opportunity lost, and of the first dawn of a hopeless task, I plodded the dreary pathway towards Akim.

As step by step, I went along, the full bitterness of how fruitless must be this long journey came full upon me. I would reach the Prah if health lasted, but the only king whose services could be of any avail to strike there the semblance of a blow against the army of the Ashantis had doggedly and determinedly refused every offer, and persisted in his intention of going 150 miles from the enemy to do "fetish."

One could have laughed at the utter absurdity of the situation. This was war; these were the poor downtrodden people whose cause we had come to give our lives for. Yes; I laughed as I walked along that afternoon, deeper and deeper into the big forest, and if in the laugh there was much bitterness and scant gaiety, the fact will not be wondered at; for there are few things more trying in life than the playing of a weariful game where life is the stake on one side, and where success is a contingency so remote that the odds against it are anything you please.

This was the fact I was now realizing; this movement on the Prah, easy of accomplishment as it seemed

on map, or minute, had almost everything against it.
This nation of West Akim, on which it hinged, was
unfortunately situated. Equi-distant from Accra and
from Cape Coast Castle, but receiving its first messages
and presents from the former place, the action of Akim
fell to the ground between the rival stools of the two
English Chiefs.

True, it was possible that time would show this stupid
negro of Akim on which side his real interests lay; but
unfortunately time was the last thing I had to spare, for
already its sands were running miserably short.

Well, never mind ! let the miserable negro go his way,
and do his fetish; there was still a shadow of a chance
left, that I would find some smaller king with a bigger
heart in Akim. Coffee Ahencora was only a day's
march from me. Perhaps he might have the spirit of a
man in him. His mother, Queen Amaquon, rumour
said, was a plucky old woman. A queen of Akim had
once fought the Ashantis, and beaten them. At Do-
downa she led her soldiers to battle with a sword in her
hand. Dahomy had its army of Amazons; the Fanti
women had already shown themselves to be vastly superior to their coward men. Perhaps something might be
done with the Queen of Akim Swaidroo.

Five miles' march brought me to the river Ahynsoo,
narrow, but deep; a cotton-wood tree bridged it three
parts across; the shoulders of the men just level with the
surface, acted like stepping-stones for the remaining
distance.

A little way off, on the north bank of the river, stood
the town of Koniako, and in its best house I took up my
quarters for the night. I had spent fully two hours in
that fruitless palaver with the coward Quabina that day ;

yet was there another palaver in store for me ere the night closed. The Chief of Koniako came to see me ; I received him in the little open court-yard, round which my house was built; the gallery at one end was hung with flint muskets, well polished, and brightly kept. "I have not come to talk," I said to them ; "we do not talk, we fight." "Ask him if he is ready to fight against the Ashantis ? I see they have guns here, and they are kept clean and bright; but a little of the rust of war is honourable. It will do them no harm. Are they ready to follow me to the Prah ? "

They answered, that they would talk it over with their king, who dwelt at Is Saban, one day's journey distant. "Talk it over with your king," I replied; "while you talk, we must act. You have had six months to talk over this war, and while you have talked the Ashantis have eaten up Assin and Fanti."

My host that night was an old and venerable-looking man. His name, Quassiquadaddie, was a curious one. His house was clean and comfortable, the walls plastered and whitewashed; the windows had small Venetian shutters; the court-yard was clean and tidy. A bed with four posts stood in the corner of the inner room.

Quassiquadaddie did the honours of his house well; more important still, he was full of valuable information of route and distance. "I am too old to fight now," he said to me ; "but I fought once too. I spent eight days in the bush." He appeared to be very proud of this eight days' feat in the bush, although it was probably the result of a severe beating from the Ashantis.

Next morning, the 8th November, I despatched messengers to Accra, to the European officer there, urging

him to use all the efforts in his power to make King
Quabina Fuah leave the place as soon as possible, and to
refuse him every dash and present. To King Ahencora
I also sent messengers to await my arrival at Eni-a-
Croom. This done, I held my way again towards the
north-west.

At the moment of my departure from the house of
Quassiquadaddie, I found I was one carrier short; I
asked the old man if he could get me another to fill the
vacant place. He brought forth his own son, a strong
young fellow, with a good expression of face. "This is
my son," he said; "take him with you. You will be a
good master to him." The young man took his load, and
left his town. He followed me for many a day afterwards faithfully and well. I called him Koniako after
his native village, and to the last, through many long and
weary hours, Koniako followed where I went.

Another day through the great forest. Never before
had I seen it as it was on this day's march. The country
was rough and hilly; the trees were of enormous growth;
matted and tangled creepers hung in heavy festoons from
the loftiest branches; a dense underwood covered the
lower forest. High above all, the gigantic cotton-wood
tree spread out summits so far above the eye and ear of
the traveller beneath, that the murmur of the breeze cast
down but a faint whisper, as it rippled the dark-green
wavelets of this forest sea.

Passing the village of Decaqua, set in large plantations
of plantains and palm-trees, I reached, after a long and
wearisome march, the town of Is-Saban, where King
Yowdowdoo, of Agoonah, held his court. I had walked
all day again; for the forest-path was rough and hilly,
and encumbered with the giant trunks of fallen trees;

nevertheless, the day's work did not end with the march.

Yowdowdoo had to be palavered; another attempt made to get the army of Agoonah to take the bush. It numbered, rumour affirmed, 2000 men; I will not go so far as to say, "fighting men."

Yowdowdoo was a very old and infirm man; so old, that he could not hear or see; so infirm, that he could not stand save with the assistance of two supporters on either side. He was seated in a chair; around him squatted a number of men of all ages; the outer circles, and the lintels of doors, tops of walls, &c., were occupied by women and children. The palaver ran the usual course, a course now becoming tiresomely familiar to me. Yowdowdoo was promised the same terms offered to the other kings—arms, money, regular payment. He appeared to catch but feebly the reiterated statements of my interpreter, Dawson, backed by those of his own linguist. He mumbled to himself at short intervals, and the only decided statement I could elicit from him was, "that he was a very great king; but too old to fight." He was not, however, too old to beg. At what age this faculty is left aside by an African monarch I have never been in a position to determine.

At last a torrent of rain put an end to the palaver, and Yowdowdoo was carried off to his mud palace.

The night came hot and sultry. Not a breath of air seemed to stir through the clay-built walls of Is-Saban. My hut was hot; its court-yard was hotter still. As if to show me the excessively warlike nature of the Agoonah nation, tom-toms, gongs, and drums were kept going all night, in close proximity to my house, and between heat and noise sleep was a mockery.

Morning brought another palaver with the mumbling monarch Yowdowdoo, and about ten o'clock I got away from Is-Saban, bound west for Eni-a-Croom, where lay that doughty chief, King Coffee Ahencora.

It was the 9th of November, hot and sultry as a zenith sun could make it. The forest steamed with noisome exhalations; the path was often knee-deep in fetid mud; but fortunately Eni-a-Croom was not distant, and little more than a two hours' march brought me to the River Aquarra, beyond which stream the village rose on a sloping hill.

We crossed the river, and entered a wide street which led up to an open space, in the centre of which stood a large densely-leaved tree. I sat down beneath this tree, for clouds had drifted suddenly across the sun, and large drops began to fall upon the red dusty street.

" Go to King Coffee Ahencora; tell him, it is my wish to see him at once, before I take shelter or food," I said to my interpreter.

I had taken Coffee by surprise. " Could I not wait ?"

" No; what I had to say to him must be said soon."

A bustle of black men followed this last message, and Coffee was declared ready. I rose and walked direct into the midst of a large crowd. The umbrella-men, horn-blowers, sword-bearers, and elephant tail-shakers, were sadly disconcerted by my sudden appearance, and the important military manœuvre known as " falling in " was most indifferently performed by the various members of Ahencora's household.

Coffee Ahencora was (relatively speaking) an intelligent-looking African. A bright black eye, shadowed with lashes which curved upwards from their lids, gave anima-

. tion to his negro face. His woolly, coal-black head was
covered by a handsome leopard-skin cap, barred with
finely-wrought gold, while a fern-leaf of the same metal
drooped backwards from the top.

Below the knees a circlet of gold and aggry beads was
strung around his legs; bracelets of the same description
were on his wrists. He wore a robe of silk and cotton,
which left bare his shoulders, chest, arms, and legs. He
sat in a Liverpool ship chair; two umbrellas of gaudy
native silk were held above his head; close beside him a
negro was squatted on the ground, whose sole occupation
was to keep assiduously wiping with a towel at the glossy
face of the king.

Again I opened the palaver, and spoke my story to the
end. I touched strongly upon the folly and infatuation of
Quabina Fuah. I showed the golden chance he had lost
of becoming a most favoured chief in the eyes of the great
English General at Cape Coast Castle. I told of the
stirring things which were being done at Cape Coast
against the beaten army of the Ashantis, and I urged on
my listener that now there had come to him a chance
never likely to come again; the chance of striking such
a blow against his most inveterate foes, as would cause his
name to be known from Coomassie to the Coast.

"Quabina Fuah has acted like a fool. Men will say he
is a coward," I said. "King Yowdowdoo is old and
feeble; you are young, your name has already been told
to the English General as that of a brave king. He has
written to you and to your mother who dwells at Akim
Swaidroo; there is the letter he has sent to you; obey its
orders, return with me to your country, and I will lead
your soldiers myself to the Prah."

It takes a long time to kill out a hope in some men's

minds; perhaps it is better it should be so, for things are
sometimes attained in the last struggles of a dying hope,
which defied the earlier bidding of more sanguine efforts.
I was yet but a new-comer at this African business.
I had but a fortnight's experience of deciphering an
African's mind on the broad page of his repulsive face;
later on, I came to know it but too well. Nevertheless,
I saw in Ahencora's countenance indications that my words
had some force with him.

When he replied to my harangue, the grievance showed
at once the drift of his mind. " A large present had been
sent to King Quabina Fuah, his near neighbour. No gun,
no rifle, no sword, or bar of lead, or keg of powder had
come to him, Coffee. Yet he was a brave king, and had
spent much gold dust, and lost many men in fighting the
Ashantis last summer."

"What, now, would I give him if he returned to his
own country, and collected his men to move towards the
Prah ?"

"I would give him a present equal to that sent to
Quabina Fuah : rifles, guns, swords, powder, lead, and
rum. Here were these four Snider rifles, and this box of
ammunition from my own private stock. He would have
ten gold pieces when we reached his town. His men
would be well paid, and he himself would receive for each
hundred men a monthly sum of 18l. Thus, for 500 men
he would get 90l. every month."

I saw he did not believe me : we, or those who have
represented England on this African coast for a century
back, had so often broken faith with the black man, that
he who now tells him truth is heavily handicapped; he
has an uphill game to play.

"When a white man speaks to a black man," I once

asked the best and most truthful African I met on the
Coast, " what does the black man think of what he is
told ? Does he believe it ?"

" No," was the prompt reply. " He thinks every
word the white man says is a lie."

And now as I recapitulated to this negro king what
would be done for him in case he obeyed my behests,
I saw at a glance that it would take many long days to
live down this distrust of the white man's truth, and to
convince these wretched people that new men had come
among them; for, alas ! the white man and the trader
had become synonymous words with them; and wherever
trade has sought the savage, be it in remote America or
innermost Africa, it has come to him in the guise of the
cheat and the liar.

The palaver ended with a kind of negative promise.
Ahencora would abandon his intention of going to Accra.
He would remain where he was until to-morrow, and his
reply would be given to me early in the morning; but he
was sorely puzzled, nevertheless. There had been many
good things given away at Accra, and perhaps he would
have got his share of them had he gone there. How hard
it was to make these West Akims look to Cape Coast
Castle instead of to Accra ! The fame of the rum
" dashes " had indeed gone far into the bowels of the
land.

Another day went by. Eni-a-Croom, or as it is often
called, Odoomtee, was a dull place to spend the long, hot
hours. Numbers of women came to stare at me; the
greater number of them were very ugly, some were very
old, all were dressed—well, the less we say about that
part of the programme the better. Still, there was one

peculiar item of dress, which, if not ornamental, was certainly useful—it was a bustle. Now, a bustle in connexion with other articles of costume is not matter for remark; but a bustle by itself, or nearly so, is, it will be allowed, a singular-looking garment.

The ladies of Odoomtee went as near reducing their costumes to the article in question as any people I had ever seen; yet the bustle had its use; astride upon it, with legs dangling down the mother's hips, sat the baby. The cotton cloth worn by the women passed round the infant's back, and kept it secure in its place, leaving the mother's arms and hands free to work as she pleased.

All day long crowds came to stare at me; through windows, round corners, by the edges of doors, black eyes and woolly heads popped and peered; whenever I moved towards the door of the hut, a rush was made in every direction.

The feeling of being stared at is unpleasant; reading, writing, or eating, the black eyes looked on. The owners seemed to be perfectly satisfied if they were let stare half the day. If there was a baby, it stared too, round its mother's side from its cradle on the bustle.

Thus passed the long day at Eni-a-Croom.

Early on the morning of the 10th, King Ahencora came to give his final answer. " He would return with me to his country. He had only to settle a dispute with the Chief of Dobbin, a neighbouring village on our way, and when that was done, he would be ready to continue his journey : perhaps I would act as arbitrator between him and the chief."

" What was the dispute about ? "

" About a goat." There had been an oath of friendship

between Ahencora and the Chief of Dobbin; the latter should have killed a goat on the occasion; this sacrificial rite he had failed to perform: hence the row.

I answered, that this goat business was a very weighty subject; so grave a matter, that it had better stand over until the termination of the war.

Ahencora now began a laboured explanation of the question. His linguists continually put in a word, or suggested another view of the matter, and all begged that I would use my influence to bring the Chief of Dobbin to a sense of his transgression. I still adhered to my opinion of the question, namely, that goats were goats, and sheep were sheep; and that this being the case, mutual concession could best advance the interests of all parties.

Ahencora seemed delighted with my logic, and triumphantly exclaimed to his retainers a kind of guttural "Hah," which I interpreted, "I told you so."

There is nothing that an African will so quickly believe as that which he can't understand. Tell him the truth plainly, and make him fully understand what you say, and he won't credit a word of it; but speak to him in mingled parable, and nonsensical platitudes delivered with an appearance of great gravity, and he will greedily swallow it all.

On the present occasion I "dashed" him four Snider rifles, and a box of ammunition, and he announced his intention of starting the following morning.

Another weary day of frequent visits, childlike questions, and more begging on the part of King Coffee passed. The black night hid the black faces at the windows and doorway, at the corners and the chinks, and

I went to sleep with the prospect of a start on the morrow; but it was idle to hide the fact, that this past twenty days of toil had told on strength and health.

The wish for food had grown less and less. A lassitude never before known seemed to cramp one's every energy, and the sleep of night brought with it, in this horrible forest, no sense of rest or of refreshment.

At last, on the morning of the 11th, after very vexatious delays, I got away from Eni-a-Croom, bound for Akim Swaidroo. The king and his retainers were also on the road. The march was only an eight-mile one, yet it taxed my strength to accomplish it; a raging thirst consumed me, the road was deep in mud, and the hammock could make but poor way; so I toiled on, on foot; whenever we reached a stream of water, thirst compelled me to drink deeply. What was this strange feeling? it was only some passing ailment I thought; I will walk faster and shake it off. So I bent to the task, and held on through the vault-like forest.

The great trees seemed endless pillars on an endless road. I reached the outskirts of another Croom. It was Dobbin. I sat down under a rough porch while a room was being got ready. The dry heat of the skin grew more intense; the thirst became greater; a weary feeling overspread every limb and muscle, and then came the pain, that seemed to be everywhere at once—the dull, dead, sick pain of African fever. I had got it.

CHAPTER VIII.

THE fever increased with the night.   I lay on a door with a blanket spread upon it, in the corner of a very small hut. I drank incessantly, and was always thirsty; the fingers seemed ready to burst into flame, the throat was parched, the mouth was filled with an odious taste, the bones and joints became painful, the head reeled with a sickness worse than that of the sea.   When sleep came, it brought terrible visions, so that one would say, awaking, "I will not go to sleep again."

Another day passed.   The fever relaxed its hold for a few hours, and the time for quinine had come; I took fifteen grains.   The morning brought a return of the fever, and another night passed in the same wretched state; again the morning came, and again the disease lightened, and again I swallowed a huge dose of quinine— this time twenty grains.

During the day I lay weak and listless, without tasting food.   Still on this day, as well as on the previous one, I was constantly pestered by my negro allies.   Coffee Ahencora came several times to visit me, and each time had some fresh request to put forward.   The Chief of Dobbin came with a sheep, a chicken, some yams and plantains, and this offering was made at a time when I could not look at food.

Again the evening brought back the fever, and the

I

long night passed in sleepless pain. A candle stuck into a bottle dimly lighted the miserable hut. When the night grew still, and the jabbering noises of the negroes ceased, loathsome things came forth and prowled my room. A large black rat ran several times across my wretched bed as I lay tossing in the throes of this fell disease.

There was not a soul with whom I could speak. I knew nothing of this fever or its treatment. I was alone in the midst of savages, and I saw my strength ebbing like a fast-receding tide; but this was not the worst pang I had to endure during that last sleepless night in the hut at Dobbin; for that evening a native runner had come to the town from the west, bringing news that made my mind feel more bitterly the helplessness of my position than the body felt the fever which laid it prostrate.

The Ashantis, the native said, had attacked Abracrampa on the 5th, and, after two days' fighting, had been driven back with great loss. They were now in the dense forest west of Mansu, retreating towards the Prah, and here lay I, sick and helpless, at the very moment when health was most precious to me. Bitterly indeed did things seem to run against me! Had all this toil and labour and exposure been for nothing? Was it all to end in this miserable hut in the depths of the dreary forest?

The night was wearing towards the day. I raised myself from the low, hard board, and staggered across the room. Three nights had sufficed to rob me of all strength. I leant against the narrow window, and looked out upon the sleeping croom; above, the stars were clear and bright; on the tops of the forest-trees a white streak of fog hung suspended over the earth.

Oh for strength to go on! anywhere out of this horrible spot. Better to be in the great forest itself than in this hot and filthy hut.

I have said that I knew little or nothing of this fever. I had left Cape Coast Castle in great haste, and had none of those things which could tempt a sick appetite to food. For three days I had not eaten; yet now, as I leant against the mud window, the cool air of the night seemed to revive me, and I felt that if I could get once more into movement, I might shake myself free from the grasp in which this fever held me.

Day was beginning to dawn; the forest-tops towards the east showed against a lighter background. I called my servant Dawson, and told him to arouse the hammock-men, and tell them I would start when it was clear daylight. For the first time they were ready quickly, and I was carried from the miserable hut, in which I had lain for three days, into the forest, which was dripping with fog and the heavy dews of the morning.

They carried me all day; once indeed I had to alight to crawl up a hill too steep for the bearers; but I had to sit down upon the ground ere half the ascent was made; and when the bearers reached me with the hammock, I saw by their faces that they thought I was in a bad way. It was a terribly long day; the path was wet and tortuous, and the trees hemmed it in so closely that there was frequently a hard struggle to get the hammock between them. At times the men staggered and nearly fell, and many a time I was knocked against the branch or trunk of a tree, or caught by the thorny tendrils that hung festooned across the track.

As usual, the fog and mist of the morning cleared off in the forenoon, and the sun came out in fiery brilliance, falling in fretted patches on the muddy pathway.

Yet, with all the heat, and knocking and dragging through the forest, I felt better as we went along. It was the first day's work I had given the hammock-bearers, and they were tired long before evening came.

I had two relays, eight men in all; but the narrowness of the path only permitted two men to work at a time. The hammock was slung on a long bamboo pole, the ends of which rested on a negro's head ; in the more open roads, or along the sea-shore, a small cross-bar of wood is placed at the ends of the pole, allowing two bearers at each end; but in the forest paths this is impracticable, and only one man can walk the narrow track.

In the middle of the day King Coffee Ahencora overtook me. I told him to pass on in front, and get to Branqua; I would follow slower; but my men grew utterly tired, and the march was at a snail's pace. Ahencora, finding that I did not appear, sent back his leopard-skin basket and two stoutest carriers for my use. It was shaped something like a coffin, or a long, narrow cradle without a hood. I fitted into it with some difficulty ; the two negroes raised it on the top of their heads with some exertion, and set out at a rapid pace through the forest. It was no easy matter to fend off the branches as the carriers ran ; but it was a great relief to get rapid movement again, even though it were in this original manner, high on the heads of two tall and powerful negroes.

As we reached the outskirts of Branqua, the carriers broke into a faster run, shouting as they went. Ahencora's drummers stood along the track, rasping the skull-adorned drums. The people of the town filled the street, firing off their flint guns, and springing like monkeys through the smoke of the discharges, and I found a house ready for my reception, with a bed laid over with native cloths of rich workmanship; for the old men of Branqua had still faint recollections of a white officer being once in their town—a man whose memory they valued still.

In 1826, Laing had made this town of Branqua on the steep hill his camp against the Ashantis at the time when Macarthy lost his army and his life in the woods of Wassaw. Laing was a man of that stamp which England has produced so often, that she has long since ceased to remember them.

He had sought in earlier days to reach the famed city of Timbuctoo—the city of golden houses and wondrous wealth—but had failed through the jealousy of the natives, and had to return to Sierra Leone from Falaba. Then came the Ashanti war of 1824. Laing retreated from Branqua to the coast, and tried again the work of exploration—this time with a greater success and a greater disaster. He reached the famous city of Timbuctoo to find —what so many explorers have found in Africa—that the tale of a golden city shrunk to the narrow limits of a mud-built croom.

He found Timbuctoo, and lost his life.

Well, this is not to the purpose of our story, save that in this town of Branqua, which I now entered, the first white man since Laing had left it just fifty years before, I found the memory of a white man was a thing that differed widely from that ideal conception which the negro forms when he trades with the subjects of the " King of Liverpool " along the coast.

Another night of fever, and the morning found me weaker than I had yet been. I managed to scrawl a few lines in pencil, and to send it to Cape Coast Castle, and then I set out again for the north. The track was now better; but the hills which divide Assin from Akim here reach some 700 feet above the sea, and our march was slow and tedious.

In the evening I reached a small plantain village of some five or six huts. I was utterly worn out by the long, hot day in the hammock, and was glad to find even this poor resting-place; but for the first time during five days I managed to eat.

I now dreaded the approach of night; it was so certain to bring with it the fever. Oh! the memory of these nights! The sense of utter darkness that came upon one when the long hours rolled by, and the hideous noises of the African forest sounded at intervals like echoes from some other world; for this grim labyrinth of trees, so silent under the sun, gave forth strange sounds at night; and as the small hours drew on, the shrieks of the sloth rang with dismal distinctness from the echoing vaults and mighty aisles of the forest, until over the fog and the vapour the light of day struggled upward, the dripping trees seemed shrouded in smoke, and the night was at an end.

That night, as I lay at the huts of Boonsu, the shrieks of the sloth sounded incessantly through the drip of rain; and once the earth shook as with the thunder of Niagara. A huge cotton-tree in the neighbourhood of the village crashed to its base, and the forest seemed to echo with a mighty thrill, the fall of one of its giants.

A year has gone by since that time, and yet the hideous reality of these nights of fever seems sometimes to live again. When the eyes closed in utter weariness, the brain still saw: the gloomy arches grew to endless length; the fog hung over a vast, dreary landscape; an endless, all-tiring toil oppressed the mind, and one woke to hear the scream of the sloth, the drip of the rain on poisonous leaves, the rustle of rats in the palm-thatched hut.

The picture is not too darkly coloured; the reality was more horrible than this pen of mine could make it. Men will read these lines who know this fever as I have known it; but few can associate its terrible hours with the scenes of utter wretchedness and the long nights of lonely misery to which I have linked it.

Eight miles north of Boonsu stands the Akim town of Accassie. I was carried into it some time after mid-day, scarcely able to lift my head from the hammock pillow. Yet was there a custom and a palaver to be gone through; for here dwelt Darco, a chief of high renown, at whose command moved 250 of the greatest cowards in all the wide realm of Fear.

It was only months afterwards that Darco (met here for the first time) showed the full measure of his coward heart. Now his subjects fired their guns, and blew their horns, and cut their capers, as though they feared no man on earth. Darco himself spoke the usual African speech:—" He was a great warrior. He had been wounded in the battle of Dunquah; his brother had been lost in the same fight. What had I to give him?"

He showed the scar of a slug on his elbow (rumour affirmed that the other traces of the Ashanti shot, borne by Darco, were of a nature to lead to the supposition that he was engaged in making a masterly retreat at the moment when the enemy fired). When pressed as to turning out with his men, he, however, declared that he was not a West Akim, but an East Akim, although his town of Accassie lay almost at the extreme west of

the Akim kingdom; but I was too weak to argue the
point with him, and, being anxious to reach Akim Swaidroo before evening had come, I once more set out on my
weary road.

A couple of hours slow marching brought us to the
outskirts of Akim Swaidroo, the goal of my long journey.
The capital of King Coffee Ahencora, the base of my
operations against the Ashantis, was no better than the
rest had been. A clay-built, forest-girt croom, over
which foul kites wheeled, and fiery sun-light streamed,
and naked, or nearly naked, men sat on their heels along
the house-walls.

I reached this goal of my journey, scarce a living
shadow; but, as I lay down in a small hut, in an inner
courtyard of an Akim's house, which had been got ready
for my reception, the sickness that comes from fruitless
labour was perhaps sharper than the fever.

I lay for three days in this inner yard of the house at
Swaidroo. My hut was eleven feet by seven in size; a
large opening at one side served as the door, and let in
the heat by day and the damp by night. Akim Swaidroo
had been so often destroyed by the Ashantis, that its
people deemed it folly to build any but the poorest kind
of huts, and they were so contrived into inner yards, and
little enclosures of mud, that if the enemy was as safely
excluded as the air was, the place must have been impreg-
nable. The yard on which my hut opened was very small
and very close; a drain of green water ran from it, and
at night the odours were foul and nasty. Altogether, it
was not the place one would select for a man lying ill of
fever.

But this poor body of ours stands queer things ere it
gives up that spirit of which it is the cage. At Swaidroo,

judged by all the rules of science, I should have died!

On the day following my arrival, Queen Amaquon came to visit me. She brought with her a large bevy of the ugliest women I had ever seen. The dress of the queen and the court at Swaidroo was peculiar. Queen Amaquon wore a necklace of beads, a stick, and a scant silk cloth; her ladies were attired in a costume which, for simplicity and economy, I can safely recommend to the talented authoress of that charming book, "How to Dress on Fifteen Pounds a Year," since it might almost be achieved on as many pence. Nearly all the ladies had babies on their backs; there were no men. Here and there in the crowd, one occasionally saw a woman with the peculiar eye and eyelash of the better-looking Akims—an eye which I have nowhere else noted on the coast or in the interior.

I was introduced in turn to the queen's daughters, to her "fetish woman," a large wild-eyed lassie, and to several other ladies of rank and quality. As the ceremony was gone through, the lady presented stepped up into the hut, and shook hands with me as I lay on my couch; and it not unfrequently happened that the baby on the bustle at her back, looking out under her elbow, and beholding a white man in such close proximity, would howl in terror at the sight.

At first, but a limited number of women came into the inner yard of my hut, and the queen alone entered the hut itself; but as the interview went on, the outsiders grew bolder, and at last the yard and opposite hut were filled to overflowing.

But the event of the day was the statement of the queen's illness. I had tried to turn her mind to war. I had spoken of the warlike deeds of a former queen of

Akim—of how, sword in hand, she had led her soldiers against the Ashantis at Dodowa, saying, " Osay has driven me from my kingdom because he thinks I am weak; but though I am a woman he shall see I have the heart of a man ;" but the effort was useless.

"That was all true," she said; but the point which grieved her most was this illness under which she suffered, and on which she wanted my opinion.

Now I was sufficiently ill myself to make the diagnosis of an old lady's ailment by no means an attractive pastime. I doubt if at any time I should have entered into such a question with the slightest interest. Nevertheless, the situation was not without novelty, and African fever was not so totally depressing as to shut out the ridiculous aspect of finding myself Physician Extraordinary to Her Majesty Queen Amaquon of Akim. Seated on a low stool she began the statement of her case. There is no necessity to enter now into the symptoms. They consisted of the usual number of pains, in the usual number of places, at the usual number of hours; but their cause and cure ?— ah, that was the question !

" Did I consider," asked the queen, " these symptoms could have had their origin in poison ? She had visited Cape Coast Castle four years before this time, and ever since her return had suffered from this ailment. Perhaps she had been poisoned by the people of the Coast ?"

I inquired " if she had consumed much rum during that visit to the coast ? Rum was a subtle poison." The soft impeachment of having tippled freely was as freely admitted; but it was a mistake to suppose that rum could harm anybody. " Surely, among the medicines which I carried, I must have some drug which would restore her to health."

Now my stock of drugs was not a large one. The specifics in use against fever were precious, they could not be spared.

Had I any more? Yes—a bottle of spirit of sal volatile. Her Majesty bent her nose to the bottle, and the hut shook with her oft-repeated sneezes.

The whole court was in a commotion. The fetish woman demanded a smell; the royal daughters grew bolder; the ladies pressed in from without, and the queen declared, when sneezing left her at liberty to articulate, that she felt immensely relieved. It was some time before order could be fully restored.

The heat meantime became stifling, and the press of women seemed to threaten suffocation. " Tell Queen Amaquon," I said to the interpreter, " that to-morrow I will see her again. Meanwhile I have to cure myself." With difficulty I got rid of the lot.

But in Akim Swaidroo there was no rest : all day long came Ahencora, or his chiefs, to shake hands, ask frivolous questions, and beg for some additional present. The owner of the house, Chief Kru, used to enter the yard of my hut, and, standing in the centre, make a profound bow to me as I lay in the open doorway, accompanying his obeisance with a "How are you?" and instantly ejaculating without pause, or wait for reply, " Quite well, thank you." Kru was under the belief that " How are you? Quite well, thank you," was the proper English salutation, and seemed never tired of showing his complete mastery of English tongue by using this mysterious sentence. I knew Kru for many months after this time, and his manner of salutation was always the same. It mattered not whether one was in fever or in health, the " Quite well, thank you," of Kru was ever an assumed fact.

But though King Ahencora came so frequently to pester me, there was one point on which he was always mute. Do what I would, I could get from him the promise of no fixed date by which he would have his men ready for the field. I had sent from Eni-a-croom a requisition for 200 guns, and stores of lead and powder for the army of this Akim king. I had got off 100 carriers from Swaidroo, the morning following my arrival, with orders to proceed to Dunquah on the main road between Cape Coast Castle and the Prah, there to receive over the arms and munitions requested. I had kept faith with Ahencora in all that I had promised him ; but still no trace of hurry could I find—no appearance of taking the bush on the part of any of the inhabitants of Akim Swaidroo. Ahencora's morning report was invariably the same, " He had sent to collect his men." " But three days have passed since I arrived here," I said ; " six days since I warned you at Eni-a-croom that all haste was necessary, and yet not one soldier has come in. Your people sit idly in the streets, and you come daily asking for another dash."

On the night of the 19th November, exasperated beyond words by the continued hesitation of the king, I sent to him a message to say that I wished to see him. He came, attended by an interpreter and two men. "Now," I said, " I have sent for you to give you a final message. Tell me at once in what time you can collect these men ? How soon will you be ready to move on the Prah ? "

The wretched negro tried many a side issue ; but I held him to the question of time.

" Not for six days after the arrival of the arms and ' dashes ' from Dunquah would his men be ready to move," was his answer.

"And these arms cannot be here under six or eight days from this time. You have arms and ammunition lying here in these huts of Swaidroo," I said. "You can get 200 or 300 men from the surrounding villages. Give me these men within two days from now, and I will lead them to Faysoo on the main road. It will take us four days to reach it; the Ashantis will not be there before that time. It is true that they will have many more men than we will have, but we can lie safely in the forest and ambuscade the road on which they are marching. It is true that I am lying here sick with the fever of the country; but I will be better carried in a hammock than in this hut. Will you give me these 300 men?"

He could not.

"Well, then, listen to what I have to tell you. To-morrow I will set out for Mansu. The Ashantis are still near that place: the English are there too. I will reach Mansu in four days, and join men who are ready to fight. I will tell the English general that I found in Akim only women and cowards. I have no more to say to you."

Seeing that I was now determined to leave him, the king became frantic. It was a move he had not anticipated. It would upset his most cherished hopes. If I stayed with him, the "dashes" would come; the money-box was there; if I died, as seemed likely enough, the money-box, the arms I carried, would all become his.

For fully an hour he begged me not to go. I was inexorable.

"Give me these men, and I will stay."

"In ten days they will be ready."

"Too late! I go to Mansu; when you are ready I will come to you again: I cannot remain here doing nothing, until I die of this fever."

Seeing it was useless to persist, he went away; but only to try another means of detaining me. A "dash" of gold-dust or rum to the bearers enlisted them on Ahencora's side, and at daybreak next morning they were in a state of high mutiny. The Accras declared they would not go to Mansu; they were engaged only for Akim. I had them brought before me; their eyes showed the orgies they had been enjoying. They all began to speak at once, and jabber and gesticulation filled the narrow yard.

Pappho, a native of Calabar, a fellow built like a small bull, spoke in Calabar, Ogi, and Coast English. The whole lot were far too drunk to listen to anything save a stick, and fever interferes sadly with the force of that reasoner's logic. In the end, they all rushed from the yard declaring that they would not go to Mansu. I now tried getting one or two of them together, and wording their interests separately. What a business it was! They were so many great overgrown children, with the passions and vices of men and beasts.

At last, after hours of difficulty, I got them together; and amidst a scene of gabbling, shouting, and fierce tumult, I succeeded in evolving from the troubled elements the semblance of a start. But, just as the loads were being taken up, the Queen Amaquon appeared on the scene, leading the ladies of her court to another interview.

"I was about to quit Swaidroo. Would I not leave her some of the precious medicine?"

"I was about to leave," I answered, "because her son would not go to war; but I would not be far distant. When he sends me word that he is ready to fight—that his men are in Swaidroo—then I will return."

"But the medicine—would I not leave her some ?"

A happy thought seized me. "Bring hither that tin case." The faithful Koniako (whose burden was always the large load which held the triple treasure of gold, drugs, and papers) approached. I unlocked the case and took from it a small box. The box held two tiny globes. I held them up before the eyes of the court. "These are very precious," I said; "their fame is spread far over the earth : the characters engraved on this box are ' fetish' symbols of great power—all pains and aches and ailments are said to vanish before the use of these small globules."

The old queen stretched out her hand, her eyes, and the eyes of all her ladies beamed with excitement. I placed in her hand the coveted treasures. "What are they called ?" she inquired.

"Cockle's Antibilious Pills," I replied, with a face of profound gravity.

Again spoke the interpreter, "The queen wishes to know when she is to take this great medicine?"

"When she lies down to sleep," I replied.

"And will she be quite well when she wakes again ? " asked the interpreter.

"Perfectly," was my reply.

At last I was free to go. The old queen toddled off happy, and my struggling cortége of semi-sober bearers was soon swallowed up by the vast forest. All this reads pleasantly enough ; nor was it even without its sense of fun at the time. In looking back since, at the toil and sickness of that time, and of the months that followed it, I have often thought that the utterly ridiculous scenes through which I went had kept intact the thread so nearly broken.

At Accassie, the residence of Darco, a fresh mutiny broke out amongst my bearers. Plantains were plenty: the damsels in an African croom are quite of the same way of thinking as the maiden in Longfellow's excellent, but somewhat idiotic, Alpine song, and Pappho and his brethren, doubtless, considered that their woolly heads were far better engaged in responding to such an invitation than in bearing the burden of hammock or baggage-load.

So in this street of Accassie there was another fight. I again tried the separate system. I caught sight of Pappho grinning from the doorway of the house in which dwelt the temporary object of his affections. Being unable to go in pursuit of him, and knowing full well that he could play a kind of hide-and-seek game for hours in the rabbit-burrow yards and mud-huts of the croom, I told my servant to approach the bull-necked native of Calabar and inform him that I wanted to speak to him, and had a dash to give him. Coercion was now perfectly hopeless; the men were dispersed all over the town, except Koniako and my personal servants.

Pappho approached me with an expression of face that reminded one of a very bold boy, or a setter-dog coming to his master's heel after "running in to shot."

"Pappho, you are a person of sense, a man of judgment" (Africa, that land of lies, must be responsible for these words of praise); "you are very different from these foolish people of Accra. You have the excellent character of the men of Calabar. Here is a dash for you; you will get another when we arrive at Mansu. Go now to these foolish men of Accra, and tell them that, if they take me to Mansu in three days, I will give them a dash of five shillings each."

Pappho, utterly astonished at hearing that he possessed a high moral character, felt, I think, bound to sustain the novel rôle.

It might have been that he looked upon himself in a new light; conscience, it is true, told him that he was as great a vagabond as the rest, but the white man had distinctly placed him upon a higher level, and it was possible that conscience, after all, had been sadly maligning him. Is it not upon some such principle that the thief is set to catch the thief, and that the whilom poacher makes the best gamekeeper? At any rate, Pappho went to work in earnest. He hunted up the various bearers in the several billets in which they had located themselves, and before many minutes I was again in movement.

The evening came down in a torrent of tropic rain; the thunder rolled over the lofty tree-tops, the large drops hissed through the upper branches, and pattered against the broad-leaved plants beneath. The hammock became saturated with water. At last, just as night began to close over the forest, we emerged upon the little clearing of Boonsu, and in the same hut that had lodged me nine days earlier, I found again a shelter and a rest-place.

The last was wanting. Off and on, this fever had still clung to me; one day I was better, the next weaker. I had actually lived for nigh fourteen days on my strength, and on the cud of bitter disappointment. Neither had proved nourishing; but there was this difference between them, that the strength lessened, and the bitter cud, chew it as one would, remained always the same.

The situation, as I had time to review it that night in the hut at Boonsu, was briefly this. No tidings whatever had reached me from the King of Akim, Quabina

K

Fuah. He was still, report said, doing a vast fetish at Accra.

My second king had, it is true, returned to his country, but had utterly failed to produce even a score of soldiers.

Youdowdoo, of Agoonah, Darco, of Accassie, were ready to beg, to borrow, to lie, or to steal, but not to fight.

The Ashantis were still, my despatches said, somewhere in the dense bush west of Mansu, making their slow way to strike the main line between the last-named place and the Prah.

For myself, fever had brought me nearly as low as it could; but the forest was ever so many times preferable to the stifling crooms. The hut at Swaidroo, with its eternal visitors; its close, fetid atmosphere, and, above all, the ever-present sense of delay and disappointment, seemed to forbid the chance of recovery. Out in this big forest, all poisonous as it was, there was life and movement—the life of the great trees, the movement of brooks and rivers.

Lying at Swaidroo, I had measured English strength against African delay, and, finding it would not last to bridge that dreary gulf, I had determined to set out again for Mansu, see again the game of war, get a glimpse perhaps of the Ashantis, and trust to action and occupation to shake off this leech-like enemy.

From Essecomah (one long day's journey from Mansu) I would send messengers to Fuah, Youdowdoo, and Ahencora, giving them a final chance of meeting me ten days later at Accassie, to attempt again the flank march on the Prah; meantime this move to Mansu would place me *en rapport* with the movements of the main body and the true position of the enemy.

Striking south-west for Boonsu on the morning of the
21st of November, I reached, after a long and toilsome
journey, the town of Essecomah. Many villages lay on
the track, and a pile of human skulls and bones close
by the entrance to Essecomah showed a battle-field of
Ashanti war some twenty years earlier.

The day had brought the usual vicissitudes of heat and
wet. In the forest, near the village of Faissoawya, the
messenger I had despatched a week earlier to Mansu met
me with despatches from the general. The chief of the
staff had drawn a neat diagram representing columns of
troops pressing back the Ashantis on the Prah, while
another set of columns were seen advancing along the
Birrum, to strike the enemy's flank and rear at Prahsu.
These last were supposed to be Akims.

A paragraph urging haste was added.

How easy and how nice it all looked on paper! These
things generally do. I sat down on a fallen tree, and
penned a short reply :—

" The paragraph urging haste is not likely to avail
much. With these people twenty days are as one day,
and haste has no meaning for them."

On the following day I sent out many messengers—one
to King Quabina Fuah at Accra, one to Yowdowdoo at
Is-Saban, another back to Ahencora at Swaidroo. All
urged different pleas to the same end, namely, to meet
me at Accassie on the 1st of December with what men
they could collect. I offered a rate of pay far more liberal
than anything that had yet been given at Cape Coast. To
Quabina Fuah I sent the following letter.[1]

When the four messengers had departed I stretched

[1] See Appendix, No. 9.

K 2

myself on my bed, and enjoyed a sense of returning
health, to which I had long been a stranger.

Looking up through the little window at the foot of
the bed, the eye caught the tops of the great cotton trees
that stood on the outskirts of the village. A fresh breeze
moved the lofty summits, and its rustle, falling down
through the sun-lit air, carried a sense of profound rest
into the mud-walled hut. The fever had gone, the wasting
heat of blood and brow had cooled; and though the battle
of the past ten days had sapped and wasted strength hopeless to seek again in such a climate, yet I felt that the
game was still alive, and another throw for success was
possible. "If things go well," I wrote that night,
in a journal filled now with brief but curious records, "I
may be at Accassie on the 2nd, at the head of some
hundreds of Akims bound for the Prah."

Early on the 23rd I set out for Mansu; the forest was
very dense, and the path a mere bush-track, overgrown with creeping plants, and filled with fallen trees.
Pappho worked like a horse, apparently bound to rise
equal to the character he had received at Accassie. He
and his comrades dragged the hammock through
trellis-work of bush, and across quagmires, which gave
forth a sickening odour as the feet of the negroes broke
through the slimy crust. There was not a croom or
hamlet on all this long forest-track. The evening drew
near, and we were still far away from Mansu; the bearers
were utterly worn out; a thunderstorm came rolling up
across the sun; the lightning flashed; the rain hissed
down in drenching torrents; the bearers staggered along.
I had taken a guide from Essecomah, as none of my band
knew the road. "Was Mansu near?" It was a futile

question. An African has two distances—one is "far," the other "not far;" one is applied to anything over three days' journey, the other to any distance that can be traversed in less than that time.

Many an hour have I spent in working out this difficult problem of distance with guides and spies; my only method was comparison. Is from such a place to such another place, longer than from such a place to such a place? When one got to know the roads and villages well, I found this a tolerably correct method of arriving at an estimate of distance. Mileage, as may be supposed, was a hopeless matter with these people.

"How many miles is it to such a place?" asked a friend of mine one day of a native.

"Twelve miles without a load, but twenty with one," was the reply.

On the present occasion all that could be extracted from the guide was that Mansu was not far; but as he had asserted this early in the day, only a frail reliance could be placed on the statement.

Seeing that the bearers were quite worn out, and being as wet as water could make me, I determined to walk the rest of the way. I staggered a good deal in the beginning, but after a bit got on better. The rain was refreshing, though the wet branches dashed unpleasantly against the face.

We entered at last large groves of plantains which had run wild. Surely this must be the approach to Mansu.

The sun was setting, the rain still poured from clouds whose "ragged rims" were edged with gold. Soon we came upon a ruined croom; a hundred different creepers grew over the wreck of what had been a flourishing village six months before. The Ashantis had burned the

place on the preceding June, when they had occupied
Mansu.

Mansu could not now be far distant. The sun set,
darkness fell quickly on the dripping forest. Still going
on foot with a strength which seemed to increase with
each step, I came to the bank of a swollen torrent.
Pappho's bull neck formed an excellent saddle, and again
we went on through the gloom.

Another rushing stream, foaming hoarsely among rocks,
lay before us ; the men formed a line across it, holding on
to each other, and steadying the now untiring man of
Calabar as again I bestrode his shoulders. More dark
path, more stumbling over roots and rocks, and wading
through deep pools of water, and at last the sounds of
voices came from the gloom ahead.

The dark trees ended, there were lights of many fires
on a sloping hill; dark figures moved before them, and a
sentry sang out a challenge as we advanced. I knocked
at almost the first hut on the roadside. A white man
came to the door. The light of the fire burning on the
threshold lit up a well-known face.

Worn, like every white man's face on that dismal coast,
with hollow cheeks and long-drawn chin, and with eyes
that looked so widely and wildly at one.

Gallant, gentle, true-hearted Huyshe! I first met him
many years before in another forest as filled with health
and life to man, as this was with disease and death. We
were twin toilers then as now on the same road. But on
this path the partnership was to end. Here to-night, as
we sat in the hut at Mansu, the goal was the Prah; men's
minds at that time did not venture farther. Well, we
will both reach the sacred river. But to you, my poor
fellow, it will be the end of life's journey !

CHAPTER IX.

IN the hut at Mansu I heard the news of the past twenty days. How eagerly I listened to the story of Abracrampa, that fight I had so long predicted. Then came poor Wilmot's death at Dunquah, and in it I recognized the foundation for the Akim's story, told as I lay in fever at Dobbin, that he had seen the body of an English "Field Marshal" carried into Dunquah.

"And where were the Ashantis now?"

"Somewhere in the dense bush north-west of Mansu. Various parties had sought them, but all to no purpose. The scent had been lost ere the game could be run to bay; and here at Mansu to-night were Wood's regiment and the 2nd West Indians. Farther up the road at Accrofoom lay the Kossohs and Gordon's Houssas, with Home and the Sappers. It was only seven miles or thereabouts to the front, and if rumours spoke truly, the Ashanti army lay but a mile or so to the west of this advanced post beyond the Oku river, where it skirts the plantations of Accrofoom.

While we spoke of all these things, somebody came to the hut door with news that a despatch had come down the road from Home. I crossed over to Wood's hut, and found him reading a letter. "There is a large Ashanti camp a mile from here," wrote Home; "I will attack it at daybreak to-morrow. I expect you to breakfast."

I went back to the bearers, who were squatted in groups, tired by the day's exertions. "In an hour's time I want to start for Accrofoom," I said to them; "It is seven miles farther on. You have had a long day and are tired; but you shall have five shillings each when you get to Accrofoom. There were a few murmurs, but the "dash" was strong, and all was settled. Then, going back to the hut, I told my companions what I had done. They were both of the same way of thinking, and at 9 o'clock, p.m., we set out for the front.

There were three of us, Huyshe, Reade, and myself. Of Huyshe I have already spoken, and Reade's name is one that claims more than a passing mention. Winwood Reade was on the coast as a newspaper correspondent; but that term would only express in a very limited degree the nature of the man. It is true that any man may act as correspondent to a newspaper, no matter what may be his rank or his literary status; but in Reade the *Times* possessed something more than a correspondent. Few men possessed a deeper insight into African character, or a truer knowledge of African history and topography than he did. Few men had struggled so often or so long with the deadly climate of this West Coast, or carried away from it a weaker frame, a stronger mind, or a richer store of observation and experience.

In Africa men usually lose mental power to a greater degree than even physical strength. But Reade had preserved intact all the great energies of his brain, and the genius which seems hereditary in his family had suffered no eclipse amid the sufferings of disease and the privations and many hardships of weary travel; but his knowledge was almost too extensive for the work assigned to him, and in his case the temptation to overstep the limits of a war correspondent was great. To record, not to teach; to tell what has been done, not to say what should be done; to picture the fight, the march, the bivouac, the life, the death of the soldier; all these are within his province.

Many men wonder why the most successful war correspondent of our times should have been a private soldier. There is no necessity for much astonishment. It is simply because he thoroughly realized the nature of his work, and did it; leaving to others the work of organization and the plan of coming campaign.

Winwood Reade knew as much of Africa as any living man. To a soul imbued with that noble spirit of romance which is the true incentive to all adventure, he added a mind richly stored with varied gifts.

It was about two o'clock in the morning when our tired bearers crept with slow footsteps into the town of Accrofoom, and came to a halt in the sleeping camp."

I lay under a large Fetish tree, amid a vast variety of boxes, casks and bags. Houssas, Kossohs, and West Indian soldiers were mingled indiscriminately. The dew was wet and heavy as rain, and the leaves of the Fetish trees dropped on the cheerless bivouac. In about three hours' time day began to break faintly through the dense clouds of vapour, and the great trees of the forest loomed out tenfold giants through the smoke-like fog.

The Kossohs, Houssas, and West Indians began to unroll themselves from the baggage, and form up into a. straggling line. I cast an eye along this curious parade, and the glance was by no means reassuring. There did not appear to be more than 250 men of all ranks and nations. With something less than the usual amount of

jabbering (it is a vulgar phrase, but the only one that
fitly expresses Africans talking to each other) we set out
for the Ashanti camp.

Down the slope into the big dripping forest; over the
Oku river, on the broad trunk of a fallen forest king, and
up an incline again, until voices sounded ahead of the
leading scouts. The voices were Ashantis calling to
each other. The scouts now went through a vast amount
of pantomimic gesture; the Kossohs ran about through
the bush as though they would play the very devil with
anything they came across. Fortunately for themselves,
they did not come across anything more formidable than
several old and decrepid Ashanti stragglers, whom they
invariably shot, beheaded, or mutilated. It was no easy
matter to keep up with these light-limbed savages; for
the strength which excitement had given me began to
ebb as the morning sun grew higher, and the deep slush
and mud of the forest told heavily against my fever-
weakened frame.

Whenever there was a moment's halt I sat down,
regained a little strength, and then ran on again, as some
new alarm took us bounding in some fresh direction.

At length a small Ashanti boy was taken alive. From
him some definite information was obtained; but just as
his interrogation was proceeding, another alarm occurred
close by, and everybody dashed off in wild confusion. I
powdered along as best I could, a Kossoh following close
at my heels, with the Ashanti boy grasped by one hand,
and his Enfield rifle held at the " trail " in the other; as
we ran a shot rang out behind me, the bullet passing
within a few inches of my side, the smoke and rush of
lead nearly staggering my already uncertain footsteps.

Was it an Ashanti in ambush ? Not a bit of it. It

was only my brave Kossoh, who had let his rifle off as he ran in my footprints. After kicking him, until I found that he rather liked the exercise more than I did, we ran on again, and finally emerged upon a vast open camp, studded over with plantain leaved lean-tos. It was the largest open space I had yet seen in the forest; all around the same low huts spread into the encircling woods, and fires smoked in many places. Here and there dead bodies lay on the ground; a few living skeletons yet lingered amid the huts; the stench was foul beyond description. Some wretched Ashantis lay at the fires, unable to rise from the ground.

The Kossohs running loose at once killed many of these wretches before we could stop them. It was impossible to restrain these merciless savages. Once I caught a ruffian with his sharp sword raised to sever an old man's head from his body. The Ashanti saw the impending blade, and bent his head to receive the blow. I chanced to be close behind; a kick and a blow sent the Kossoh flying along the track, and saved the old man's life; but saved it only for a moment; for, coming back the same trail a few minutes later, I found the headless trunk lying by the wayside.

As we entered into the vast camp, the smallness of our numbers became apparent. In the intricate forest the party had separated, and the portion with which I found myself did not number more than seventy men.

It was now nearly midday. The Ashantis had vanished. There was nothing to be done but to return to Accrofoom. But where in the meantime was Accrofoom? No man could tell. Every body pointed in different directions. Home alone guessed right. At last we fell in with two more Ashantis: their lives were spared; they said the

fallen tree over the Oku river lay in another direction
altogether from the one we were pursuing. Again we
marched through the huge deserted camp, and again came
to a stand, uncertain how to proceed. At length the
small Ashanti boy, who had been taken early in the day,
volunteered the information that we were going altogether
wrong ; that he had often been to Accrofoom in the last
few days to gather plantains for his master, and that he
would show us the right way if we would spare his life.
As it had not entered into our calculations to take it, the
promise was easily given.

Retracing our steps in an opposite direction, we reached,
after a toilsome march, the tree-bridge over the Oku,
and got back to Accrofoom, exhausted by incessant movement and constant disappointment.

Looking back now on that fruitless day, and remem-
bering the immense camp in which we found ourselves
with only seventy or eighty wild Kossohs at our backs, it
seems a fortunate thing that we did not find the foe we
sought ; for assuredly there could not have been less than
20,000 men in that huge camp, and into this hornet's
nest we would have run, had not Amonquatier betaken
himself a few marches nearer to the Prah on the day
previous to our coming.

I went back to Mansu that evening for the triple purpose of getting a few days' rest, seeing a doctor, and
being near the 100 Akim carriers who had gone to
Dunquah for the arms and munitions promised to Coffee
Ahencora.

Futile as my mission to Akim had proved, useless as
had been my efforts to raise even a single fighting man,
or stir to the faintest show of enthusiasm the cowardly inhabitants of Swaidroo, I nevertheless had not abandoned

the scheme, nor relinquished the intention of going back to Akim.

I had reckoned the speed of the Ashanti retreat, and calculated that twelve days would still elapse before they reached the Prah. If Ahencora had even 400 men at Accassie, we might strike from there to the main line at Amponsie Quantah ere the Ashanti rear-guard had passed that place.

My health was now fully on the mend; three days' rest would bring back much strength, and then I would be off into the big forest again to Essecomah Swaidroo, and I hoped—the Prah.

A small sketch will best put before the reader's mind the plan I now meditated.

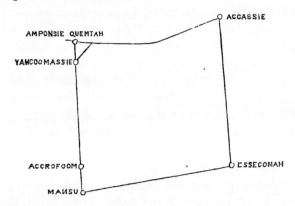

Mansu, Essecomah, Accassie, and Amponsie Quantah formed the four corners of a large square, the sides of which would be about twenty-five miles long.

The Ashantis retiring leisurely from Accrofoom by Yancoomassie, would be off Amponsie Quantah in ten or twelve days. I would march from Mansu to Essecomah, and thence to Accassie. Here, gathering up all the Akims

I could find (it will be remembered that I had appointed this place as the rendezvous for Ahencora's men, and had written to Quabina Fuah at Accra, urging him to join me there), I would move on Amponsie Quantah without delay.

It meant a long and arduous march by tracks deep in swamps and water; it meant, in all human probability, only disappointment and vexation at the end; but it had the fascination which ever attends a well-designed plan, and which often hides from us the feebleness of the material which is to work it to a successful issue.

In England the material which we call man never fails ns. Be the scheme ever so hazardous, the chances of fight ever so much against us, the soldier or the sailor never fails us. Nay, often, when the plan is faulty enough; when incapacity and official bungling have accumulated against us odds overwhelming; when the venture has become desperate, out from the chaos of bad plan or no plan comes the British soldier or blue jacket victorious and conquering, rolling back by his matchless courage the odds multiplied against him, no matter what may be the astuteness of his enemy or the incapacity of his chief.

We have got so much into the habit of relying on our own men that this question of the dependence to be placed on our material is never entertained by us their leaders; but if any English soldier wishes to know the novel feeling of being in command of a body of men on whose courage or discipline it is impossible to calculate for the duration of a single hour, let him go to Africa, and, enlisting an army of West Coast Negroes, take the bush as their commander.

Three days passed away at Mansu, the 27th November

came. I made arrangements to start on the morrow for
Essecomah and Accassie. The arms and powder had
been sent to Ahencora, and with it another message to
that king to be at Accassie on the appointed day.

Suddenly all this was changed. Almost in the middle
of the night of the 27th there came a despatch from Wood
at Sutah (now the advanced post) giving tidings of a
repulse which he had met with at Faysoo from the
Ashanti army encamped there under Amonquatier. He
wrote briefly and in haste. The Ashantis had almost
surrounded his column, his men had retreated in confusion, baggage had been lost, ammunition was running
short. He wanted men and munitions to be sent to
him immediately. The commandant at Mansu was ill of
fever; I went to his tent. "Would I take command of
the party up to Sutah?" "Certainly I would. When
will it be ready to start?"

"In an hour," was the reply, and in an hour's time I
was striking north again for Mansu along the high-road.

I had with me twelve West Indian soldiers, sixty Cape
Coast volunteers, and sixty carriers with rifles and rocket
ammunition.

After a forced march we reached Sutah at half-past
eight o'clock a.m. The scare was over; rifles, pouches,
jackets and bags were being distributed again to the
valiant Kossohs and Houssas, who had cast them away
into the forest in paroxysms of terror on the previous
evening. A tent, a hammock, a case of shell ammunition,
some pots of jam and tins of *pâté*, and half a dozen
bayonets still remained in the hands of the enemy.

The pursuit had been carried on with great vigour by
the Ashantis. For four miles the invisible warriors had
poured through the bush, driving well along the flanks of

the Kossohs and Houssas, who several times became totally unmanageable, firing their guns into the tree-tops as they rushed wildly, five or six deep, along the narrow track.

There were many and various opinions afloat that evening at Sutah as to what caused the Ashantis to stop the pursuit. Some said night-fall, others fear ; for myself, I have always thought that the case of condiments from Fortnum and Mason stopped the pursuit. A flock of geese saved Rome ; but it was reserved for a *pâté de fois gras* to save Sutah.

Never before had such a prize been taken by an Ashanti army. Fancy the face of Amonquatier, as he dipped his fingers into the jam, and flourished a Bologna sausage over his head in his camp at Faysoo. Truly were these things trophies of victory over the white man !

Absurd though this may appear, it has nevertheless more than a germ of truth in it. Months later, when the King of Ashanti wrote to Sir Garnet Wolseley on the subject of the threatened invasion of his country, special allusion was made to the capture of condiments or other luggage at Faysoo as proof of the prowess of the Ashanti arms.

After the Kossohs had received back their arms, and recovered their wonted spirits, they determined to avenge the defeat of yesterday. And how do you think these brave fellows did it ? Swore solemn oaths of vengeance ; asked to be led at once against the enemy ? Not a bit of it. They proceeded in a body to the guard-hut, took by force a helpless Ashanti prisoner, and, bringing him into the forest, proceeded to hack him into pieces with their swords.

News of this outrage came to us as we lay in a large

hut of plantain leaves in the middle of the rough clearing of Sutah. Some officers at once went to the spot, and found the wretched Ashanti still breathing, but at his last gasp. He was horribly mutilated, the Kossohs had vanished, and all attempts to trace the perpetrators were utterly fruitless.

The repulse at Faysoo told plainly enough that the Ashantis were in no mood to be trifled with. Their 20,000 fighting men would have made short work of any few hundred Houssas, or Kossohs, or West Indians that it was possible to bring against them. Before this affair at Faysoo a term had arisen as to the proper tactics to be pursued against the army of Amonquatier. It was called "prodding." They were to be "prodded" here, and touched there; but after this little experience "prodding" became at a discount; and "touch" was voted a dangerous game, until there was at hand something better than the West African to touch the Ashanti with.

Finding that there was no prospect of an advance from Sutah for some days, I again turned my attention to West Akim, and on the evening of the day of my arrival I returned to Mansu.

About a mile from the latter place there was a small clearing, where, previous to the Ashanti invasion, had stood an Assin village. It was nearing sunset, bright and tranquil; the great forest looked its best, for shafts of golden light shot through its vast arches, and many a gleam lighted up the red-leaved orchids, and the great grey stems that rose so silently and so loftily above. The clearing was bright with flowers—flowers ran wild over the ruins of the mud-built croom; a hundred creepers had twined themselves over the overturned houses, and the mounds were rich in white and yellow blossoms, and

L

great crimson petals hung along the path. The village had borne the name of Appiagoe, or the "Lover of Life." It was well named.

Under a broad-leaved tree on the wayside there was a tent; as I came up the narrow path, a well-known friend came forth to meet me. I had some dinner at the tent door, and then we walked together into Mansu.

"You look weak and thin, old fellow," said my friend to me, as we parted at the foot of the hill on which the camp was built. "Take care of yourself. Don't do too much; it is the best service you can render to the Expedition."

Poor Huyshe! These were the last words we were ever to speak together. He went back to the flower-covered Appiagoe, the "Lover of Life," to continue his road survey to the North; but death had already set its seal on him, and the road which he was then surveying to the Prah was the pathway to his own grave.

On the 1st of December I set out once more for Akim. It was night-time over Mansu. The camp was fast asleep. As I passed out from the huts, I heard close by the voice of a man in pain; he was calling to his servant, but no servant came in answer. I took a light and went to the hut from whence the voice proceeded. Stretched upon a rough bamboo-frame lay an officer; the fever was on him, and from the dry, swelled lips came forth the sounds which I had heard. A cup which had contained some drink lay overturned beside him, his negro servant lay asleep in a far corner of the large hut; and for all he cared, the sick man might rave as he pleased for drink or assistance. I got him a cup of water with a lime-fruit in it, and set out on my journey.

We soon turned off the road into the deep forest, the night was very dark, and morning seemed yet a long way off: now and again, a deep shriek issued from the unseen depths; it was the sloth, whose cry ceases when the dawn approaches. Half an hour brought us to the banks of the Oku river, foaming and tumbling down its bed of rocks. The crossing-place was deep and rapid, and we had to wait for daylight to effect the passage.

"How many hours to daylight, Dawson?"

"More than one hour, sir."

"How do you know?"

"By that call in the forest; it is never heard after five o'clock."

More than an hour to wait. I was sleepy, so, spreading a cloak on the rock by the edge of the rapid, I lay down to sleep. The trees began to drip; the forest sent forth its poisonous vapours, but I slept soundly on my rocky bed to the rushing of the river. We crossed the river when daylight showed the ford, and held west at a rapid pace. It was the same rough, tangled road I had crossed just a week before; but a few days' rest had brought back more strength than I had deemed possible in such a time, and when I stopped to take food, the hammock and bearers were far behind, and full seventeen miles lay between me and Mansu.

Striking north from Essecomah, and passing Benin, Yamoura, Faissoanza, and Kukissoo, I reached the town of Accassie on the afternoon of the 3rd. Along the forest-path nigh the entrance to the town, I found Coffee Ahencora's drummers waiting to rasp their skull-drums in my honour, and some half a dozen rascals bowing and gesticulating in the road. This proceeding I felt sure indicated delay and excuses of some kind, and, without any ceremony, I sent the lot flying into Accassie with a message to their master that I did not want "Custom," or drumming, but fighting-men for the Prah.

My arrival was followed by the usual palaver. Ahencora was indeed present, but his followers did not number thirty men. The fortnight which had elapsed since I had parted from them had been thrown away, and despite warning, promises, threats, and entreaties, Accassie was destitute of soldiers.

It is needless to repeat what I said to Ahencora and his few chiefs. To call a king a coward, and to tell his nobles that they were so many old women, would be deemed strong language out of Africa; but, alas! it seemed perfectly identical whether one spoke of these kings to their faces as brave and mighty soldiers, or as cowardly rascals.

I have been thrown among many peoples, tame and wild, all the world over: robbers, rascals, scalpers, worshippers of sticks, stones, and devils; but never had I met a race so utterly hopeless to move by any influence recognized by man, so perfectly defiant in their apathetic animalism, to all that the toil and ceaseless endeavour of one man can achieve with other men.

Summoning Ahencora at once before me, I set to work at the hopeless task. "There was no further use in talk; enough, too much, had been already said. True to my word, I had come back again to Akim—where were his soldiers? I had marched more than 150 miles, seen the Ashantis retreating along the main road, and come back again only to find the Akims as I had left them—like women and cowards.

"Here, now, was what I had to say to him. I would start for Amponsie Quantah on Friday. He had talked long enough of his soldiers. Let him produce fifty men on Friday, and I would take them to the Prah. If these men were not forthcoming, then I would quit Akim for ever, and seek some people who would fight."

"Yes," said the valiant Ahencora. "The fifty scouts would be ready, and he himself would start on Saturday and overtake me ere I reached the Prah."

So this seemed settled. Now came the proof of Akim energy and Akim bravery. "See," said Ahencora, "my soldiers have caught two Ashantis." And, as he spoke, two wretched Ashanti slaves were produced. They had been captured by a party of Akim scouts near Amponsie Quantah, a few days earlier; such, at least, was Ahencora's account of it. The scouts had come upon a party of four, they shot two, these prisoners were the others. One of the men killed carried on his head a wooden box which contained two human skulls; the skulls of Ashanti chiefs who had fallen in battle, or perished by disease, and now were being carried to Coomassie for interment.

The prisoners, two very wretched-looking youths, were now examined. On the previous Thursday, Amonquatier had quitted Acumfudie for the Prah with the bulk of his army. Supplies of ammunition had been received from Coomassie; an order had come from the king to recall the entire force from Fanti-land; and there were rumours of war on the north-western frontier, where lay the kingdom called Gaman, and the city named Bemkatoo.

A tremendous down-pour of rain put an end to palaver and examination, flooding out the motley concourse from the little square yard into which my whitewashed hut opened. •

The chief of the scouts, a shrewd-looking little Akim,

took off the prisoners and the box of skulls. "Let him keep these prisoners safe," I said to the king, "I may want to examine them again." Ahencora promised they should be taken care of; but their fate was only too certain.

Ashanti prisoners were rare things in Akim, and the first "custom" at Swaidroo was the last of the prisoners. Of that, however, I was not told until long after.

On the 5th of December I set out for the Prah—alone.

Neither Ahencora nor his fifty scouts appeared. Quabina Fuah was still at Accra; not a soldier had come in from the dotard Yowdowdoo; the valiant Darco, of Accassie, averred that he belonged to East Akim, and could not think of fighting in any other part of the world. Unfortunately, East Akim lay many days' journey from the nearest Ashanti, so Darco, returning there, could rest in peace and plantains.

Striking nearly west through the big forest, I reached a town called Apradie in the evening. Here I was overtaken by messengers from Ahencora, assuring me that their master would reach Akrapon on the 8th, with all his followers.

"Very good! Go back, and tell Coffee Ahencora that if he and his followers are not at Akrapon at the time promised, I will give to Quabina Fuah, now on his way from Accra, the whole of the rifles and supplies of ammunition sent originally to Ahencora."

Next morning, at daybreak, I set out for the west, and, after a long and very fatiguing march, reached the ruined croom called Akrapon. I was now close to the main road at Amponsie Quantah. The track was very bad; it led over steep and rugged hills, through many swamps, and across numerous rivers, over which the forest closed in gloomy arches. Hammock-travel was, of course, impossible, and I had toiled all day through swamp and thicket, until evening found me thoroughly exhausted.

The next day came, and with it came my old enemy the fever. All day I lay in a ruined hut, until night came to shut out the big spiders and many-shaped creeping things which careered along the crumbling mud wall, and dodged in and out of the innumerable rents and fissures around me. This African fever has many methods of attack; sometimes a fever of sleeplessness; sometimes one of heavy, apathetic slumber. To-night at Akrapon it was the sleepless phase, and all the night I lay listening to the forest cries, and to the drip of the leaves as the dense fog rose towards morning, to blot out the starlight and the tree-tops.

Next day I rallied, the fever went, and with a dose of quinine sufficiently strong to deafen a dozen men, I set out for the main road at Yancoomassie, only a few miles distant. As I was about to start, Ahencora arrived; he was covered with mud, and full of protestations of bravery. His soldiers were " all coming in," he said.

Soon some sixty or eighty rascals came slouching in; some with flint guns, so long in barrel that the muzzles stood several inches higher than the man; others with hair twisted into ringlets to denote their amazing bravery; others carrying loads of green plantains, and balancing above all, the gun and the shot-bag.

They were a grand host! and, despite the remnants of fever, I laughed a hearty laugh as they defiled past to the sound of Ahencora's horn, and took up their quarters in the ruined croom.

" ' These be your soldiers,' Ahencora ?"

" Yes."

" ' Ay, in the catalogue they count for such.' " And Ahencora nodded his negro head in happy acquiescence.

I left the " army," and reached Yancoomassie after sunset. The advanced companies of Wood's regiment were there. Wood was four miles south at Faysoo. No white man had yet reached the Prah, but two West Indian soldiers had gone on, and returned with news that no Ashantis were to be found on the banks of the river. Some straggling parties of Ashantis were still supposed to be in the neighbourhood of Prahsu, either on their own side of the river, or on ours.

Early on the following morning, the 9th December, I sent my trusty servant, Dawson, back to Ahencora at Akrapon, and pushed on myself along the main path to Amponsie Quantah. Here I waited for the band of Akims which Dawson was to fetch from Akrapon by a path which led direct to Amponsie Quantah.

Noon came, but no Akims. I turned down the path leading to Akrapon, and sat down to listen. At last, I heard sounds of men approaching through the forest, and out into the sunshine, that glinted on the stream of water on the banks of which I sat, came my army. I counted it as it passed the ford; eight-and-twenty men—" and the king ?"

" Oh ! the king is behind at Akrapon. He is very lame."

" All right—we will go on without the king ;" and I turned my face to the north along the road to the Prah.

It was not a pleasant road to travel. In all my wanderings I do not think I had ever trodden such a road as this road to the Sacred River. Many dead bodies lay along it in advanced stages of decomposition. The stench at times was horrible ! One had to spring across the fearful mass of putrefaction that lay on the narrow track, and run for some yards ere breath could be inhaled, so deadly, so sickening was the odour. And as one rose at the jump, crowds of foul flies sprang from the dead body and buzzed around the living one that had so suddenly disturbed their repast.

I halted for the night at Acumfudie, and my army found shelter from the evening thunderstorm, in the plantain huts of the Ashanti camp.

In another Ashanti lean-to I lay down for another night of fever. This Prah seemed to grow more difficult, as bit by bit I drew nearer to it. The thunderstorm rolled away, the stars came out over the forest, an incessant jabber filled the air. My army of twenty-eight men made as much noise as two brigades of British infantry, and I lay on the ground, drawing those short sharp breaths, rapid as the respiration of a broken-winded horse, which tell that the fever has for a time clogged the machine of life.

At last the camp-fires died out, and all was quiet. This short and laboured breathing, with a sense of smothering, was a new phase to me of African fever. The skin was dry and burning, and seemed to rise in lumps, to be rough and rugged under the touch. What was this? I asked myself. What horrible form of the ills that flesh is heir to, was this new kind of fever?

There had been much smallpox along the road; the Ashanti camps were full of it; even that very day, as I came to Amponsie Quantah, a wretched Ashanti had come forth from the forest, where for ten days he had lain sick, hideous with the fell disease. If this was it, then the game was up, and everything had been to no purpose —all my hopes were ended.

I got a match, struck a light, and looked at the rough skin with anxious eyes.   No; smallpox had not come to add its loathsome name to the long catalogue of African suffering and disease.

I took a huge dose of quinine, and lay down again. Towards daylight the drug conquered the disease, and though hardly able to stand when morning came, I felt that the Prah at least was safe.

I set out, as usual, leading, for not one Akim would stir until I left the camp, and then the army straggled after in twos and threes.   By the ruined sites of Barraco, Damsam-su, and Asampanya, over the fallen trees that crossed the path, alternately walking and being carried, I drew near at last to the Sacred River.

The forest was now a vast Ashanti camp, rotting bodies lay on the pathway ; a wide space opened before us, and the ground dipping abruptly at its further edge, disclosed the Prah.   It ran, a turbid, mud-coloured mass of water, deep and swift, between the sombre forest shores. Nothing else spoke or moved in the picture, and the low rushing of the river made monotonous sound in the intense silence.   This deserted Ashanti camp on the high river bank had over it a sense of vast desolation.

Beyond the river lay the great forest of Ashanti, dark, silent, and mysterious.

On the nearer shore, raised high above the water, a fast-decaying skeleton lay on the land, with arms outstretched before the head, and fleshless hands pointing forward—a grim finger-post, set up by Death, to point the road to Coomassie.

CHAPTER X.

I HELD a review of the "Army" on the high bank overlooking the river.

From its numbers, as well as from the condition of the
Ashanti soldier alluded to at the close of the last chapter,
my force realized all the essential requisites which go to
form what is called a "skeleton corps." The parade
showed one Akim chief, three Assin scouts, and twenty-
six Akim soldiers. The arms consisted of twenty-three
Enfield rifles, and three flint guns.

Upon attempting a *feu de joie,* fully twenty out of the
twenty-three Enfields declined to go off; upon being duly
hammered, recapped and re-adjusted, some eighteen or
nineteen still refused to comply with the wishes of their
owners—the reason of this was soon apparent. Enfield
cartridges rammed bodily into the rifle, bullet foremost,
became even more harmless missiles than the iron stones
of the Ashantis, and it was in this manner that my army
had prepared their arms for war.

It took some little time to get matters right, and to convince the braves that the rifle was a better weapon than the
flint "Dam" gun, carried by the Assin scouts. With a view
to correcting the bad impression entertained of the capa-
bilities of the Enfield, I caused many shots to be fired
across the river, at marks on the opposite side. The
bullets went, goodness knows where; for, treated on the

principle of the "Dam," in the matter of elevation, the
Enfield invariably poured its deadly fire into the summits
of the highest cotton-wood trees ; while the effects of
the flint were always visible to the excited auditory in the
water of the river. At last I took the weapons, one by
one, from the hands of the Akims, and fired at a log far
away down the river, which projected from the water;
then, as the bullets cut the water close about the tree
stump, the Akim cries of wonder rose loud and strong,
and the flint was left very far behind in popular estima-
tion, but the climax of the review consisted in the per-
formance of the fourteen-shooter. This weapon, fired with
great rapidity across the river nine or ten times without
reloading, had a marvellous effect upon the "Army."
Stopping at the ninth shot, I would lay down the rifle as
though I could have continued the amusement for a
lifetime, had I been so minded; then quietly resuming
the weapon again, three more shots would still further astonish the wondering Akims. "Ho," would
jabber forth some sceptic brave in his native language;
"that is all, there are no more shots." "Indeed, my
friend, you are wrong. See—" and another would splash
into the river, until the last doubter grew silent, and the
magic weapon became a first-class "fetish."

When the firing ceased, and the forest echoes became
silent again, some Akims averred that they heard at
intervals the cries of men calling to each other. We
listened, and from up the river came sounds plainly
enough. What were they? No one knew; but when,
four weeks later, the English camp was formed at
Prahsu, the explanation was found. About a mile
higher up the river there was another crossing-place in
the forest; at the Ashanti side the sick and wounded had

been left, while the army of Amonquatier moved on to Coomassie. It was the shouting from this camp, alarmed, doubtless, by the firing of my braves, which they heard. From whatever cause the shouts proceeded, the Akims soon changed their demeanour. Many had been swimming to and fro in the rapid current; this pastime was now abandoned, and all lined the high bank to listen, but the forest echoes remained unbroken.

A glance at this swollen river and its forest shores told the story of the disordered state in which the Ashanti army had reached the Prah. They had tried every means of crossing the flooded river; two huge cotton-wood trees had been felled from either bank, in the hope that their branches interlacing in the centre of the stream would have formed a kind of bridge for the soldiers to cross upon; but the trees did not meet, and between their separated tops ran a current of great strength. It was afterwards known that many Ashantis had essayed to swim this dangerous chasm, and had paid with their lives the penalty of their rashness.

Day and night thousands of knives had been employed hacking out other huge cotton-wood trees into large deep canoes, and by means of these the greater portion of the Ashantis had finally succeeded in crossing over.

All things showed the traces of hurry, confusion, and pressure. Everything around told the story of the opportunity which had been lost, never more to be found; the chance of overwhelming this frightened host during the last hours of its stay in Fanti-land. Nor could I look upon these signs without experiencing more than a pang of disappointment. Here was the goal to which my steps had long tended, through so many weary hours of sickness and miles of constant toil; I had at last reached it

—reached it to find that the most sanguine pictures I had
often drawn of the stricken state of the Ashanti army at
the Prah had been more than realized in the actual event.
But the army which was to have struck a blow at the
enemy thus placed, where was it ?

Far away by the Volta mouth, preparing for a bootless
and futile struggle with unknown, and until now unheard
of, tribes beyond the Volta.   Croboe and Aquapim carried
away to another struggle; East Akim kept idle at home
at Kebi; West Akim led away to Accra by the " dashes "
of gold, and the scent of rum; while I, after a bitter
fruitless toil through swamp and forest of fully 300 miles,
found myself worn down by repeated fevers, almost alone
by this red river—the first white man whose eyes during
this war had caught the gleam of the water beyond which
lay the dark forest of the Ashanti-land.

It is very easy to be wise after the event, but in this
case there had been no want of wisdom in the beginning;
one month and six days earlier I had set out for this spot
by a long circuitous route; and, at the Prah, on this 10th
December, I realized how feasible was the scheme for
whose fulfilment I had toiled so hard.

I do not hesitate now to affirm, even with the experience of all that has happened since, that had I possessed
but one eighth of the force of disciplined Houssas taken
away to form the camp at Addah, or had even the
miserable West Akim chiefs been free from the influences
of Accra allurements, I would have more than realized the
most sanguine hopes of my mission.

In a memorable phrase, which caused much sensation
in England at the time, the English general spoke of the
" humiliating position " in which he found himself;
without troops in the presence of the retreating enemy.

It is not too much to say, that had he possessed the native levies lying at Accra, or had the operations which had their base at that place been directed on the Prah and not on the Volta, the Ashanti army of invasion would have left its bones in the Fanti-land.

Following the road which I had taken, Captain Glover might have brought his 800 Houssas and Yorubas to Akim Swaidroo in eight days. At least 5000 Akims would have followed his march. Emerging at Damsam-su, close to Prahsu, and only two short marches from Swaidroo, he would have struck the Ashanti flank with fearful effect. His own base would have been perfectly secure. The head and the rear of an Ashanti army are equally strong; the flank is helpless. There is, in fact, no other flank than that presented by a long line of men in single file passing along a forest pathway, and upon such a line would an attack from the east have fallen. I am as convinced as I can be on any subject, that had Accra been used as a base from which to attack the Ashantis at the Prah, instead of being as it was, put to a diametrically opposite purpose, the destruction of the Ashantis pent against the Prah would have been complete.

As it was, the first phase of the war was now over. The cloud of Ashanti invasion had rolled off before the determined front presented by the English leader with his score or two of officers, and his four or five hundred native soldiers; but the work, which was afterwards done at Amoaful and Ordahsu, might have been effected at Faysoo and Prahsu at a tenth of the cost, had there been 500 English soldiers on the coast in November, and had the vision of trans-Volta war remained a dream.

In the evening I marched back to Damsam-su. I

found a crowd of men assembled there ; two English
officers, Home and Buller, on their way to the river, with
their servants and a small escort, and more than 100
Akims under the valiant Ahencora.

We camped on the site of a ruined hut.

Next morning my companions set out for the Prah, and
I held a grand review of the entire Akim force. It
numbered a little over 200 men. I had promised that
each soldier should receive 6*d*. per diem, and every subordinate chief 2*s*., and every chief of 100 men 4*s*. per diem.
This scale of payment put chiefs at such a premium that
the demand for them became very brisk. Every one
wanted to be a chief, to abandon his musket and
assume the long cane, which was symbolical of chieftainship.

At last the matter was arranged in due proportion.
King, chiefs, and warriors were paid ; and I dismissed
the lot back to Akim to cut a road to Swaidroo, promising
to rejoin them in a short time. For myself, I turned
south along the main track to Yancoomassie to communicate with head quarters ere the second phase of the
campaign—the conquest of Ashanti—opened.

And now there was a dull time to be got through
before that second phase could open. One whole month
had to be lived through ere the white soldiers would be
ready to cross the Prah and march upon Coomassie. It
was a gloomy prospect—a whole month in this poisonous
forest, expectant but inactive.

Wood's regiment of disciplined natives came up to
the front, and passed on towards the Prah ; Russell's
regiment followed close behind ; and on the 15th
December, fifty sailors of the Naval Brigade marched into
Yancoomassie. It was time that I too should move,

and on the 19th I set out for a third and last visit to Akim.

I had been asked if an independent movement was practicable from Akim direct upon Ashanti, and I was anxious to revisit the country before giving a positive reply.[1] I wished to test thoroughly the nature of the people, and to see if, under the more favourable circumstances of their king's presence (Quabina Fuah had returned from Accra at last) they would show any disposition to fight.

So I set out again on the same toilsome road. My baggage-carriers had dwindled down to scant numbers from sickness and desertion. Now and then I had been able to add a new recruit to their ranks; but on the whole I was considerably below the strength I had taken from Accra.

I reached Akrapon with double loads on the evening of the 19th, intending to hire villagers at that croom to carry loads to Akim; but the men bolted into the bush upon my arrival, and I was on the point of abandoning some loads, and pushing on for Akim with the remaining carriers, when an unlooked-for event put me in possession of additional bearers.

Suddenly there emerged from the forest, on the side of the main road, some eight or ten Assin warriors, with the usual long gun and load of plantains balanced on their heads. I called to these braves to approach the spot where I stood; but the only reply they made was to bolt as fast as they could along the track leading towards Akim.

"After them," I shouted to my men; "they are deserters from the camp on the road; they are running away. After them, and bring them back."

Away went Pappho, Boppho, and a tall Abra called

[1] See Appendix, No. 17.

M

"the long scout," going like the wind. The result was the capture of four Assins. Upon being brought before me, they pleaded guilty at once; it was true they were running away from the camp.

"Tell them," I said, "that the punishment of this crime is death; but in this case it shall be commuted to carrying four loads from this village to Accassie."

Thus recruited with four additional hands, 1 set out for Accassie. I camped in the forest that evening, and towards evening on the 20th entered the town of Apradie after a toilsome march.

I was scarcely settled into my quarters when a messenger from King Quabina Fuah was announced, preceded by a couple of gentlemen bearing two-handed gilt iron swords. The doughty Fuah had returned from his "fetish" at Accra; but perhaps it will be better to let the monarch speak for himself. Here is his despatch :—

> "Insuiamu,
> "Western Akim, 1873.
> "To W. F. Butler.

"My Good Friend—I have the honour to inform you these few lines to say that I have reached my town from Accra and I herewith send my clerck with these post from Captain Gloverd to you but now only waiting to see your face with twelf rifles Snider for my children specially English flag which will go first with me And some tobacco which are I have none to smoke hoping you will not disappoint me

> "Yours respectful
> "King Quabinah Fooah
> "Western Akim"

The heroic Akim had not truly spoken his mind. He had put the English flag before the fragrant weed; but there was not a king or chief in all the wide Protectorate for the freedom of which we were fighting, who would not gladly have sold his devotion to the English flag for a pipe of the commonest "Negro head."

As I lay in the dark hut at Apradie that night, I had something better worth reading than the letter of the Akim King.

"The post" he wrote of meant letters from far-away lands, and among them was one written in the previous July, from the shores of silent Lake Athabasca, away in the great wilderness of North America. What a change! Here, as I lay in this foul croom, midst the ceaseless jabber of these miserable beings, how vividly came back the memory of that day when the snow clamped under the snow-shoe, as we swept over the frozen surface of Lake Mamoway, and beheld for the first time the great Athabasca, spreading far and faint into the endless east! Snow, ice, the wail of winds through pine-trees; the streaming of the coloured lights across the zenith; such were the scenes that rose before me, as for a moment the mind tore itself away from such different surroundings, and sought again the dim pine woods of the north.

How far off they seemed! And yet it was only eight short months since I had built my camp along the frozen shores, and lay down to sleep in the snow-drifts of the Peace River. No wonder these nights seemed far away, for I looked back on them through full 15,000 miles of varying travel.

Fuah's envoy brought another letter, which, though short, was suggestive. It ran thus:—

"Pong, Nov. 9th.

"DEAR SIR,—I hear that you are on your way to Swaidroo, with King Western Akim.

M 2

"I am bringing a *picked force* of fighting men—5000 Eastern Akims, 1500 or 2000 Aquapims—7000 good men in all, and hope to be at Swaidroo, to aid in any movement that may be contemplated against Amonquatier's army, on the 21st instant.

"Yours truly,

(Signed)   "REGINALD SARTORIUS."

On the 21st November, to be at Swaidroo, with 7000 picked men—yes, that would have answered—but now it was the 21st December, and the fighting force of *picked men* were picking sea shells at the Volta estuary.

In the morning I despatched King Fuah's "clerck" (a gentleman rejoicing in the name of Bambin) back to his master, and set out myself for Accassie. Bambin bore a message to the King to the effect that I expected him to meet me at Accassie on the 23rd, to hear the General's wishes.

While I was dismissing Bambin, the sounds of firing came at intervals over the forest from the north-east. It was a "big custom," the "clerck" informed me, to commemorate the death of Fuah's nephew, at the royal town of Insuiam. King Attah of East Akim had written to Fuah, saying, "Let your nephew come to my town and eat 'fetish' with me; then there will be peace between us."

The nephew went, ate fetish, and came back poisoned. Hence there was a great "custom" for his death. "What was the cause of the dispute," I inquired, "between King Attah and King Fuah?"

"About a wife," was the reply. "Formerly King Fuah lived in a town three days' journey to the east of his

present place of abode; but King Attah had a dispute
about one of Fuah's wives, and Fuah swore the great
oath, and moved his household to Insuaim."

" And the wife—did she come to Insuaim also ? "

" No, she remained with Attah."

" Oh ! and then there was war, of course ? "

" *No, but Fuah and Attah spoke very much, and were
not friends.*"

Fuah was evidently a sagacious prince. It did not
appear that he had done anything of a more belligerent
nature to avenge his honour than the swearing of the
big oath, and indeed it would seem that that manifestation
of vengeance had been amply sufficient to satisfy the
African code of honour. Gathering up his sixty or
seventy remaining ribs, he had fled to Insuaim, and
maintained a dignified reserve until the present war had
caused Attah to propose a reconciliation on a mingled
basis of fetish and poison.

I listened to all this as I plodded the muddy path
towards Accassie. Repeated assurances were given that
Quabina regretted his past misconduct in going to Accra,
and that henceforth he should be filled with a spirit of
loyalty and obedience.

" Well, go back; you have your message : I have
nothing to send, to give, or to see, until I see Quabina
Fuah himself at Accassie"

I reached Accassie that night, and took up my quarters
in the same house as before, a clean, whitewashed hut,
with three small windows looking into the street; the
" fetish " tree of the village stood close by, and I often
watched from my windows the natives as they sat beneath
its shade, and spent the long hours in what sounded to
me a ceaseless gabble.

At daybreak I received the following letter from Fuah:—
"Insuaimu, 23rd December, 1873.

"MY GOOD FRIEND—I have the honour to receive yours with all contents but I am quite sorry I cannot disappoint you but on the time when I meet you I close the Accra and as my old uncle put me on the hand of the Accras and since I take the stool I never see theme at all and also Captain Gloverd wrote me that I must see him before he whent down to Addah.

"But I cannot disobey you at all never I shall be shake your hand this morning soon asppossible and anything that you want me to do I must do I am not a coward man that I tarnish my name.

"Your sincere obliged friend
"KING QUABBINAH FOOAH
"Western Akim"

The 23rd of December was a great day for Accassie. Early in the forenoon the horns of Fuah began to echo in the surrounding forest, and from the tree-arched pathway to the north a crowd of natives poured into the town; at last came my old acquaintance Fuah. He was borne in a kind of chair, set on poles, and carried by four stalwart slaves. A large concourse of the usual description preceded, surrounded, and followed him; the horns blew, the drums beat, but I had become too well accustomed to this thing, and I waited the approach of my doughty monarch in my hut, without movement or preparation of any kind.

Soon the long procession began to file into my little courtyard; and to occupy every coign of vantage on the premises. At last Fuah appeared. He looked very solemn, and seemed fatter than before. He wore a gorgeous green and yellow window-curtain of damask stuff, passed once round his fat body, and hung loosely over one shoulder.

Advancing with quick strides to the lower step which led to my little room, he stopped abruptly before it; then, stretching out his right hand to his sword-bearer, he took from him a short, two-handed, gilt sword, and, holding it towards me with outstretched arm, he swore the great oath.

In a deep, firm, set voice, he poured forth a lot of varied imprecations. His father, his mother, and many of his relations were called upon in this oath, severally and collectively, to witness his sincerity. Every fetish, from a boiled papaw, to the blue coat worn by the unfortunate Sir Charles M'Carthy, was appealed to in touching and eloquent terms.

Whatever I said, that was to be Fuah's law. Whatever I ordered, that Fuah was to perform without let or hindrance. Wherever I went, he would lead the way; though all should run away, he, Fuah, would remain; and finally he swore by the Sacred Cock, to consent to lose his head, if he failed in any portion of this tremendous programme.

At the mention of the Sacred Cock the bystanders seemed visibly affected.

Fearful lest the infatuated monarch would swear himself away altogether, I arose from my seat, took him by the outstretched hand, and led him into my little apartment. It was fully open on the courtyard side, so that the meeting was visible to the crowd of courtiers who thronged the place.

I cannot say that I was at heart much impressed by this scene. As for Fuah's father, I knew that he had, in common with the majority of Africans on the coast, a very indefinite idea of that relative. Sir Charles M'Carthy's coat I knew nothing of, and the Sacred Cock failed even to stir my enthusiasm. But I knew that this Akim King could turn out some 2000 men, and on him alone could I rely for the means of invading Ashanti by a distinct movement on my own account.

People who read this may wonder how it was that I hoped ever to bring these coward tribes face to face with the long conquering Ashantis; but that will appear in due time. Enough now to say that as before, every element of success, so far as the feasibility of the undertaking was concerned, was to be found in this movement except the material *man*; but even that difficulty, important though it was, I hoped successfully to overcome. By and by we shall see how that hope was realized.

Fuah, having seated himself in my hut, was sedulously mopped on the head and face by two attendants, and soon recovered his wonted equanimity. He heard all that I had to say, with an expression of face which seemed to indicate that he was prepared to repeat the ceremony of the great oath, as soon as his breathing was fully re-established; I had enough of that sort of thing, however, and endeavoured to keep him to detail as much as possible.

" What number of men could he turn out ? What date could they be all assembled by ?" and much more to the same purpose.

" All his men would come ; but as to their numbers, that was impossible to say ; in twelve days' time they would be all ready."

" Well, then, at Tribee in twelve days I will expect you with all your men. You will have 200 more rifles, thirty barrels of powder, fifty bars of lead, six Sniders, and tobacco at Tribee in twelve days from this date. Let me see how you can keep the oath you have just sworn. At Tribee I will tell you the wishes of the English general. All he says to you now is to collect your soldiers at Tribee. He will himself be at Prahsu in ten days, at the head of his army, ready to reward those who serve him, and to punish those who disobey his orders."

The Great Oath, I said, had given me much satisfaction; but I had noticed that there was one portion of the ceremony which he, Quabina Fuah, had not observed. He had omitted to place a bullet in his mouth, and to put a flint between his teeth at the solemn moment.

It was true, Fuah remarked; but acts of that kind were only necessary in the case of a young monarch unused to war. He was a veteran brave; war was to him an habitual pastime, and therefore he had dispensed with the formula of the bullet and the flint; but if I wished these adjuncts to the oath, he was fully prepared to throw them in.

As I had always regarded these accessories to the great oath of Africa as precautionary measures to prevent the swearer from being choked by the fearful falsehood he was pledging himself to, I dispensed with them on this occasion, and assured Fuah that the Sacred Cock was amply sufficient to convince me of his determination to act in a brave and loyal manner.

Thus we parted. I was to visit his capital city of Insuiam on the morrow, and he went off in his pole chair, a mingled mass of perspiration and perplexity.

At a later period of the day Coffee Ahencora appeared from his city. I ordered him to assemble at Tribee on the same day, the 3rd January, and I promised to visit him at Swaidroo in two days' time.

The rest of this eventful day passed quietly. Chief

Darco, evidently sorely puzzled and perplexed by the
great oaths, palavers, and press of business, appeared in
the evening to assure me that he too was brave beyond
the power of words to express it; that he could not see
his brethren girding themselves for the fray while he
remained amidst his plantains, and that he too was prepared to do good battle, if I would give him some of
the arms and munitions I had promised to the other
kings.

I accepted Darco's offers of service, and set out on
Christmas morning for the city of Insuaim.

It was a short march of six or seven miles, and the
morning was yet young when I drew near the king's
town.

It stood in the largest forest clearing I had yet seen in
the land, but the huts and wattle-houses scarcely filled
half of the open space. Some years before the Ashantis
had come down on Akim, and ravaged Insuaim ; the town
was destroyed, and this was a new city, built on the ruins
of the old one.

Passing through large plantations of plantains, my
cavalcade entered the maze of huts which forms an
African croom. Shots were being fired in all directions,
for the " Custom " for the king's nephew was still at
its height. In the centre of the town dwelt the king;
in fact, it would be perfectly true to say that the entire
centre of Insuaim belonged to Fuah. His palace consisted of some ten or twenty groups of huts—some
separate, some communicating with each other.

In these huts dwelt the many wives of Fuah. There
was not, that I could see, a single hut that had the least
pretension to size or comfort; nor did Fuah appear to
have any State apartments of his own. He seemed to

lead a sort of "all-round life" among his many huts.

His State reception took place in the open air in the midst of the huts. Beyond the horn-blowers, drummers, and interpreters, a vast concourse, principally of women, filled the ground; at times the women became very noisy, and talked, or rather chattered, so much that the eloquent speeches of Fuah or his interpreters became inaudible; upon which a crier shouted, "Yo-ho," in an authoritative manner, and order was restored.

Whatever may have been the native eloquence of Fuah (and I have been told that the fame of his tongue was great in Akim), his speeches were sadly marred by being rendered into English by his "Clerck" Bambin. That functionary had been for a short time an inmate of a German Missionary Establishment near the Volta. His English had therefore been attained under considerable difficulties. In endeavouring to express his master's words in the English tongue he thought in Akim and spoke in broken English, with a strong German accent; the effect was peculiar; and if, as has been stated on the authority of a certain great statesman, language has been given to man for the purpose of enabling him to conceal his ideas, Bambin of Akim fully succeeded in utterly bewildering his hearers, and must, therefore, ever stand prominently forward as a master of the art of elocution.

I have alluded already to a small Fanti boy whom I had brought as a personal attendant from Cape Coast. He was not only a precocious youngster for a negro, but he would have been quick, lively, and clever for any race or colour under the sun. He was not more than twelve years of age; still he was able to speak English fluently, and to read and write it too. I had been so frequently

deceived by the so-called interpreters of the country, that
I had long ceased to have any faith in their services, and
kept little Quabina, the Fanti boy, as a check upon the
erratic freaks of those worthies.

At palavers he always stood beside my chair. " Small
boy, is that fellow speaking my words rightly to these
people ? "

" He is talking quite different, master," Quabina would
whisper. Then there would ensue much confusion.

" Come, sir ! " I would shout at the interpreter, " what
the deuce are you saying ? "

" Me, sa—me say what master says."

On the present occasion the small boy in an aside informed me that Bambin was playing the very deuce with
the interpreting. " He is saying everything quite different from master. He is making plenty confusion with
the king," was the small boy's graphic account of Bambin's eccentricities of speech. It was full time to stop
this work; and, amidst much laughter, Bambin was
declared utterly ignorant of English, and the small boy
was put forward as the true interpreter.

When the palaver had ceased, I retired to my hut to rest,
for the heat had been intense, and the atmosphere of the
great crowd stifling. But for me that day there was no
rest. Fuah came himself, and sent presents of sheep,
plantains, eggs, and palm-wine; then came a deputation
of old men, then a deputation of old women; these people
had nothing particular to say; they simply stood round the
little square yard, and stared at one with unblinking eyes.

The deputation of old women was peculiarly devoid
of interest. Each old lady generally brought a plantain
or an egg as an offering, in reality as an excuse for coming
to gaze at the white man. The younger ones mustered

strongly outside the wattle fence, and their black eyes glittered in every nook or crevice of the mud walls; but the older dames seemed jealously to deny them a closer inspection of the wonder within; and I could not help thinking that, if circumstances had made an exhibition of me, the glances of younger eyes would perhaps have reconciled me somewhat to the infliction.

As it was, the damsels were kept out, the old women flocked in. "Age before beauty" seemed the first rule of Akim etiquette; indeed, no lady appeared entitled to presentation to the white man while she had any of the charms of youth remaining.

Meanwhile Pappho of Calabar, and Sambo of Accra, and Boppho of Jellah Coffee, were having a very festive time outside in the crowd; these worthies had long ago settled into excellent retainers and trusty bearers. They had grown accustomed to the life of change; they were regularly paid their subsistence-money (threepence a day), and their hire was kept steadily in arrear. Wherever they went, they managed to get good quarters; sometimes they got drunk on deep potations of palm-wine. On these occasions the trio might be seen rolling over each other in the throes of a seemingly fierce contention, but not otherwise doing much damage to anything.

When Pappho became inebriated, he invariably used all the English of which he was master, to express his over-burdened feelings; and as this knowledge was limited to the language used by Liverpool sea captains—the English most in vogue along the coast—the effect was not edifying.

On the present occasion Pappho was, vulgarly speaking, the cock of the walk at Insuaim. I could see him through the open doorway of my house, swaggering up and down

among the women, as though he had been a young sub-
altern, just enlarged in the Burlington Arcade, from those
admirable training-cages, Aldershot or Chatham. With a
highly polished skin, and a small scarlet skull-cap set
jauntily on the very edge of his big, woolly head, he grinned
unutterable sweet things at the bevy of unadorned dark
ones who crowded the road in front.

It was a curious Christmas-day! but, like every other
day, it wore away, and night came down upon the forest-
city of Insuaim. The " Custom," however, was pro-
tracted far into midnight, and the air reverberated with
the oft-repeated discharges of flint-guns.

" If these brutes," I often said to myself, " would only
burn as much powder against the Ashantis as they con-
sume here so uselessly, the war would have been over
long ago."

At length the noises died away, and the quiet of the
night was only broken by the dismal sounds of the forest.

The river Birrum flows close to Insuaim. It is a large
deep stream, with a strong current. It is to the Akims
what the Prah is to the Ashantis—a sacred river. In the
daytime we will see our fat friend, Fuah, performing a
vast " fetish " on its shores, preparatory to his taking the
field. Our old acquaintance, too, the Sacred Cock, this
time actually in the flesh, will appear during the ceremony;
but in a manner not at all in keeping with his traditional
repute.

On the evening of Christmas-day I visited the Birrum
river, and, on returning through the forest from its
shores, met Fuah on the pathway. " I have been looking
at your river," I said to him. " It is a fine river; but
you should have a boat on it." (It had occurred to me
that a boat would afford an easy means of reaching

Prahsu by water, in case this Akim Expedition proved a failure.) Fuah replied that the "fetish" of the river would not permit a boat to sail its waters.

"Never mind the 'fetish,'" I said, "I will give you 5*l.* if you hollow a canoe out of one of these trees." But Fuah was obdurate, and a boat they could not or would not make.

On the morning of the 26th December I set out for Akim Swaidroo, for the purpose of giving the light of my countenance to that valiant monarch, Ahencora, who all this time was supposed to be making frantic efforts to place "his last man" in the field.

Fuah wished me good-bye near the outskirts of his town. He looked as though he had been very drunk on the previous night, and his last request was for "a little rum, as this was his Christmas too. The last rum I had given him was very good."

Here is a specimen of a correspondence which I had now frequently to engage in:—

"Insoyemu, 26th, 1873.

"MY GOOD FRIEND—With much glad to inform you these few lines to say that as all my friend kings which are going to this war they have their subsistence before they move therefore I beg to know mine at once I know that you shall give me all ammunitions but particular these I wish to know of it by your favour as Commandant of Accra gave me order that I musk ask something which I need to ask you.

"Good morning Thank you Sir
for yesterday Brandy
"I am quite well hoping you the same
"Your reall friend
"KING QUABINA FOOAH."

To this I replied,—

" MY DEAR KING,—You do not understand Sir Garnet
Wolseley's wishes. He can give far more to his kings
than any Accra king or chief has received ; but he gives
when the army is fighting, and not before it goes to
fight.

"Have the Accra kings fought yet ? They got their
subsistence ; but what have they done ?

" The English general is great, and good, and powerful ;
but he gives his kingdoms and his riches in the field
when the enemy has been beaten, and not in the towns
when men are at peace.

" If you are wise, you have now an opportunity of being
a great king, greater than ever reigned in Akim, in
Croboe, in Aquapim, or in Accra. I once wrote to you,
saying that you might make your name a terror in
Coomassie. I say it to you again now.

" Whatever I have said to you has been good. When
you went in opposition to me, you went wrong. In all
things be guided by my voice, and you will be rich and
powerful.

" Your good Friend,
" W. F. BUTLER."

I reached my old quarters at Swaidroo by mid-day, and
was again lodged in the house of Kru, whose " How are
you, quite well ? thank you," was uttered as solemnly
as ever.

Ahencora soon appeared. He had, he said, great news
to tell. There was an Akim man, who had long been
a resident in Ashanti ; this man had lately appeared at
Beronassie (a frontier town of Akim). He had left
Ashanti, he said, because the people had grown cool

towards him. He was now at Swaidroo ready to answer my questions.

The Akim runaway then stepped into the crowd, and told his story.

There was much confusion, he said, in Coomassie. The skies had spoken. In the middle of the day, a large stone had fallen in the centre of the roadway opposite the king's palace; it had come out of the sky while the sun was shining. The fetish priests had killed a sheep and a man before this stone, but the portent was bad.

But that was not all. There had been a child born in Coomassie, one week before he (the Akim) had left Ashanti; from the moment of its birth the child spoke. "Make ready a room for me," said the child, "put me in that room; close the door and windows, and to-morrow I will speak and tell you many things." The people, much alarmed at these words, did as they were directed. In a cleanly-swept room the infant was put to rest, with doors and windows fastened.

The morning came, the door was opened, the child was found dead, and a dense mass of bush filled the room. It seemed as though the place had been for ages deserted. The fetish men shook their heads; the power of Ashanti is on the wane, they said; "with bush and forest shall the cleared places and cities of Ashanti soon be covered."

So spoke the Akim, and the crowd listened with greedy ears.

"What do you think of it?" asked Ahencora.

"I think," I replied, "that the stone which fell from the skies shows that the English shot and shell will soon fall into that city, and that Coffee Kerrikerri will be a fugitive in the bush."

But there were other things of greater interest which

N

the Akim knew, and which I now learnt for the first time :
the paths and forest-tracks which led from Akim to
Coomassie. What work it was to get at the names of
the different villages, and some approximate idea of their
size and distance from each other.

There was Amantea just beyond the Prah, then Branqua, then Abemassie, then Gademwaah, then Yancoma :
at Yancoma the road forked, one branch-path led to
Dadiasso, a very large town, which could turn out 1000
fighting men; the other road led to Ennoonsu, Akina,
Cocofoo, and Coomassie, with many villages and people
along it.

To all this I listened with the greatest interest. Here
at last was something definite, something tangible, where
before all had been vague conjecture; and the mystery
that hung over this darksome forest, where no white man
had ever gone, was beginning to be dispelled.

Giving my Akim informant a handsome dash, I dismissed him for the present. In the evening the old
Queen Amaquon came down with her ladies. In the course
of the day I had been introduced during a palaver to a
venerable-looking Akim; he was called Coffee Ahencora's
father. He had, in fact, spoken of himself as such.

Now, Queen Amaquon was well known to the world at
large as Coffee Ahencora's mother, and with such data in
my possession it will not be considered rash if I ventured
to surmise that this old Akim and Queen Amaquon were
husband and wife—alas! this was entirely an error on
my part—I had already found that conversation between
even an African queen and a European commoner was
limited; and more from a desire to say something, than
from any expectation of solving the somewhat difficult
problem of the domestic relations of an Akim household,

I observed to the old queen that I had during the day met her husband; but to my surprise she replied, that she had had no husband for two years.

"But is not the old man who is called the father of Coffee Ahencora—" here I stopped; for it suddenly occurred to me that I was putting what lawyers would call "leading questions;" so I adroitly turned the conversation into another channel, and hoped that the health of Queen Amaquon was better?

"It was something better," she replied. "Perhaps I had some more of these wonderful medicines to give her?"

"Alas! no. But there was soon coming from the main road a doctor of great repute, and it would be his business to pay particular attention to her case."

On the morning of the 27th I set out to return to Accassie. I had determined to make it my head quarters until I struck my camp for the North. If I lived at Insuaim, Coffee Ahencora became jealous; if I stopped at Akim Swaidroo, Fuah grew suspicious. At Accassie I could send messengers to both potentates, and play one against the other to some purpose. I therefore took up my residence in the town of Darco.

I had much to do, and many things to arrange in these few days. Before the end of the year three officers were to join me from the main road, and to remain until the termination of this Akim invasion of Ashanti. They had but recently arrived on the coast from England, and it was not without some apprehension that I looked forward to their coming; knowing by a too bitter experience the lesson which a new comer in Africa has got to learn.

I had also to receive the final instalment of rifles and

N 2

ammunition from Mansu for the use of the Confederated
West Akims. This work I deputed to Lieutenant
Macgregor, of the 50th Regiment, who had orders to
bring the consignment of rifles, lead, and powder direct
to Tribee, at which place it will be recollected I had
notified Ahencora and Fuah that they were to assemble
on the 3rd of January with all their men. One officer
was to remain at Insuaim to bring Fuah to the trysting-
place; another was to do the same by Ahencora, at Akim
Swaidroo; Macgregor coming up with rifles, &c., from
Mansu, was to propel old Darco from his city of Accassie
to the common point of assembly; while I, moving on
New Year's Day from my camp, would proceed direct to
Tribee, and there await the coming together of my army
from all parts of West Akim.

Such was the plan. After that we should see.

On the morning of the 30th December I sent my
bearers to Apradie to meet the officers as they approached
from the main road, and to conduct them to Accassie.

About mid-day Pappho came racing past my little
window, shouting as he ran. After him there followed
two officers; two men so full of health and strength and
life, that my first thought as I gazed at them was, "These
men have come to kill me. I can never match their
English strength in marches now."

Until I looked upon them I had not realized what a
wasted skeleton I had become. They were both officers
of the Household Brigade, and both had quitted England
but three short weeks before.

How full they were of this venture, and of its chances!
Failure was impossible. A hundred questions had they
to ask about the Akims. How would we skirmish?

How we would attack this town and that town. How the word of command was to be given; and fifty more of a similar kind.

Skirmish! Fire! Advance! word of command, wheel, countermarch—alas! the thing was very simple in Akim; or for that matter, in all the States of Fanti-land—very simple, as they would know full soon.

The last night of the old year came. I sat in my hut with Brabazon, waiting for it to die.

For the first time the Harmattan blew across the forest the cool wind of the desert; the first *dry* breath I had felt for many months.

On the morrow I was to begin, with the New Year, a new campaign.

CHAPTER XI.

On New Year's morning I struck my camp at Accassie, and set out for the North.

I had not proceeded far before a messenger in breathless haste overtook me. A dire calamity had fallen upon the Chief Darco. His Queen had gone to the main road at Barraco with some of her handmaidens, bearing plantains for sale to the many natives who crowded that line. Some Houssas had seen her; they had carried off the plantains, and detained the Queen. The handmaidens had come back to Darco with the news of his double loss.

Soon he arrived; and jabbered incessantly. I told him that I would write to the officer of the Houssas on the main line; his Queen would be restored to him.

"And the plantains," put in Darco; "will not they be given back too?"

"Alas! I fear not. The appetites of the Houssas are keen, Darco. The fruit has been eaten long since. Is it not sufficient that the wife of your bosom should be restored to you?" On this point he did not seem to agree with me; and I fear, that had I given him the choice of Queen or plantains, he would have chosen the fruit.

I dismissed Darco to his unhappy home, and continued the march to the village of Avissa. Here my party was to separate; for here the pathway for Insuaim branched to the right.

Sending one officer to Quabina Fuah, at the latter place, I held on to Swaidroo with Captain Brabazon. I introduced Brabazon to Ahencora in full palaver; telling the king that this officer was, but a short time since, one of the guards of the Queen of England, and that he had come to fight the battles of the Akims against the Ashantis.

While the palaver was going on, news came that the village of Avissa was the scene of tumult. Upon which Ahencora, his mother, his interpreters, Kru, and the other chiefs all spoke at once; finally, through the crowd, came a woman in a state of high excitement. She was the wife of the chief of Avissa, one Cobra Ahencora. This chief owed a kind of divided allegiance; on the one hand to Quabina Fuah, on the other to Coffee Ahencora.

Fuah had sent to summon him to Insuaim with all his men to march under the banner of West Akim to the war. But Cobra, doubtless, thinking that he might altogether escape service in the field, pleaded that to Coffee Ahencora, and not to Quabina Fuah, was his fealty, if any due, and declined to obey the summons from Insuaim.

Upon this Fuah had declared that he would go to war with Avissa if the refusal was persisted in. With the rifles and ammunition he had received for service against the Ashantis, he would, it was averred, soon carry destruction into the hamlet of Cobra Ahencora. Hence the alarm at Swaidroo, for Avissa lay only a mile or so distant.

I despatched a Fanti policeman to Avissa with a summons to Cobra to join me forthwith with all his men, and that he should march with me against the Ashantis. But scarcely had this been done, when there arrived a messenger from Insuaim, saying that Fuah had refused to stir an inch from his city unless the chief of Avissa marched under his command.

Here was a pretty quarrel !

I saw at once that little could be done through messengers, and on the morning of the 2nd, when I should have been starting for the muster-place at Tribee, I turned my steps once more towards Insuaim.

What heart-breaking work this was! Roll up the stone as I would, down it came to the starting-point again; for every ten miles of calculated toil there was ever another ten of unforeseen disappointment.

I reached Insuaim, and went direct to Fuah. Palaver followed palaver. I sent a summons to Cobra Ahencora, and backed it with three Fanti policemen (I had six of them). Late in the evening Cobra arrived, and I lodged him as a prisoner in an outhouse at the back of my hut; then, summoning Fuah, I delivered judgment on the case.

This cunning old Akim Cobra had taken advantage of the quarrels of Fuah and Coffee Ahencora to assert his independence of each ; I had, therefore, decided that he should march to the war with me, and that when the war was over the question of his allegiance would be settled by the English general, who alone had power to settle all disputes. Keeping Cobra a prisoner with the intention of starting on the morrow for Tribee, I thought at last that all was settled. On the morrow Brabazon would go back to his post at Swaidroo, and I would cross the Birrum and march to Tribee ; but when morning came fever had laid its hot hands on my Swaidroo envoy, and Brabazon was not able to stir from his hut.

The day passed away; the next morning came; Paget was down with the fell disease beside his comrade. Fuah heard with delight the news of this disaster. I went to his labyrinth of huts, and demanded to see him. He was seated upon a low bed in a hut six feet by five. He was sorry to hear that sickness had attacked the officers; but they would be well in time, as his Christmas had yet to last eight days, and he could not stir until it was over.

I answered that sickness mattered nothing to us; that I would go on to-morrow, and that if he failed to keep his original promise, the vengeance of the English general would fall upon him.

On the morning of the 5th, having lost three days by these unforeseen occurrences, I set out to cross the Birrum.

Finding that Brabazon showed no symptoms of rallying, I decided upon sending him in my hammock to Prahsu, and I left my eight carriers at Insuaim to bear him on his road. Paget had rallied, and I directed him to see Quabina Fuah out of Insuaim, and then to follow me to Tribee, at which place I would await his coming. The other officer, Lieutenant Macgregor, had not yet arrived from Mansu, but he had orders to bring Darco and Ahencora along with him; so on the morning of the 5th I set out with a few carriers, my two servants, and three policemen.

The 5th of January had come. In ten days I was to cross the Prah, and not a soldier had yet rallied to my call! It was a darksome look-out.

In the hollowed trunk of a tree I crossed the swift-running Birrum, and held my way through dense forest to the north.

Mossoo was reached at mid-day, the usual useless harangue given to the wretched apathetic denizens who flocked forth at my arrival, and then I held on for Abenassie.

With the sense of movement my spirits (in no brilliant

mood as may be supposed) grew lighter, and I strode along the forest track with hasty steps. It was a day of the Harmattan; cool and fresh the north breeze blew through the great forest, curling the tree-tops, and bringing down showers of dry leaves on the pathway, which at last was dry and firm under the foot. The lungs for once seemed to inhale with a sense of freedom from poisonous oppression. I had the rascal Cobra Ahencora nominally as a guide, but in reality to remove him from the neighbourhood of his rival claimants. He was a man of about fifty or sixty years of age, ill-looking to an extreme. His right eye had totally disappeared; but as if to compensate him for its loss, nature had given him a hole in the centre of his right cheek. He kept close in front of me on the path, and when we came to any stream or forest opening he muttered imprecations to the fetish, and looked the most diabolical old villain I had ever set eyes upon. He had originally lived far north of the Prah river, and not far from Coomassie; but his parents ran away in the time of Sir Charles M'Carthy, and carried him with them to British territory.

Towards evening I reached the little town of Abenassie; the place was full of women and grey parrots, and both made much noise.

As I entered the town several women executed a war-dance before me, posturing their figures in a manner which caused that singular garment, the bustle, to gyrate very much after the fashion of a loose pack-saddle on a restive mule.

When this ceremony was over, I was conducted to a hut, or rather to a maze of huts—all low, dark, and communicating with each other by numerous and intricate passages. Then came the usual presents — plantains, bananas, poppies, and a few eggs, or a debilitated-looking cock, whose decapitation at the hands of Dawson was but a hasty prelude to his appearance on the supper box. Yes, there was no table, and a small packing-case did duty for one. Another case acted the part of chair; and thus, seated in the open air when it was fine, under the low hut-roof when it rained, evening after evening I discussed my solitary meal.

Dawson was by no means an indifferent cook; but, unfortunately, he had not much range of material to try his skill upon. Fowl for breakfast, fowl for dinner, fowl for supper, varied occasionally with stringy Australian beef and dry biscuit.

The small black boy stood beside my box seat, and talked his quick but childlike talk as he waited; sometimes questioning me on England, with a strange mixture of cleverness and simplicity. " Master, tell me, does the sea end at Liverpool? Is there a king at Liverpool? Are there any poor people in England, master ?"

" Yes, small boy, a good many."

" But how is that, master—isn't all the money made in England ? How can people be poor there ? "

This boy had been educated by the Wesleyan Missionary Society at Cape Coast, and was, as I have said, the best and nicest African I met on the coast. He was a credit to the mission. He was for months the sole person I could exchange a word with. When I got a budget of newspapers he used to read them line by line, but the picture papers were his great delight.

One day he came running to me in high glee : " Oh, master, look ! here's a picture of one Fanti boy."

It was a page of " Punch " which he had got, and the

caricature of a Fanti soldier, in a paroxysm of terror, offered him immense fun. Yet, while his Wesleyan masters had done so much to improve this little Fanti, they had not been able to rise superior, in their zeal for the conversion of the heathen, to those feelings of rancorous bigotry which prevail against some other fellow-Christians at home. They had not failed to transplant these into his mind.

"Master," said this small boy to me one day, "are there not Christians in England who are like the fetish people here in the bush?"

"What do you mean, small boy?"

"Are there not some Christian people in England who have pieces of sticks and stones for their gods? The ministers always told us at the school that there were plenty such people in England. He said they were called Catholics."

Poor little ignorant Fanti boy! This part of thy tuition might well have been left alone. There were foul lies enough growing rank in this dark Africa of thine without transplanting more from the hotbed of European bigotry.

Early on the morning of the 6th the old rascal Cobra came to me; this Abenassie was one of his villages, he said; there was a man in it who wanted to marry his daughter; perhaps I would allow him to stay behind for a few hours to do "Custom." I was tired of the old wretch ; and as the track had been tolerably direct on the previous day, I gave him leave to stay, and set out myself for Tribee. A tall slave bearer of Fuah's led the way. Shortly after leaving Abenassie he turned along a bye-path, and soon hopelessly lost his way. I retraced my steps to the main track, and then sent back two policemen with orders to bring out the wretched Cobra, if necessary, by the neck, custom or no custom.

He soon appeared. " Now go in front, and keep it until we reach Tribee."

Again the procession started, this time Cobra leading. He was even more garrulous than on the previous day, and his invocations to the " fetish " were frequent.

All at once he stopped, and turned towards me.

" A short distance ahead there was a very good fetish on the pathway," he said.

" All right—let us go on." A few hundred yards more brought the forest path which we were pursuing to a spot where it joined the larger track, which led from Akim Swaidroo to the Prah. Almost at the point of junction there stood a grim sight. The skeleton of a man stood upright against a large tree; the feet touched the ground; the body seemed supported against the trunk of the tree; the skull had fallen from the neck, and lay upturned on the ground close to the feet.

I approached this figure; the bones were held against the tree by long strings of a forest creeper, coiled often round legs, arms, and body; along the inner edge of this creeper or tendril there ran a close-set row of long, sharp thorns; these thorns still clung to the fleshless bones : altogether the sight was not a pleasant one. I guessed its explanation even before the jabbering sentences of the grinning Cobra could be rendered into English.

Here was the story of this fetish which this old one-eyed demon had to tell.

Some time last wet season, in June or July, the valiant Akims, then, fighting in Fanti at Jouquah or Dunquah, took prisoner an Ashanti soldier.

In common with the other brave confederate kings and

clans they shortly afterwards ran away, and finally came back to their own country. Fuah entered his capital in triumph. Ahencora did the same. It is true that the persons of the Akims bore many traces of the Ashanti slugs. It was evident from the position of many of these scars that the Ashantis had carried out flanking movements against their enemies. However, the Akims brought with them as a token of victory the wretched Ashanti whom they had taken prisoner. Having shown him round the country for some time, a bright idea seized them; they brought the miserable being to the spot on the road to the Prah, and here they bound him firmly with the thorny tendril round neck and body, arms and legs, to this tree, and there they left him without food or water, with hundreds of sharp spikes entering his flesh, until he died.

This atrocious story Cobra recounted to me in a voice and with a manner which said plainly enough, " Ah ! it was an excellent idea this ! We Akims are a fine people."

" How long did he live ?" I asked.

" Three days," answered Cobra ; " and this was such a good fetish that not one Ashanti appeared on the track."

As he recounted this exploit, in which, doubtless, he had borne a prominent part, his single eye winked gleefully, and the round hole in his cheek wrinkled with a demoniacal delight.

Truly, my soldiers were fine fellows !

" Lead on, Cobra, or I shall kick you before me."

The path now led up the side of a steep incline, and we stood on the summit of the divide between the Birrum and the Prah. The track was dry and good; but, at times, the ground was covered with large round fruit which had fallen from the lofty trees, and from which an unhealthy odour came; as we passed such places the natives quickened their steps, saying the smell produced sickness amongst them.

It was past noon when we entered the town of Tribee; the Harmattan was blowing strongly, and Tribee lay under a burning sun.

A question often arises in my mind as I write, "Will those who read, see this land as you have seen it?" Here, while the pen runs swiftly along, telling its story of what memory recalls, I sometimes pause, and ask myself, "Are you faithfully reproducing the same image which you saw twelve months ago in reality, and which you see so often still in memory, stamped indelibly there by fever, and fruitless toil, and disappointment?" I look back over this manuscript, and as I read the names of towns and forest crooms scattered through it, there rises before me a long panorama of time and event, set in the scenery of this vast forest; but, the reader! ah, that is a different thing!

A single name recalls to the traveller so vivid a picture, that he is sometimes liable to forget that those who follow his wanderings in thought are not seeing with his eyes.

Well, let me try to put down one or two of these pictures here, as they stood before us full many a time, when weary and exhausted we toiled on to the croom where the hot day's work was to end.

Morning. A dense white steam fills the forest; the eye cannot follow the great grey tree-trunks more than half way to their summits; there is the ceaseless drip or rain-drops on the broad-leaved undergrowth, and a clammy cold clings to the air; there is, the natives say, "a bad smoke" out to-day, and yet, long before mid-forenoon this smoke has vanished, and the fiery sun has come out—the clammy chill has changed to suffocating damp heat.

Mid-day. The great sun blazes in sullen fury down upon the silent forest, but the fierce rays fall only in nets of gold on the great grey stems which raise their buttressed trunks 100 feet without a branch, and then fork in massive limbs whose every length would make a forest tree. One hundred feet higher still, the waving surface of this ocean of foliage lies outspread before the glare of day—a vast sea of tree-tops whose waves ripple in a middle region seemingly set between earth and heaven.

Evening. There is the splash of water upon the topmost trees; the rain hisses down in ceaseless dreariness, and the roll of the thunder crashes loud and long over the reverberating forest.

But, though the hours may pass as they will, and sunlight, fog, and lightning, ring their changes over this sea, still all unchanged, set in an eternity of sombre gloom, rests this huge equatorial forest. The day and the night are the same to it; noiseless rivers steal along under dense layers of tangled foliage; huge poisonous fruits fall down from lofty close-set trees, and lie beneath the undergrowth, emitting noisome odours; great orchids hang over the pathway, spiral creepers, hundreds of feet in length, twisted like huge serpents, cling from tree to tree; and far down below the mass of foliage, amidst these tangled and twisted evergreens, beneath the shadow of the great grey tree-trunks, man moves as though he slowly picked his way at the bottom of some mighty ocean.

This forest of Akim and Ashanti is the only forest I have ever seen which defies man; you could not clear it, for the reason that long before you could cut it down, a new forest would have arisen. During six months there is continuous rain; during four months more, heavy tropical storms occur almost daily; for five or six weeks the weather is dry : but all the twelve months through, the heat is very great, hence there is produced on the Gold Coast a vegetation such as one sees nowhere else on the globe.

So vast is this vegetable kingdom, that the animal world sickens and dies out before it—this immense forest holds scarcely a living creature. For months I have trodden its labyrinths, and seen only a diminutive deer, a grey monkey, and a few serpents. How little we knew in England of the true nature of this forest! "It will burn," wrote one wise man to a daily paper. "Take plenty of petroleum oil, pour it over the forest, and then set fire to it."

"I know tropical forests well," wrote another, "the underbush will burn when the dry weather comes, as it does in Burmah and Tenasserim. Then you will be able to march through it with ease."

But, alas! the African forest is always green, always wet, always fire-proof.

There is a lighter opening in the forest gloom ahead—all at once the trees end abruptly, and low, mud-walled houses, thatched with reeds, appear before us. The forest treads upon the very skirts of the croom—there is no cleared space, save where the houses stand, these houses form little clusters of huts, each cluster having a tiny, square yard in the centre, upon which all the huts open; bye-paths lead out at the corners into the street, which is usually broad, clean, and adorned with a fetish tree, beneath which the gossip of the place is carried on. The women are nearly always engaged in household work;

o

the men are always idle, sometimes gambling with sticks, sometimes with old cards, seldom doing any useful labour.

" Why do you not clear the forest for some distance all around your croom ? " I have asked the people of a village, " and plant the open space with corn and plantains ? " " It would be no use," they have answered, " other people would come and take our grain and fruit. We could not refuse them, so we go three or four miles off, and make our gardens there, and then it is too far for people to go to look for food."

So closely does this forest hem in the crooms, that if it were possible to walk along the tops of the trees, one would look right down into the huts from the edge of the clearing; but often the croom stands upon a knoll, or sloping hill, and the surrounding forest looks somewhat less impending.

I reached Tribee after mid-day, and the following morning saw Fuah to the fore. He had not quite twenty followers with him; but he spoke with confidence of his people being " on the road ; " and having taken up his quarters in a hut some little distance from mine, settled himself to smoke with a composure eminently calculated to infuse serenity into his few followers.

The high fetish ceremonies which had taken place on the passage of the Birrum River by Fuah, on the morning of his departure from his city, were afterwards detailed to me by an eye-witness.

It would appear that the greater portion of the population of Insuaim accompanied their monarch to the banks of the river. Arrived on the high ground overlooking the stream, Quabina took in his hand the sacred cock, and twirling that bird two or three times over his head, he endeavoured to cast him towards the centre of the stream. The bird, however, appeared to have a marked disinclination to take the water, and invariably managed to flutter back· to the shore from whence he had been projected. Several of Fuah's subjects then pursued the sacred bird along the shore, as he fled with neck and wings outstretched, quite after the manner of an ordinary fowl when pursued by an anxious hen-wife, captured and brought him back to the monarch; again Fuah let him fly, with so inadequate an aim that he regained the shore.

At last he was safely consigned to the waters of the Birrum, and Fuah set forth to the war. It was long afterwards that I was told of this proceeding, and it was also some time after the event had taken place that another occurrence was related to me, as horrible as this was ludicrous.

On one of the nights preceding the mustering of the Akims, two Ashanti slaves, or prisoners, whose presence I had never been allowed to know of, were put to death in Insuaim as an offering to the war fetish.

Truly, my soldiers were queer ones! as low as animals, as cruel as the Ashantis; but without a vestige of their bravery.

Later on the same day, bad news came from Insuaim. Paget, Brabazon, and Macgregor were all down with fever, without attendance of any kind, lying in the same wretched hut.

I gathered together a few medicines, and told Dawson to make ready to go back to Insuaim. I paraded the remaining bearers, the eight who had originally started from Accra with me, Pàppho, Boppho, Samtee, Koniako,

and Co., and I told them that they must return to the
assistance of the sick men, to carry them to Prahsu if
necessary.

There was much murmuring and discontent. Pappho
asked if he might speak.

" They had," he said, " been good boys; those who were
bad had long ago run away; but the eight who were now
present, had they not followed me for many months, and
obeyed all my orders ?

'' When I sent them to the coast, had they not come
back again ? wherever I turned, were they not ready to
turn too ? They would go with me anywhere ; but now
I wanted to send them to work for other masters, and that
they did not like."

" No matter, Pappho ; you must go. These officers lie
sick at Insuaim. It is necessary that you all go to help
them, for they have no bearers.

" See, I am keeping with me only the small boy, and this
man who cannot walk. When you have taken the officers
to Prahsu you will return to me again ; I shall then, I
hope, be far north of here, but you can join me there if
you wish."

They shook hands with me, one by one, promised
obedience, and went their way; but, excepting Pappho
and Koniako, I never saw them again.

When they reached Insuaim, that place was in a
tumult. One of the officers, driven desperate by the
conduct of the first lot of carriers I had left with him,
had, in an unfortunate moment, drawn a revolver and
fired at a runaway bearer. After this nothing could be
done with the natives.

It would appear that upon the arrival of my second
lot from Tribee, a free fight took place outside the hut in

which two of the officers were lying ill; and in the midst
of this fight my Accra men disappeared. They had stood
by me through many vicissitudes; and, from whatever
cause they now deserted, their loss was a sore one; I
was in fact made completely helpless by it. My eight
bearers were employed carrying one fever-stricken man
to Prahsu; six of the others had run away, and I was
left with only three servants at the moment when baggage-
carriers became of absolute necessity. The hour of invasion had come, my baggage-bearers had vanished.

I don't think I had ever lived through days of more
killing weariness than those days spent in Tribee.

The Akims came in tens, where I had expected hundreds. My three officers had all been struck down almost
at the same moment by this deadly fever. I was, for the
first time in three months of travel, left utterly without
carriers; and, worse than all, each day brought from the
head-quarter camp (now pitched at Prahsu) letters that
made me realize but too distinctly, the impossibility of
keeping time with African natives to the plans of English
chiefs and the footsteps of English soldiers.

Hour by hour did I waste in reiterated harangues to
Fuah.

" Our days are as fixed as the sun," I would say to
him. " When we fix upon a day to move, nothing turns
us from our resolve."

" But the other white officers are sick at Insuaim,"
would reply the smoking negro. " They will have to get
well before we move."

" No, not a bit of it. We go on, no matter who is
sick or who is well. The English General crosses the
Prah on the 15th at Prahsu, and on that day I cross it
too at Akim, even though not another white man is there

to cross it with me. To-day we are at the 10th, in four days more our time will be over; and your men, where are they? You have not two hundred soldiers, all told, around you. You have not ten for every one hundred you swore to bring me. Do you see that chest of silver? Ten—twenty—such as that await my orders. They are yours and your soldiers when you march and fight; but not a shilling shall go to you or them while thus you hesitate and delay."

This, and much more did I pour forth to the wretched king; sometimes in my own hut, where he came at early daylight to give me " Good morning," and sometimes in his hovel, when I sought him in his lair.

At last came Coffee Ahencora with some 200 followers, and much noise of horn-blowing. Prominent among his chiefs stood "Kru," now beaming with the light of battle; but still prouder than ever of his complete mastery of the English tongue. Kru made his profound bow, said, " How-are-you-quite-well-thank-you," and passed on to the war.

The next day brought Darco, also arrayed for war. Behind him marched two atrocious-looking rascals, carrying each a huge horse-pistol, with flint locks. Darco's wife had come back to him, he said; but his plantains had been irrevocably lost.

On the 11th of January Macgregor and Brabazon came in, weak and exhausted, but still free of fever. Paget had been sent insensible to Prahsu ; the bearers all, save those who carried him, had vanished for ever.

On the 13th I struck my camp at Tribee, and pushed on for Beronassie and the Prah. It was a long, hot march ; the sun blazed down on the forest ; the road or track was rugged, filled in many places with stagnant water, and cumbered with the twisted roots of trees laid bare by rain torrents. It was a four hours' march; and long before it was over, throbbing brain and faltering step told me that the fever was again upon me. At times I sat on a fallen tree, but then came the feeling that in a little while I would not be able to move, and that I must push on, while even a faltering step remained to carry me to my destination.

At last Beronassie was reached, and I lay down to suffer the old routine, now so painfully familiar. Again came the wakeful night, the fog, the rank, dank smell of poisonous vegetation; the lifting of the darkness, the lightening of the fever; the day of languor that followed, messages from Ahencora, from Darco, from Fuah; all secretly glad that the white man had got the fever again; all rejoicing in another chance of delay.

At last came the 15th of January.

I rose from my bed on the floor, and sent for Ahencora. "I am going to the Prah," I said to him. "You have 200 men here. March them with me to the river."

"He could not," he said. "His men were not yet all come in."

"Will I end the work for once and all, and strike the brute with my stick with all my strength across his head?" I thought. "But no—better not—we will try this game of patience a little longer. By force I can do nothing. Whatever is to be done with these people must be done by other means." I turned from him; "All right," I said, "I go to cross the Prah. Perhaps the Ashantis are as cowardly as you are."

I set out. Brabazon and Macgregor followed, an old chief led the way. The Prah, he said, was but a few miles off. · Half a dozen Fanti policemen brought up the rear ; some Akim women, hired at Tribee, carried our scanty loads. Three miles brought us to the Prah. It lay in the dense forest, a yellow, slow-moving mass of water, not one-third in size of what I had seen it one month before, some thirty miles lower down its course. On the south shore some fifty or sixty Akims, the advanced guards of Fuah's and Ahencora's forces, were camped in small huts of palm-leaves. Some were smoking, some fishing in the yellow stream, some cleaning their guns or Enfields.

I summoned the chief in command of this guard.

" On this day," I said to him, " the English General invades Ashanti. To-day he crosses that river, thirty miles from where we stand. I mean to cross it too ; move your men over, and make your camp on the Ashanti shore."

" They could not cross, they were too few ; the Fetish held the river ; they could only cross when all had come up."

" Very well—the day has come—the order of the General must be obeyed, and the white men who have come to fight for you will cross the river alone."

The Akims squatted on their haunches upon the edge of the steep clay bank which overhung the river.

Having rested awhile in their midst, I told the policemen to carry a few loads down to the edge of the ford. There was a ridge of sand in the centre of the stream, and beyond this ridge the current ran deep and strong. We waded to the sand island ; and then, divesting ourselves of nearly all our clothes, took the deeper water. At one point it rose to our lips, then we barely touched the bottom ; in another second the outlying branches of a

6.

fallen tree met our grasp, and, climbing through its submerged branches, we gained the farther shore.

It was some time after mid-day. Not a sound stirred in the great forest of Ashanti. The Akims stood in groups upon the south side, gazing vacantly at the white man's doings. They might well look ; the sight was a curious one.

Three white men and six Fanti policemen, carrying baggage, had invaded Ashant.

CHAPTER XII.

"THE Prah rolls to the sea," says a proverb of Ashanti.
" It's waters do not come back again; neither can the
white man come hither from the sea."

Well, we had come hither.   But, what then ?

The breadth of the river did not matter much, Coomassie
was a long way off; and of my Akims, there did not seem
even the vestige of an army.

We made our camp on a ridge of sand, ran up a lean-to
of leaves, lighted a fire, and cooked our dinner.   When
night came I put three of my six policemen on sentry,
and lay down for another night of fever under the shade
of an evergreen tree which had its roots in the sand.
The leaves dripped plentifully during the night, the fog
rose from the river, and the sleeplessness of fever made
me aware of the peaceful and profound slumber enjoyed
by my three sentries towards the small hours of the
morning.

The morning of the 16th found our positions unchanged, a few more Akims came up to the south shore,
but none would cross except to fish or gather plantains.

At mid-day came a letter from Sir Garnet, and
despatches from the chief of his staff.   On this day, the
16th, Russell's regiment was to reach the foot of the

Adansi Hills. In ten days more the entire force would be concentrated at Quisah and Fommanah, holding the road to Coomassie as far as Detchiasoo. I was to advance north-west from the Prah, scouting as I went, and spreading in all directions the alarm of a large force along my route.

Another night passed, and the 17th brought distinguished arrivals. Fuah, Ahencora, and Darco appeared upon the south shore, built huts, and smoked themselves idiotic; messengers passed and re-passed the river; the Akims came in batches of tens and twenties; an incessant noise of hammering filled the air, it was the braves beating out the lead into slugs and pellets.

Later in the day a doctor arrived from Prahsu. The news of so many officers being down with fever had induced the despatch of this officer. He carried a small medicine chest, and a large guitar. He was a powerfully-built man, full of energy and life and vigour; wore a Scotch cap in defiance of the sun, and laughed at malaria.

"Malaria is only a convenient name," he frequently observed. "There is in reality no such thing." I was happy to hear it; but, as I had already suffered to the extent of many days fever, and the loss of between two and three stone in weight, I might be pardoned for thinking it an *inconvenient* reality.

The last limit of patience had now arrived: we could wait no longer.

On the morning of the 18th I summoned Fuah, Ahencora, and Darco across the river. Seated on a sand-hill under the big tree, we held a stormy palaver. A hundred excuses were put up; the old, old reasons for delay were refurbished. Darco added his lies to the innumerable falsehoods of the other kings. More arms, more time, more money, white soldiers to assist them—these, and fifty other demands were put forward.

In vain I read to this triumvirate of cowards the general's letter, in vain I pictured to them in glowing colours the plunder of Coomassie, they would not move. " Then the game is over !" I said after an hour of this fruitless labour. " We leave you to-morrow morning, and return to the main road at Prahsu. We cannot lose this war because you are cowards."

The palaver broke up in storm—the kings went back to their camp on the south shore, and on the morning of the 19th, after a final appeal, we set out for Prahsu. I had stretched human endurance to a point not easy for others to comprehend; not easy even now to realize myself, and the long weary game seemed at last over. As I quitted the Akim camp, and moved towards Bero- nassie, Ahencora, Darco, and Fuah came quickly after us.

" Surely, I was not going to leave them ? If I would stay they would do all I wanted."

How they begged and implored !

" Too late—too late," was my sole reply to them. " I gave you to the last moment—the time has now gone by." Then I turned south with a heavy heart, and plodded on towards Beronassie.

That night, as I lay in a small hut near Beronassie, I think I spent the bitterest moments of my life. Health, strength, toil, name; all set upon this venture, all perilled or lost—the result—nothing. Yet I do not think that the sense of failure, bitter though it was, was the keenest sting felt that night. Injustice, so easy to inflict on others, is the hardest of all things to bear ourselves; and paramount above every other feeling, was a sense of the injustice of these coward kings. If ever a man had spoken truly to them, kept faith with them, acted to the last letter of what he had promised them—I had done so. In meetings and palavers most monotonous to repeat, I had harped ever on the same subject. " We are not as the traders by whom you have been so often deceived. What we promise is as fixed as the sun."

Little by little I had seen the effect of this policy tell upon these savages; I had, as it were, lived down their prejudices. Three months passed in their midst had taught them at least the lesson, that the white man could tell the truth. I do not think that it set their ideal of truth or honesty one jot higher. I do not think that they regarded me at the time in any higher light than had I cheated, tricked, or duped them; but when I spoke they believed my word, even though their own innate cowardice and falsehood remained unchanged.

Well—as I have said, it was the sense of this success with them, dashed now by the wretched end of the expedition, that made the moments of that night so bitter. I had not tricked them—they believed me—yet they had utterly failed me. It had been hard to see the earlier energy of three months ago, regarded by my black kings as a cause of suspicion.

" If he toils thus what sinister objects must he not have in view ?" was an unasked question which I had frequently read on the broad faces of my surrounding negroes; *that* was an unpleasant attendant upon labour; but harder still, was the reflection that even with suspicion partly overcome, the negro had utterly wrecked the cause I had striven for. Enough of this : it is not easy to write of it calmly, even now !

On the morning of the 20th, I arose with the dawn to find Darco and another chief present.

Darco had come from the Akim camp during the night as the bearer of an urgent message from the kings. " If I would go back again to the Prah, the Akims would cross the river that day, and move into Ashanti, halting when I wished, going on when I ordered. He had brought with him the Chief Phim-phon, a man whose knowledge of Ashanti was excellent. Phim-phon would act as guide. Phim-phon knew the paths : all would yet be right." So spake Darco, of Accassie, with an amount of gesticulation and gesture needless to dwell upon. I listened with ears that drank greedily, and mind that doubted gloomily. What if this were true ? What if these men would even now go forward ? it was not too late. The object of the expedition might yet be accomplished.

" Listen, Darco. I will go back to the Prah, and test the truth of what you say."

Right or wrong, I made the resolve quickly. It meant but a day's delay, if still the Akims would not move. It meant in a great measure the fulfilment of the general's object, if they would move for even three days into Ashanti. It meant still a chance of success where already the cup of failure had been deeply tasted : so we went back to the Prah.

I took up my old station on the sand-bank on the north shore, and awaited the result of the day. Our latest arrival, the doctor, remained on the south shore in the midst of the Akim camp, and began a series of manœuvres with Ahencora and Fuah, of a singular character. He insisted upon their moving at once—they began slowly to cross. The doctor became more urgent—we could hear him from the north shore, using language the strength of which must have made it easily intelligible to any savage or civilized race on the globe.

At last he seemed to be running a-muck amid the lean-to's and leaf-huts, and the disconcerted Akims came over more quickly.

I sat on the sand-ridge counting them as they emerged from the water. As the valiant kings came up they made a low bow to us, and passed on into the forest. Ahencora's men led the advance, Fuah brought up the rear.

Darco came up with a sort of "I-did-it" air and expression on his sable countenance. Phim-phon was got up regardless of clothing, arms, or ammunition, as the " guide, philosopher, and friend" of the expedition.

This passage of the Prah was irresistibly ludicrous. It was terrible work to get the fat form of Fuah over the river without immersing him in the water. Darco was a tall and attenuated savage, who, as I have already mentioned, bore upon his person indubitable proofs of the "flanking tactics" of the Ashantis. The Akims themselves were strange figures; some tall and strong, some small—all muscular—all shining like liquid tar, as they came from the water.

Every kind of weapon was represented in the force. The king's attendants carried Sniders; about half the force had Enfield rifles, the other half had the long flint native gun, polished and in good order. The lead was carried in small bags upon their heads. A load of " Kanke" meal being likewise borne in the same manner.

We kept the score pretty regularly as the dusky warriors passed our stand-point. Never shall I forget the appearance and costume of No. 311. He was a large

powerful negro, armed with a long flint-gun; he was utterly
destitute of clothing, unless a square black Dutch bottle
could be construed into a garment. He took the field, in
fact, with a flint-gun and an empty Holland's bottle, for
clothing, arms, and equipment; the gun was balanced
upon his head; the bottle was worn after the manner of
the old Hussar jacket, suspended from the left shoulder.
His whole appearance fulfilled the requirements of what
is termed " an Irregular." He was, I think, the most
irregular-looking soldier I had ever seen.

It was impossible to look gravely on as this warrior
" marched past," and we greeted his appearance with
shouts of laughter.

'These be soldiers,' I thought again; 'aye, in the
catalogue they count for such.'   So No. 311 was duly
registered, and passed on to the war. When the last
man had passed, the fighting doctor came over, and we
set out for Embronem.

It was a fine bright evening. The ruined village of
Amantea was soon reached, its masses of plantains lying
still in the flood of golden sunlight, its orange-trees long
run wild, hanging thick with over-ripe fruit.

By sunset we reached Embronem, and the long deserted
and ruined croom was busy with strange and unwonted
life. Men were cutting wood, lighting fires, building leaf
huts, clearing the old ruins of their tangled foliage.

The scene was the first satisfying sight I had looked
upon for many months ; and later on, as I penned a short
despatch for Prahsu, announcing my advance at last into
Ashanti territory with even this scant semblance of a
savage force, I felt as one who, after a long weary night
of doubt and disappointed longings, sees at last the faint
gleam of the dawning.

We laid our dinner that evening in the open moonlight of Embronem. It was one of those nights so bright with yellow lustre, so blue with the shadow of the vast vault above, that the sense of sight, satiated with the fulness of beauty, long carries without effort the fragrance, and coolness, and refreshment of their memory.

Moonlight is to Africa what it is to the ruin and the graveyard :—the kraal, the croom, the forest, or desert, change their natures beneath this flood of yellow light; and morning comes as a cruel awakening from the dream of beauty which the night has brought to us.

To-night, at Embronem, we looked on such a scene. Not a breath of wind stirred the tree tops, on the topmost rim of which Canopus lay like an immense brilliant, throbbing with pulsations of coloured light; the blue smoke of the wood fires rose into the large open space in which we were camped, in fragile pillars of vapour; high in the zenith hung the great globe of the moon, standing out clear and distinct in the sky, its light so vivid that only the larger stars could pierce its lustre.

It is little wonder that in such a scene, and with hopes growing fresh again after many disappointments, our spirits rose as lightly as the grey smoke that curled above Embronem.

We ate our dinner, and when the Australian meat and a guinea fowl had been disposed of, and the time for the fruit had come, we summoned Fuah, Ahencora, and Darco to join the festive board. It is almost needless to say we had no fruit, but the fighting doctor had brought from Prahsu a demi-John of rum; Brabazon was the fortunate possessor of some cakes of chocolate ; and some knowledge of native tastes had convinced me that, even without the last-named condiment, we possessed in the

P

first-mentioned article a substitute for every other food, fruit, or drink known to the African.

"Go," I said to Dawson, "tell Quabina Fuah, Coffee Ahencora, and Chief Darco, that we will be glad to see them here, to drink a glass of rum to their success in this war."

Presently came the three doughty leaders. A mob of henchmen followed them, half in fear, half in curiosity. Fuah drank his rum as though it were the weakest water; only after repeated potations, did he appear to relax under its influence, and then merely to that degree which is implied by the somewhat vulgar but expressive term "Squiffy." It was dreadful waste of liquor, but justifiable under the exceptional circumstances of the case. I think that if I had the power of placing a ten-gallon cask every day ten miles in advance of my army, Fuah would have gone boldly forth day after day to the uttermost bounds of Africa : such was his love of drink.

While Fuah's broad face began to wink blandly at the moon, the indefatigable fighting doctor performed a series of fantasias on the banjo. He informed Fuah and the other kings and chiefs that " Love was like a cup of tea." He melodiously " ran them in " several times, and finally he addressed the now half-inebriated monarch by the title of " His lady love," and besought him to " Look down on me."

All this time Fuah sat on his stool the picture of inebriated perplexity. The banjo was a "fetish" of unwonted power; the doctor was a fetish man of a high order : the song was evidently an incantation of unusual potency, and between rum, song, and the " fetish," Fuah was utterly bewildered. At last there was no more rum, and they went away to their respective bivouacs.

About nine o'clock on the morning of the 21st of January I got some one hundred men together, and sent them on along the path towards the south-west. An hour later the entire force straggled out of Embronem for a farther advance; but the halts and delays were incessant, and it was late when the second village beyond Embronem was reached—Branqua on the hill. Here an altercation occurred, which well-nigh sent the whole force flying back to the Prah.

Not satisfied with the progress made, I was desirous of pushing on three miles farther to the village of Abramassie; with this object I directed the fighting Doctor to proceed to the front, and superintend the movements of Ahencora's men. As we descended the hill from Branqua I came suddenly upon Fuah, and then Darco, making a retrograde movement from the front. What were they doing? What was the meaning of this strange conduct?

They jabbered an unintelligible reply, and pointed forward.

"There was much confusion," said the interpreter, "between the white officer and Coffee Ahencora in the front."

I pushed rapidly on to the front. The rounds of incessant jabber filled the forest. I reached the scene of disturbance. There stood Ahencora with his chiefs, the picture of fear. His face wore that peculiar green tinge which the African assumes in moments of terror. Before him stood the fighting doctor in the act of replacing his revolver in his belt.

The story was soon told. The doctor had found Ahencora camped, or in the act of camping. He had urged a forward movement to Abramassie. Ahencora had demurred, out came the revolver, and hence the hubbub.

Fuah and Darco hearing of the row, were making "the best of their way home."

The moment was critical. I stopped the tumult, ordered that on no account should a weapon ever be drawn upon king, chief, or soldier, and quieted the outraged honour of Ahencora. He was bad enough, but he was the best of the lot; and in any case I had long learned the utter uselessness of coercion, where at any moment my whole force had but to step into the bush from the pathway on which they marched to be irrevocably lost to me.

I ordered Ahencora to send on his scouts to Abramassie, and we camped that night on the borders of a small stream at the foot of Branqua hill.

Late in the evening came letters from head-quarters. Among them was a note to each king, threatening him with the severest displeasure of the general if he persisted in his refusal to cross the Prah.

I sent these letters unopened to the kings, and shortly afterwards they came to request that I would read and explain them. I was already made aware of their contents by a copy enclosed to me; but I now read them aloud as for the first time.[1] When the reading of these documents was over, I said to my audience : "These are the words of the English general. He wrote them during the days you remained inactive at the Prah. By this time he knows that you have crossed the river and advanced into Ashanti; but remember, he expects you will keep moving, and moving quickly. On the one hand, he offers you his friendship and his rewards; on the other, if you fail he gives you rockets and ruin."

Rockets and ruin ! Fuah funked a rocket as much

[1] See Appendix, No. 30.

perhaps as anything, save an Ashanti soldier. Having heard and inwardly digested this matter of rockets and ruin, my kings withdrew to their camps.

The next morning we got away after the usual delay and two hours' labour. Ahencora (who now led) blew his horn; Darco "too-tooed" upon his; Fuah brought up the rear in stately dignity, marching after three of his wives. As the campaign was supposed to be one of great personal danger, the remaining seventy-seven wives were left at home. One of the three selected to share the perils of war carried on her head the gold dust or cash box of her lord and master; in camp another performed the duties of cook.

Fuah's face bore a striking resemblance to portraits of Henry the Eighth; in figure and proclivities he also resembled that monarch. Black, however, as the Tudor king has been painted previous to the era of Mr. Froude, he could not have been as black as the Akim monarch; and, in the matter of wives, Fuah certainly surpassed the great Reformer.

The Akim, too, was fond of the block as an institution in his kingdom; in fact, his executioner always accompanied him in war and peace; but whether this functionary was a prominent feature of his domestic economy or not, I cannot with certainty aver.

On the 22nd of January we pushed on from Branqua by the ruined croom of Gademwaah to deserted Yancoma. The distance was about eight miles, the path good, the country deserted. As we approached Yancoma evidences of Ashanti scouts were met with, and the ashes of fires lighted since the last rains showed the recent presence of people on the now quiet pathway.

Yancoma was a pretty spot. The forest had long covered the vestiges of the croom, and clumps of huge bamboo trees rose on the margin of a broad river, which rushed with impetuous torrent over immense rocks. This river was called the Ennoon—a name destined to appear frequently in the remaining pages of my story. It was a stream larger than the Prah when I had last crossed that river; it was as wide or wider than the Birrum, but it differed in every way from these waters. It foamed along in the bright flashing of many rapids, and the noise of its waters filled the forest with that sound which of all others falls with a soothing, lulling charm on the troubled mind, and nowhere falls on the ear with such a charm as in the hot lands of the tropics.

After this vast, dense, soundless forest, in which water was stagnant, muddy, and filled with forms of death, it was refreshing indeed to look upon this snowy torrent of the Ennoon, and to lie lulled by the ceaseless roaring of its torrent.

Under the great clumps of bamboo, whose tops rose up high above us, and drooped downwards again, forming as it were an immense canopy beneath which the light was darkened, we made our camp that night.

Beautiful as was the spot, it had its drawbacks. With nightfall came the fog, and the leaves of the bamboos dripped as though a heavy rain was falling; chill and damp came the midnight, and in the morning my latest accession, the fighting doctor, was down with fever.

At this place (Yancoma) I was well into Ashanti, but as yet no living enemy had been met with—all was silence in the vast forest; all was ruin and overgrown creeper in the croom or village.

So, far for this eighteen or twenty miles to the Prah it

was new Ashanti and old Akim; and though more than forty years had gone by since Ashanti had conquered it, it had been suffered to remain a wilderness without people. Here, however, at the Ennoon this state of things was to end; beyond this rushing river the villages of Ashanti began, and grew denser as Coomassie was neared. Two roads led from Yancoma—one, crossing the Ennoon river, led in the direction of Quisah to the west; the other led nearly north to the villages of Ennoon-su, Akina, and Coomassie.

Before deciding which road is the best to follow, we must glance aside a moment at the movements of other columns. By the last despatches from head-quarters, the advance of the main column was at the Adansi Hills; by the 26th, now four days distant, the whole force was to be massed at Fommanah and Quisah, preparatory to a direct advance upon Amoaful and Coomassie. Amoaful has since become a well-known name; but then it lay in that shroud of obscurity which hung around fifty other names along the onward pathway of our little army. Yet months before this name of Amoaful had caught my attention, as I lay one evening in an Assin croom, studying the itinerary of scant information, which a Wesleyan minister journeying years ago to Coomassie, had compiled as he was carried.

"Amoaful," said the guide, "from here there is a branch road to Akim." Two other places bore the same notice, one was at the foot of Adansi Hills, the other somewhat nearer to the Prah. Both these last-named spots were now in unopposed occupation by the main column, and consequently were useless as points upon which to move from Akim, if the line of advance was to be an independent one.

While it was yet a matter of doubt as to whether the Ashantis would oppose the passage of the Prah, or defend the line of the Adansi Hills, these two last-named routes from Akim had engrossed my attention; but when news came that the adventurous Gifford with his few scouts had climbed the steep ridge of Adansi, and looked down upon the old kingdom of Ashanti from its rugged frontier, it was evident that a line nearer to Coomassie must be followed, if my Akim horde could succeed in deluding the Ashantis into a belief in the existence of another column of invasion.

That native help could ever be made of use in actual conflict with his enemy, the English general had never for a moment allowed himself to believe; but that the presence of a column of Akims along the route which led from Accra to Coomassie, by the Lake Boosumaque and the holy city of Cocofoo, would tend to embarrass the plans of the Ashantis, and probably cause them to divide their forces, thus weakening the resistance they would oppose to his main advance, was a contingency, the probability of which, in his opinion, was most likely to arise; and it was this aim and object which he had in view, when he ordered the enterprise I am now relating.

Events had now rendered it imperative that to make this expedition felt by the enemy, a road must be followed which led well into Ashanti; one of the four great paths by which the Ashantis traded with the sea—the road from Cocofoo to Accra.

It was therefore along this path that I was now moving, intent on striking the main line of advance at Amoaful, at which place the two paths converged. Let us now turn a moment to the right flank of my advance, to a line still farther to the east, along which another column had been ordered to move.

Captain Glover had raised in the eastern districts of the Protectorate an immense force. It numbered between 40,000 and 50,000 armed men. It was composed of the natives of many tribes, acting, in a semi-independent manner, under the leadership of their several chiefs; but in addition to this horde of undisciplined negroes, he had a force of some 900 trained Houssa and Yoruba soldiery, armed with the Snider and bayonet.

As we have stated in an earlier chapter, he declared war against certain tribes on the Lower Volta, and in the month of December moved his forces against them. The war was the usual description of African campaign. Time, so precious to the European chief or soldier, is the last item thought of by the negro.

Croboe or East Akim, Accra or Aquapim, were in no hurry whatever to settle matters with their enemies beyond the Volta. To drink rum, to fire off powder in their camps, to eat "fetish," to do all that we have seen my army doing for the past two months, and in addition to that, to draw good pay or presents for doing it, were occupations singularly in unison with African predilections.

War upon such a scale will ever command a considerable following in negro-land, and will be filled with examples of heroic persistency and long-continued fortitude. I do not think the African would ever grow weary of such a struggle, or wish to exchange it for more peaceful scenes.

But on this occasion time would not wait for the Croboe, or the Krepee; Coomassie had to be taken in the first week of February, and already January was at hand. This Volta war might last a negro lifetime, and not be much nearer its end then; so, late in December, Captain Glover received urgent orders to abandon his trans-Volta campaign, and to move his forces to the Prah.

To the Croboe, the Krepee, or the Aquapim war on the Volta and war against the Ashantis were too widely different affairs. Of the many thousand warriors of these tribes, none would obey the order to change the scene of conflict, only the trained Houssas and Yorubas answered the command to move upon the Prah, and with these men Captain Glover prepared to carry out the orders which he had received.

Moving quickly from his camp upon the Volta, he reached, by dint of hard marching, the neighbourhood of the Prah, on the 13th of January; and on the 15th, crossing the river with 800 or 900 trained soldiers, captured the village of Obogoo. His line of advance at the Prah, was about as distant from mine, as mine was distant from that of the main column. At Obogoo we were still closer together—the estimate is one of conjecture; but I do not think that from my camp here at Yancoma to that of Captain Glover at Obogoo, was more than fifteen miles as a bird would fly. Fifteen miles is a short interval between two columns; but in such a forest as this of Ashanti, the distance of such a measure becomes vastly increased; one mile through this dense tangled wood is more than equal to ten miles of any ordinary land. Nowhere is it possible to strike to the right or left, from a forest path, so filled with obstructions of rock and fallen tree, is the surface of the ground; so matted together is the immense vegetation which darkens the earth, that he who would strike out for himself a track through the bush would come hopelessly to grief.

No pathway led to the east from the line of my advance from the Prah; here at Yancoma, as I have said, the main track divided into two paths, one leading west-north-west; the other north-north-west. I was desirous of following the first-named road, which led to a place called Dadiasso, a town of many inhabitants; for, by doing so I would be drawing nearer to the main column, at its point of concentration at Fommanah. But some ill-defined feeling of fear seemed to weigh upon my black kings; they dreaded to meet the English general, of whom they had heard so much; and although I constantly reiterated to them that their reception would be most flattering if they advanced, even at this hour, with resolution and energy, yet I was never able to over-come this dread of the main line, and they persisted in their avoidance of it, even though it promised them security from the Ashantis.

On the morning of the 23rd January, many signs were apparent of another delay. The guides were absent, and no search could trace their whereabouts. Phim-phon, who had sworn every oath in the fetish calendar to guide me truly in Ashanti, had vanished. The Akim, whose long residence in Ashanti had made him valuable as a source of information, had also hidden himself, and the three kings kept dodging to and fro in the forest avoid-ing my presence.

I saw it was another case of the Prah, and prepared to meet it as best I could. It is needless now to detail the substance of another palaver; it was the old story, so often repeated.

Pretexts were put forward as frivolous as they were false; ignorance declared of every path or road, distances distorted, anything and everything done to effect the one great object—delay.

Towards mid-day I so far triumphed that I succeeded in starting a body of scouts along the path leading north ; they were to be out all night, and great things were predicted of their doings.

At daylight they returned. They had attacked the village of Akonwherry, on the Dadiasso road; the inhabitants had run away ; the village was set in flames—it was a great triumph !

" Where are the prisoners ? " I asked.

" Ah ! the Ashantis all ran to the bush; there are no prisoners."

I had offered a reward of three pounds for every prisoner taken. This was to stop, if possible, the barbarous practice of decapitating all prisoners, and to obtain some information of the country before me ; but the reward was offered in vain.

That these scouts had entered some village during the night was evident, for they carried with them as loot some wooden stools, half a dozen fowls, and a few eggs. Never before had such an event been known in the memory of the oldest Akim. The soldiers of Ahencora and Darco had actually entered in war an Ashanti village, and got out again. The rejoicings were very great. All through the mid-day the camps were in confusion, and at length things culminated in a row.

The soldiers of Darco and those of Ahencora quarrelled over the spoil. The jabber rose to an infernal din ; guns were seized from their forked sticks ; and everything promised a very pretty fight.

At this moment Fuah appeared with a large whip. For the first time in his life he exerted himself. He lashed about him with the whip, and after a few minutes the braves, who never had the least idea of letting their fight pass the limits of jabber, dispersed to the different camps.

Somewhat elated by their success, in this daring capture of defenceless Akonwherry and its decayed eggs, the kings seemed emboldened to another move. Ten miles to the north lay a village called Ennoon-su. We would push forward a party of 150 men, with two officers and the rocket trough, and occupy the village.

The scouts of Fuah averred that they had been to this village, and that like Akonwherry, its inhabitants had deserted it; we would occupy it while thus deserted; and when the inhabitants returned, as they assuredly would, we would meet them in the village.

After a deal of talk this was agreed to, and a couple of hours before sunset the party got away,—Macgregor, Brabazon, a rocket trough, a bundle of rockets, and about 100 Akims. It was my intention to follow at daybreak with the bulk of the Akims, and I expected to reach the village in time for the morning's skirmish, an event which I looked upon as certain to occur.

At dusk I sent messengers through the camps, warning the chiefs to be ready for an early move, and long before daylight I was stirring in our wet bivouac under the dripping bamboos.

The fighting doctor was very bad. He lay in his hammock utterly reduced in two short days from extreme strength to complete weakness. I had no carriers, but I could not leave him behind. After several ineffectual attempts to procure Akim carriers, I succeeded in getting three tall slaves of Fuah's household to carry the sick man; and having arranged matters for his safe transport, I set out for Ennoon-su.

Not an Akim chief or soldier had stirred from camp, and I was forced to lead the way alone along the forest track.

Long experience had shown me that it was just possible by this means to shame them into following, and in this case I was right. Before I had gone a mile from the camp, a chief and six men overtook me ; then more and more, until at last I had a couple of hundred warriors. We walked fast to recover the time lost in getting carriers for the sick man.

All at once there was a shout in front, and presently an Akim came running back along the track carrying something on his head. He brushed by me as he ran. The something on his head was a half-earthen dish or water-vessel, in the hollow of which lay a freshly-severed human head. I stopped the rascal as he ran ; his news was soon told :—

" The Ashantis had come to the village; there had been a fight. This head had belonged to an Ashanti ; he was taking it to his king, Fuah."

The pace quickened, and in less than an hour I saw before me a wide river, beyond which stood a group of huts on the farther shore. It was Ennoon-su : the fight was over.

I forded the river, and listened to the story of the skirmish.

Led by the two officers, the party had reached the neighbourhood of the village at sunset, on the preceding evening, a few Ashanti scouts falling back before them as they advanced. Expecting a volley from the village, the two officers dashed into the water followed by the Akims, but no stand was made by the retreating scouts, and Ennoon-su was found deserted.

The Akims were placed in line along the forest edge; the officers occupied the village, in the centre of which the rocket-trough was placed. The night drew on : suddenly, about midnight, a portion of the Akim line came at full speed into the village, shouting that the enemy was approaching; then all the other Akims turned tail, and bolted in wild confusion for the river; forms rushed past the officers' hut in the darkness, and everything seemed to betoken that they would be left alone to do battle with the enemy; but no enemy appeared, and the fugitives halting at the river edge, gradually reoccupied their old positions.

Morning came, and the light seemed to reanimate the spirits of the Akims. They cleared away the bush in their front. All at once the sound of men approaching was heard : the sounds ceased, the men had stopped, then a voice was heard through the trees thus :—

" Ho—who are you on this road? We have come to see if there are white men on this road."

Two shots were now fired in the bush, it is asserted, by the newly-arrived party; the Akims returned a volley of buck-shot from their Enfield rifles. The effect was deadly —three men were shot, several others were wounded, and the attacking party instantly fell back.

One of the officers was bathing in the river; the other rushed from his hut to the front to find his soldiers busily engaged in cutting off the heads of the fallen. The first head taken was by a soldier of Fuah's. Fuah, as we have seen, was far away from the spot, fulfilling to the letter the regulated position of an Akim king in fight, namely, eight miles from the nearest firing; but the head was sent at once to the Akim generalissimo, who doubtless received it as another token of his unbounded bravery.

Soon upon the opposite shore appeared Darco at the head of his braves. Darco crossed the river, and at once suggested the propriety of his removing again to the shore whence he had come, and there making his camp.

Had an Ashanti shot been fired at that moment, I have not the least doubt but that Darco would have fled ignominiously across the Ennoon, nor ceased running while life and legs lasted. I endeavoured to reanimate his spirits by assuring him that we had gained a most important victory. He smiled a ghastly acquiescence, and Ahencora's arrival convinced him that for the present his position was secure.

Lastly came Fuah, seemingly the hero of the day. "His men had cut two heads," he said. "He had placed his feet upon the skulls of his enemies!" After this the destruction of Ashanti must be only a question of time.

One fact became very apparent from this skirmish, namely, the power of the Enfield rifle to throw buck-shot with deadly effect. In one instance, the gun held by a man who had been killed was found with its barrel shot through and through by a pellet. I am strongly of opinion that for close bush fighting, such as this of Ashanti, there is no weapon so effective as a double-barrel breach-loading gun throwing buck-shot.

We must now travel in imagination a few miles to the east, to the head-quarters of Glover's column, at a village called Conomo.

From this village of Conomo, on this same 25th of January, a party of East Akims started with the intention of attacking a small croom, which they said lay some distance to their west. They reached this croom : shots were fired, a loud volley broke suddenly from the bush, and the East Akims ran away, leaving three of their party dead, and carrying several wounded along with them. They fell back at once to their camp at Conomo, and reported to their commander that from the loudness of the fire which had greeted them they were of opinion that the village was held, not by Ashantis, but by " West Akims of Cobra Fuah;" and they requested that an English officer and a bugler might be sent back with them to the village for the purpose of ascertaining if their supposition was correct.

Upon reaching again the neighbourhood of the village a panic seized the Akims, and they fled in disorder to Conomo; but it has never been explained how it came about that no more determined effort was made to solve the question, for most undoubtedly the East Akims were correct in their assertion that the loudness of the fire at Ennoon-su proved the occupation of that place by my column. Yes, ridiculous though it may appear, there can be little doubt now[2] that the three men killed were East Akims of Glover's force; and that on the 25th day of January there did not intervene between Conomo and Ennoon-su more than eight or ten miles. Of that proximity I had no clue. It was only long months after, that, in reading the despatches of the commander of the right column, I saw the supposed Ashanti attack at Ennoon-su had in reality been made by a portion of Captain Glover's column. So that on this and the two following days, these two columns were in near proximity to each other, but to one only, was the clue revealed.

Eight days later a detached force of Captain Glover's

[2] See Captain Glover's Despatches of January 28, 1874.

Q

column did attempt to form a junction with my force on this river Ennoon; but it was then too late to do so.

Two days more brought a considerable accession to the number of my braves.

On the 26th I held a rough kind of muster, and found I had got together about 1400 men; more were yet coming in, and others were reported farther back along the road; so that the estimate of numbers made by me some months before as to the probable strength of a West Akim force was nearly realized, and I might confidently look forward to having 2000 naked savages assembled within one day's march of Coomassie by the 1st of February.

In spite of delay, of falsehood, of deceit, things began to look better. Here at the Ennoon river I was but two days' march from the Ashanti capital, and Amoaful, the spot towards which I was tending, lay but one day distant. So far nothing had occurred to cause panic amongst my braves. In cutting off the heads of their cousins, the East Akims, they had fancied they were having a signal triumph over their Ashanti enemies. Even Darco seemed to have recovered himself a little under the influence of this unusual success; and as for Fuah, he only wanted a demi-John or two of rum to set up his standard within four miles of the nearest skirmish.

To still further enhance the value of this signal victory, I caused a day's pay to be distributed to the force; and the whole of the night of the 26th passed in a wild scramble for the pieces of silver scattered through the now numerous camps.

It would be no easy matter to give even a faint idea of the noise and jabber attending a payment of my army.

When I first entered Akim, silver coin was almost unknown. I carried with me a considerable sum of money,
all coined in threepenny pieces—all as new and as shining
as the Mint could make them. These bright silver bits
were in vast repute for some time; upon receiving his
threepenny, a native would usually wear it as a ring upon
his finger, and each day's work would result in the addition of another ring upon his fingers, until upon the fifth
day his immense thumb would shine resplendent with its
"bit." But after a while the novelty wore off, and threepenny rings were at a discount, and were gambled freely
against gold; but the love of bright silver never departed,
and at last when another consignment of coin reached
me, I found it almost impossible to circulate the older-
looking shilling, and the half-crowns of the Georges and
the last William. Often there waited a deputation outside
my hut to offer back some dull-coloured florin or leaden-
looking sixpence, under the impression that it was "no
good;" and "this no queen's money" became the invariable accompaniment of every payment.

But I stoutly combatted the idea by declaring that the
coin was even still more valuable than the new one, as it
bore the image of the queen's grandfather, and was becoming every day more scarce in the kingdom. On the
present occasion at Ennoon-su the payment was on a
scale larger than it had ever been before, and the noise
and jabber were quite in keeping with the magnitude of
the time.

Had a hundred Ashantis appeared at this moment, I
have little doubt that the entire Akim force would have
executed a rapid movement upon the Prah; as matters
stood, however, the day passed away without alarm of any
kind, and in the evening I received a promise from the

kings that they would move towards the Amoaful path on the morrow.

We were now in one of the great gold-fields of Ashanti, the richest, perhaps, of any known to man on the African continent. This river, called Ennoon, rolls through a rough country filled with indications of gold. Around Ennoon-su the whole surface of the country is excavated into wells, or circular holes, long since sunk in search of the precious metal; these wells are placed frequently quite close to each other. It would appear that the negro miner had never mastered the common knowledge of sinking a shaft, and then running a tunnel along the " bed rock," on which the gold dust of necessity lies densest. He sunk his well, took what gold he could find at the bottom, and then, abandoning that spot, sunk another shaft close by, until the entire surface of the land became pitted with wells.

Of quartz-mining I could see no indication, although the reefs were numerous enough. The turbid current of the Ennoon in times of flood crushed on its own account, and with the subsidence of the water the natives still find upon the rocks the small nuggets which have fallen from the broken fragments, as they were rolled along the river's bed.

If ever a time shall come when the climatic conditions of this land shall change, and human life be able to sustain itself in this vast forest of death, the skilled labour of the white man will still find in this long-worked gold-field a rich harvest for its toil.

For four hundred years Ashanti has sent its gold to the sea. Four hundred years again there will be gold in that land of death. I had seen in far northern lands gold locked in great cañon caverns, treasured by nature in the

midst of rocks, behind mountain masses, and in the depths
of vast solitudes. But man had hunted out the hidden
metal, and possibly his life in the venture had unlocked
the secret safes of the earth.

Here, in Ashanti, Nature had seemingly guarded her
treasures by a process more completely effective than
that of great distances and giant mountains encompassing
them.

The grim figure of Fever stood sentry over the mine of
wealth, ready to wither with his burning touch the adventurous white man who would dare to seek this gold
lying close beneath the red surface of the earth.

By the evening of the 26th of January, the scramble
was over. More Akims had joined me; the faithful
Pappho had come from Prahsu beaming with smiles, and
grinning from ear to ear. He had picked up two other
carriers on the road.

Everything looked well, and I turned into my Ashanti
hut that night with hopeful anticipations of an early move
to the north-west on the morrow.

CHAPTER XIII.

It was the 27th of January. At nine o'clock in the
morning I got about 100 Akims together, and started
them on a path leading to the north-west, a path said to
conduct to Akina, Mansuah, and Dadiasso.   Brabazon
commanded this advanced guard.   Macgregor and Lowe
were still suffering from fever ; the latter, being unable to
walk, was borne by the faithful Dawson and two policemen.

I felt certain that we should fall in with Ashantis, and
gave orders for the entire force to move in support of the
advance.   Ahencora got his men away in tolerable time.
Darco and Fuah hung lazily along the road.

It was the usual day of sun above the tree-tops ; of
mingled shade and fretted light beneath them.

The country north of the Ennoon was broken and
rugged, many watercourses ran between steep and lofty
hills, but hill and valley lay clothed in the same dense
foliage, and shadowed by the same gigantic tree-tops.

Filled with a sense of disease and the presence of death,
that forest wore to us who toiled beneath its shadow, a
gloom the memory of which long months have failed
to dissipate ; yet was it a very beautiful earth-covering,
and as one sees in the tiger symmetry, despite savagery,
and in the cobra beauty beneath the reptile form, so, in this
forest of fever, the eye rested at times upon vistas so

filled with the marvels of vegetation, gigantic leaf, fragile fern, rare exotic, tree-trunk so great that only California's mammoths can vie with them—and the mind forgetting for a moment the skeleton ever lurking beneath, and seeing only the beauty, exclaimed, "This forest has no equal!"

Other thoughts than these had I to con over that day on the path to Akina.

About mid-way on the road I stopped awhile to ascertain how my army was following, and to close up the scattered links a little. While sitting by the pathway a pencilled note was put into my hands. It was from Brabazon. He had come upon a camp of Ashantis deserted, but with fires lighted; the enemy had retreated before his Akims without firing. I wrote a reply and sent Pappho at full speed to the front to deliver it. My orders to him were to await the closing up of the main body and my arrival before proceeding forward, then I hurried on with all speed to the front.

Half an hour's rapid march brought us to the Ashanti camp; some of Darco's men had occupied it and seemed loath to quit it. Motioning to them to follow at once, I pressed on, for everything betokened an ambuscade, and I feared lest Brabazon's impetuosity might hurry him too far from support. All at once the sound of musketry broke through the forest; loud and long the echoes caught up the discharges, and sent them ringing through the deep vaults. I pressed forward at a terrific pace, followed by Macgregor, who staggered as he ran from the effects of the fever. Over the hills, through the watercourses we swept, while the sounds rolled on as before. The sole thing to dread was a panic in the front; if the Akims with Brabazon took fright, or fancied them-

selves unsupported, they would run to a man, and leave
their leader to his fate. If they knew that I was approaching with a large body of men, they would stand.
Among my Fanti policemen there was one who acted as •
bugler. He had formerly served under the Dutch at
Elmina, and he blew the Dutch bugle-calls with some ,
precision. The small boy, whose ear for music was
wonderfully acute, whistled most of the English calls,
and the Dutch negro was in the habit of taking lessons
from him in the evening when the march was over; so
that a delightful medley of the war-calls of Holland and
England had resulted from the practice.

On the present occasion I bethought me of the bugler
as a means of conveying courage to the Akims with
Brabazon, and, while continuing the rapid pace to the front,
I shouted vociferously for the Dutchman. He was some
distance in the rear, and evidently in no hurry whatever
to advance.

In language impossible to transcribe, the wretched
blower was now summoned to the front; at last he
appeared in sight, but his gait and manner showed that
he was making the most of any obstacle on the road to
retard his progress. When he finally reached me, I was
not in an amiable mood towards him. "Blow the advance, you vagabond!"

He blew a note so utterly at variance with any known
call, that it would have been sufficient in itself to alarm
the bravest soldiery. I could stand it no longer, and by
a vigorous application of my cane to the bugler's back, I
made him produce sounds from his bugle which were
satisfactory. The "advance" was blurted forth with a
vivacious distinctness impossible to picture. The faster I
beat, the better he blew, and thus we proceeded at a

rapid pace up the steep incline which led to the village of Akina, on the top of which the fusilade was growing fainter.

As we pushed up the rugged path at a run, we passed Ahencora's men extended along both sides of the track, prominent among them being our old friend Kru, now doing duty as a private soldier with a full-cocked rifle in his hands, his chieftainship having vanished under the pressure of a great fear.

He nodded to me with a ghastly smile, but the usual " How-are-you-quite-well-thank-you " died upon his lips.

A few yards brought us to the summit of the hill; the firing had ceased ; the Akims were busy looting the huts. Two of Fuah's soldiers lay dead at the far end of the village, and a small group of their friends stood round their bodies smoking and chatting.   Overhead blazed the zenith sun, for it was nearly mid-day.

Akina stood upon the crest of a very steep, conical hill, around three sides of which flowed a small stream. Dense forest covered the slope, but the top was bare of trees and half covered with mud and wattle huts.

Over this hill the Ashantis had retreated, abandoning the village to the advancing Akims who spread at once through the houses in search of plunder.   At the far side of the small village where the ridge sloped abruptly to the west, and the dense jungle recommenced, the retreating Ashantis turned upon their pursuers, and a thundering volley from out of the green leaves showed the Akims the position of their foes.

The Akims at the front were the bravest in the army, and, though taken somewhat by surprise, they held their position well, firing back at random into the bushes,

jumping and skipping about as they loaded and discharged their Enfields, while their leader, Brabazon, well in
the front, continued to empty his revolver pertinaciously
into the trees.

The Akims had the advantage of numbers, the Ashantis
of position; lying concealed by the slope of the ridge,
they were perfectly safe from the bullets of the Akims,
which invariably passed over their heads; but it was
fortunate for Brabazon and his men that the force before
them was a small one, for, standing out well in the open,
close to hidden foes, they must have suffered severely
from a heavier fire. Two of their number were shot dead
in the front, a circumstance which showed how close was
the fire of their opponents.

All at once the fire from the trees ceased, the iron
pellets stopped their flight, and Brabazon, gathering
together a few braves, pushed down into the bush with
the intention of following along the path to the west.

Just at that moment I reached the summit of the
ridge and stopped a further advance. It was not a
moment too soon. These Ashanti tactics were easy
enough to read. Ambuscade after ambuscade, with ever
increasing numbers, and a constantly decreasing pursuit.
Fuah miles away in the rear with the bulk of his
men.

So far all had gone well. We had taken Akina, a
croom where an Ashanti war captain held his post, and
we had lost only two men; we were within a few miles of
Amoaful, and it was only the 27th of January.

I threw out a line of scouts around the base of the hill,
and as the different bodies of Akims came up they made
their camps along the stream and up the slope of the
ridge. I kept a few men upon the summit, and made my

own camp in the houses, clearing away all but those required for our use; then the usual despatch was written to the general, and the day's work was over. The quiet time, the evening, had come.

On the top of this hill we stood more than one thousand feet above the sea; through open spaces among the lower set trees the eye looked over deep valleys of forest-tops, and hills such as this of Akina stood out around us. It was a bright, pleasant sight to see the slanting sunlight of the evening streaming along these green valleys, and turning the rippling summits of the forest to liquid gold. We had so long been beneath this great forest that it was pleasant to get even partially above it for a little.

Many tracks and paths branched from Akina. The Ashantis had retreated along a well-beaten path leading towards the west, towards the main line of advance; their camp lay evidently in that direction; so far as we had gone the main column of invasion had not reached a position on the road to Coomassie parallel to the one I now occupied at Akina.

Among the articles found in the huts, there was the stool of the Ashanti captain who had charge of the district. It was a very curious article; its original colour had long vanished, it was dull and deeply stained with human blood. Many a life had been shed above it; it was of great age, and from the manner in which the Akims regarded it, it was evidently of the highest reputation. They brought it to me as a present, but I did not desire their blood-stained gift, and I told them to keep it themselves.

I lay down that night to sleep with a belief that we should be roused during the night by an attack; weapons were placed ready for use upon a sudden awakening. All at once, in the depth of sleep, a loud volley of musketry broke upon our ears, and I awoke to find my anticipations realized.

I dashed into the open, the shots sounded close at hand, just beneath the first dip of the ridge on the northern slope. There was a loud volley, and then a few scattering shots, and again all was silent. I ranged my eight or ten policemen round the huts to guard the baggage, and sent messengers to the camp, telling the Akims to remain in their places. Never had I known such a silence through the ranks of my army, not a man moved, not a voice spoke. At last, up the hill-side, came envoys from Fuah and Ahencora, begging that I would sound the bugle for the purpose of scaring away the Ashantis. I sent them back to say that I would *not* sound the bugle, that nothing better could happen than that the Ashantis should attack us here in this strong position, and that we relied upon other means than the bugle for the purpose of carrying dismay into the ranks of the Ashantis.

From whatever motive the attack was made, it was not followed up, and silence reigned over the forest hill. We were about to lie down to rest again, when two Akims appeared at the huts, they had been struck by the Ashanti slugs as they lay asleep in their camp, and they wanted their wounds dressed by the surgeon. . A party of Ashantis had stolen well into the camp and fired suddenly upon them. They had answered with a random volley, and that was all they knew.

When daylight came I examined the ground; the Ashantis had stolen in by a secret path winding through the camp, and had actually reached undiscovered within sixty yards of the huts; here a fire was smouldering, and by its flickering light they could discern the forms of some Akims stretched upon the ground wrapped in their white clothes. At these figures they had fired, and then vanished in the darkness.

What was the object of this night attack, of this stealthy creeping of a small body into the heart of the Akim camp? The guide whom I have mentioned, the Ashanti-Akim, gave the answer :—

"The Ashantis had come in the hope of recovering by stealth the blood-stained stool so sacred in their eyes. By this secret path they knew that they could approach the village unseen. The fire had frustrated their design, and in a moment of panic they had fired at the sleeping forms around it and fled."

There was a large Ashanti camp near, somewhere to the north-west, between Akina and Cocofoo.

I passed the whole of the 28th of January in strengthening the position of Akina; the vacant spaces were occupied by men; the low brushwood was cleared away in front; paths were cut, bringing the camps into closer communication with each other.

In the evening a thunderstorm rolled over the hills, and a few drops of rain fell. In the pauses between the thunder, another sound caught the ear; the Akims spoke to each other, and I saw them listening intently; this other sound resembled the roll of musketry, it was fainter than the thunder, and it came from the west-south-west.

"They are fighting on the main road," I said to my companion.

The Akims still listened; but upon asking them what the sounds were they answered "Thunder." Yet I was not convinced, for though blended with the distant rumble of the thunder, the other sound had in it a peculiar sharp roll such as musketry alone can produce.

As usual, the Akims lied; that distant roll came from Borborassie, on the west of the main road, where, shortly before sunset on this day, Nicol was shot dead leading his men into the village.

Later in the evening shots were fired in our rear, along the path by which we had advanced from Ennoon-su. Shortly afterwards the small boy, ever on the alert for news, ran in to announce that "white officer was on the road," and presently Paget walked in upon us. He had made a forced march from Prahsu in four days. He looked pale and emaciated from fever, very different indeed from the picture of health and strength he had presented on that day, just a month earlier, when he had first joined me; but this African fever finds in British pluck its most obstinate opponent, and long after health is sapped, and strength has vanished, the staggering limb and wandering brain are kept to their work by the spirit which will not declare itself vanquished.

Paget had fallen in on his road with some small parties of Akims coming to join me. As he approached Akina his party was fired upon by our men, these were the shots we had heard in our rear. A ridiculous scene had thereupon taken place. Paget and his Akims occupied the crest of a hill, the supposed Ashantis were in a valley; both sides, believing the others to be enemies, prepared for battle. Neither would advance. At last some of Paget's braves, bolder than the rest, crept down the slope and captured an outlying Akim belonging to the opposite side. Then the mistake was discovered without further strife.

Strange though it may seem, it was no easy matter to know an Akim from an Ashanti—language, voice, and even accent, are identical, and so unable were the Akims themselves to note the difference between their foes and themselves that they wore around their necks pieces of tin as a distinguishing badge.

I spent the 30th of January in urging upon the kings the necessity of another movement. In the evening I succeeded in getting a scouting party as far as Mansuah on Lake Boosumaque, a lake famous in the traditions of the country, and one which has been heretofore placed on all maps of Ashanti many miles from its true position.

To the south of Mansuah there is a high hill, and from its summit the eye ranges over a wide view to the north; at the base of the hill lies the village, and just beyond it the Sacred Lake, then a vast ocean of tree-tops; and far off, when the day is clear, there is seen a faint, blurred speck, a brown island midst the green waves—it is Coomassie.

Yes, from a spot four miles from this camp at Akina, the goal of the expedition was in sight.

At that time I had not much of that physical strength left which holds distances of little account, every mile was a matter of consequence, each step was sometimes a labour; but had I the power to see a few days deeper into my life, to know even the events that the next fleeting hours would bring forth, I think I would have crawled on hands and knees to look from that hill-top on the city towards which my steps had toiled through all this weary forest—but which I was not to see.

The Akims had requested to be allowed to conduct this scouting expedition to Mansuah by themselves, and according to their own methods. Upon their return to Akina they told the following story.

They had found Mansuah deserted; they had entered

the village, and roamed through the houses.   Suddenly a
voice was heard calling to them ; they had run away at
the sound ; but seeing no one, they had again entered the
village : the voice called again ; going cautiously to the
place from whence the sound proceeded, they had found an
old blind man lying on the ground unable to move.   He
was an Akim of the old Akim kingdom which had once
been subject to Ashanti, and he had remained in Mansuah
years ago, when the Akims had fled beyond the Prah and
formed their present kingdom.

The Ashantis, he said, had abandoned Mansuah five days
earlier.   He was too old to go, he had remained behind
alone in the hut until the voices of the scouts had sounded
in the deserted village.   Then the following dialogue took
place between the old man and the Akims.

" Who are you ? "

" We are Akims."

" To what king do you belong ? "

" To Coffee Ahencora of Akim-Swaidroo."

" Where is your king ? "

" He is at Akina, a short way from here."

" Go back to your king and say to him that the Ashantis
are in a large camp at Cocofoo ; that the King of Ashanti is
there ; that there is another large camp at Amoaful on the
main road, and yet another on the Duabin road to the east."

Such was the story which was brought by the scouts to
Akina, and which was at once carried to me.

I was puzzled : it had about it a certain air of probability ; yet so often had these Akims lied to me, I
might say so universal had been their habit of falsehood,
that it was almost impossible to bring oneself to credit
aught they spoke.

This story brought back by the scouts was eagerly seized

upon by the kings in answer to my frequent demands that they should march forward.

"I will not ask you to go to Cocofoo," I said to them ; " but let us move to the west on Dadiasso : the villages along the path are many, but they are small. Already the General writes from Fommanah—his soldiers are by this time at Amoaful. Let us move to Dadiasso, and we will there be close to the main road."

But they answered, " We do not know where the General and the white men are. We cannot move until we know where they are." Vain was it to tell them that every day would make a change in the position of the white men, that long before we could hear of them they would be in Coomassie, and out of it again. This news from Mansuah had filled them with fear. Darco was positively in a terror so great that he threw off all semblance of courage. His teeth chattered at times when he urged in palaver the terrible danger we were in.

"Where is this blind man ? " I asked. "Why did you not bring him with you from Mansuah that I might question him myself.

Then twenty men volunteered to go to Mansuah and bring him back a prisoner.

On one point the Akims were right in their estimate of the Ashantis. On the evening of the 29th of January I received a despatch dated "Fommanah, 25th January," announcing in a hurried postscript that the King of Ashanti had acceded to all the demands of the Major-General, and that in consequence of his submission there was every probability of a speedy termination of the war.

Upon communicating this news to my kings they took quite a different view.

R

" The Ashantis would fight," they said; " they were a very bad people."

By mid-day on January the 30th the scouts returned from Mansuah, bringing with them the blind Akim.

When he came before me he told pretty much the same story which the scouts had repeated on the previous day. I questioned him very closely, but he generally managed to evade me by rambling off into a long statement of the fetish which had lately appeared to him. This fetish was called Cauthawherry; he dwelt in open spaces in the woods; he was equal in rank as a fetish to Kikawherry.

This is what Cauthawherry said to the blind prisoner :—

" This country is to belong to the Akims, as it did in times gone by. Coffee Ahencora is to rule over it. He will soon come to this place. When you hear that he has come, tell him to beware of the Ashantis; if he goes too far they will entrap him, and destroy him."

This and much more did the old Akim pour forth whenever I tried to pin him to date and place as to the movements of the Ashantis. He still, however, maintained that there were three large Ashanti camps formed to resist the three columns of invasion, and that Coffee Kerrikerri had been present at Cocofoo three days earlier.

When I dismissed the old man I went round the camps once more, and tried separately to move the kings to Dadiasso. I promised money and large reward, I spoke with the earnestness of a man who sees almost within his grasp the consummation he has long striven for.

There over the tree-tops to the west lay the main road, how near I could not say, but certainly not a day's march distant.

" You get up in the morning and leave Dadiasso," said

the Akim guide many a time to me. "The sun is not much above the trees when you are at the main road." And here was Dadiasso only a little way to the west; no wonder, then, that I strove by a last effort to bridge that short intervening space, and by one other day's toil to carry this long severed chain to its link of union with the main column.

Looking back on that day from the stand-point of the present, it is not easy to make the mind recall the varying threads of thought which, woven from long hours of doubt and toil, drew together here in a final anxiety. It would be still more hopeless to attempt to place them before the reader. It was not that in all things in life success is ever sweet, and failure ever bitter; or that the fact of success in this particular instance could affect in any degree the fortunes of the campaign. It was not that the feat of marching these 2000 reluctant and cowardly savages from the Prah through that (to them) fetish-guarded forest, was in the remotest sense a military achievement; but it was—that here at Akina the long months of labour, of doubt, of sickness; of hope dashed by disappointment; and disappointment lightened by hope; of falsehood from without; of success just sufficient to make failure always possible, always bitter—it was that all these things culminated here into a focus of intense and absorbing earnestness, making the last move of a long wavering game, a stake in which life and all it contained seemed of little moment.

Here at last it seemed that in another day I should hand back to my General, completed and fulfilled, that trust which he had placed in my hands three months before.

Well, if it be pleasant work to fight our battles over

again, they should be the winning ones, and not those of lost ventures.

As I reached my hut on the hill-top after a final fruitless effort to stir the kings into action, I noticed groups of Akims engaged in tying together small bundles of dry reeds, the inner fibres of the palm-leaves; others were engaged in packing together the bundles which they carried on the march.

Before many minutes men began to move off by paths through the trees towards the south.

The Akims were retreating.

For a moment I was stupefied. Surely it could not be !

Then came a ghastly procession of the wretched kings to speak to me. " The Ashantis were surrounding them on all sides. That morning an Ashanti, one who had long dwelt in Akim, and had joined them in this war as their comrade, had deserted to his people. He had gone to tell the Ashantis how weak were the Akims, and to bring them upon them. They must go back while there was still time."

I heard all this as one might hear something in a dream. It was different from any excuse they had ever made to me, not in its sense, but in the manner in which it was made. While they spoke the Akims were already moving off in long lines for the Ennoon: the whole game was over !

It does not matter much what I spoke to this craven throng; I remember but little that passed now—though the surrounding scene stands forth in my memory, and I see as vividly as though they still stood before me the crowd of men who could not look me in the face, the dark figures moving away into the forest, and the bright sunshine on the orange-tree in the open space.

I had some vague idea of staying at Akina by myself and letting the others go away. I went mechanically into the hut and sat down; the few bearers had got their loads together, and were moving away; Paget, already in a relapse of fever, was being carried out by the policeman. I sat there alone for some time in a kind of stupor, then my two comrades came, and, taking my arm, roused me, and we went out into the open.

The greater number of the Akims had gone; but Fuah and a select body still lingered on the edge of the forest. The moon was high over the forest when we reached the Ennoon, the silver river was black with long lines of men wading to the south shore, and it was long after midnight when the yellow torches ceased to pass beneath the dark vaults of the forest.

We slept that night in the forest not far from the river; but the panic-stricken horde pressed on, and many did not pause until Yancoma, twenty miles distant from Akina, had been reached and passed.

In the grey of the following morning we again moved south.

There was but one hope left now, and that was by a rapid march we might reach the front ere Coomassie was taken. Possibly we might be able to strike across from Embronem or Yancoma to the foot of the Adansi hills, and thus save a longer round.

But this latter course depended upon Akim assistance, and in that I had no faith.

About the time that we left our forest bivouac that morning, many men were moving from a croom called Egginassi, a few miles to the west of Akina on the main road to Coomassie; below them lay a swamp, and farther on a hill and a large Ashanti town. The swamp was nameless until that day, but since then, and for long years to come, it will be remembered as the battle-ground of Amoaful.

It was the 31st of January.

CHAPTER XIV.

THE next few days are a dreary record.

We plodded on, some weak and faint, some strong, all silent and gloomy as the forest which lay around us.

We crossed many streams and rivers, fording them as we came to them, and going on again as our clothes dripped dry. Sometimes it was fierce sunshine; sometimes a torrent of rain; and sometimes we lay down at night in the wet to sleep.

Paget was very weak from the fever, the doctor was scarce stronger, still both struggled on in some kind of way.

We could find no path at Yancoma. No path at Embronem leading to the west; so, following the longer track to the south, we emerged at last at Prahsu on the fifth day.

At Prahsu little was known of the state of affairs at the front. There had been a great fight at Amoaful, and then the army had pressed on towards Coomassie, and all was silence. So, after a night of sickness at Prahsu, I turned north again with a hope that I might reach the front before Coomassie was taken. The companionship of my little expedition was ended at Prahsu, and each one pressed on for himself.

The track was now broad and open, a veritable road; hammock-travel was easy, and, sick or well, movement became possible.

At Fommanah, on the 6th, I heard of the capture of Coomassie; but the news was meagre in the extreme, and rumour vague and conflicting filled up the want of definite tidings. Stray parties of Ashantis were still hovering along the road.

An hour before daybreak on the 7th I got away from Fommanah. It had rained all night unceasingly, but with the dawn the clouds had cleared off, leaving the brooks changed to torrents, and the rivers running deep and turbid.

At Kiang Boussou the temporary bridge had been swept away; and it took us two hours to cross the rushing flood which filled the river channel.

All day I toiled on; rapid marching had used up the carriers, and they lagged far behind along the road. After mid-day I began to pass bodies of men moving to the south. Convoys of sick and wounded, where, from swinging hammocks, men with large, lustrous eyes and long-drawn faces, looked vacantly out at the shifting mass of light and shade through which they were being borne.

Towards evening I drew near Amoaful; the forest sent forth a deadly odour; bodies, horrible to look at, lay at intervals along the track, and, as one passed them, myriads of flies rose from the sickening mass and struck against one in their random flight.

On I went through Egginassie, through Amoaful, through Cocofoo Quantah, until, as the sun went down beneath the trees, I gained the last hill croom called Aggemmaum.. It was dusk when I entered this village, in which for the night of the 7th the English army had encamped.

Along the path on either side white men—soldiers— were busily engaged cooking and eating their suppers. English soldiers! It was pleasant to see them again; one felt inclined to stop and shake them by the hand. Soldiers at last! They looked at me, wondering, no doubt, why I should be marching the wrong way now; for their work was done, and their faces were turned to the sea. At the far end of Aggemmaum, the head-quarters occupied a group of Ashanti huts. Near the entrance to the court-yard of these huts I met the General.

Four years earlier, far away in the great wilderness of North America, I had met him once before on my return from another expedition, as his Iroquois canoe shot from the outlet of the Rainy Lake down the rapids of the Rainy River.

The times were changed.

Then a great success was awaiting at his hands its final development; now a campaign filled with the difficulties which lie beneath enterprises which have no parallel, and which are without precedent, had been accomplished, and Wolseley was leading back his army to the sea—the most successful British soldier of the age; for never before in our times had a war been entered upon under presage of disaster so loudly prophesied, and so widely believed by the outside world; and never before had promise of success given by its leader been more fully and completely verified. Almost to an hour he had kept time with his friends and with his enemies.

A strange unwonted war had this been, too. Looking for its counterpart, one must seek the record of by-gone strife, when Latin Europe first moved into the New World, and the mailed chivalry of Spain scaled the sun-shrines of Cusco or pierced the mountain-passes from whence the mysterious Mexico lay outspread at their feet.

Not to Wolfe, not to Clive, not to Napier, had a more singular success been given.

Far in the depths of this forest—a crimson island in a sombre ocean—lay hidden away this city of blood. The forest was filled with poison and death—men withered beneath its dismal shade. The city was red with the blood of countless victims, shed through long years of crime; the ghastly drum of death beat daily in the streets, colossal vases filled with human gore stood before the fetish fanes, and day and night the scent of death hung foully over Coomassie.

No wall or rampart defended this city; but fifty leagues of fever circled it; a vast superstitious dread protected it, and thick set in the forest swamps of Amoaful, and along the slopes of Ordahsu crouched 20,000 of the bravest soldiers of Ashanti.

And now the crimson city lay a charred ruin in the silent forest, and with faces turned to the sea the little army and its young leader struggled on towards home.

It was thus at the last moment of his triumph that I met the General. Many things had changed with me: he was the same: ready with kind word and smile; as little moved by success, as he had been cool and confident when difficulties impended.

To few men Fortune gives the gift of fame; to fewer still she gives the mental power—the tact and manner which has nothing to learn from success.

This meeting in the forest of Ashanti brought vividly before me the memory of that other meeting in the rapid

of the Northern river, making the weary struggle through
which I had just passed, look all the more dismal. Still
there was enough in the leader's voice and glance that
night at Aggem'maum, to make even the follower who had
failed a prouder man.

Next day the little army continued its march to the
south. Silence reigned again in the vast forest; the
vultures wheeled above Amoaful; the great trees lifted
aloft their arms to the sky as though fierce waves of fight
had never ebbed and flowed beneath their dusky shadows.

Thus the English regiments and their leader left this
dark spot of Africa to its wonted gloom and short-broken
desolation; but they left behind them, too, other record
of the work which they had done.

Buckle at Amoaful, Eyre at Ordahsu, Nicol at Bor-
borassi, Huyshe at Prahsu, rest for ever in the endless
silence of this vast twilight. Nothing marks their forest
graves; the long dim tree vaults close their arches above
them; the leaf falls through the still, dank gloom, and
the night dew drips its endless tears through the long
watches of the tropic darkness.

Thus they sleep—better there in the forest, where
they met death doing brave work, than in the hum of
cities or in dim cathedrals their last resting-places had
been made.

And here it is fitting to close this history. For, as I
write, the sandy ridges of Kaffraria rise over the Indian
Sea, and a great war-ship, under clouds of canvas, bears
swiftly to a new sphere of action the chief whose mission
it ever seems to sustain at the farthest confines of the
empire the honour of the crown he serves so well.

On the 17th of February a worn-out man reached the

summit of one of those low jungle-covered hills which lie
behind Cape Coast Castle—the moan of surf—a sound long
unheard—was audible, and a vague blank upon the
southern horizon showed where lay the road to England
—the sea. As he reached the crest of the ridge, lights
gleamed out from ships at anchor, and one broad flash
shot forth into the darkness, followed by the sullen sound
of the evening gun.

"The sea at last! the work is over!" thought the
traveller; "there is nothing more to be done but to go
on board a ship, lie down and rest, until England is in
sight."

Such rest was not to be. A fever—compared to whose
deadly strength all the previous fevers had been as nothing
—burst suddenly upon him, and the long-pent poison of
these weary hours of toil found at last expression in overwhelming illness.

During many weeks he lay on the confines of the two
worlds—a waif, flung more than once from the sea of life
upon the dim shore that lies beyond, and sent back again
to life by a Mightier Power.

Then came a long period in which the sick man looked
at life as some bird prisoned in a cage, or, maimed of
pinion, might look upon the sunshine and the blue sky
where so long had been his home.

And then, as the dark memories of toil and fever and
failure faded away, health came back with a brighter picture. A great hill-side, at the base of which an isle-set
sea broke in dreamy ripples; far out a deep blue waveless
ocean; above, the purple hill-top sleeping in the sunshine, and around the lazy hum and scent of summer in
far-stretching heather.

APPENDIX

CONTAINING

COPIES OF INSTRUCTIONS, DESPATCHES, LETTERS, &c., RELATING TO CAPT. BUTLER'S MISSION TO AKIM.

No. 1.

HEAD QUARTERS, CAPE COAST,
2nd Nov., 1873.

INSTRUCTIONS for Captain Butler, late 69th Regiment, who has been selected by the Major-General Commanding to proceed on a special mission to the King of Western Akim:—

You will proceed on the 3rd instant, in one of her Majesty's men-of-war, to Accra, en route for Western Akim, to the king of which country you are accredited as a "special commissioner" in connexion with certain correspondence that has taken place between his Excellency the Governor, Major-General Sir Garnet Wolseley, K.C.M.G., C.B., and the kings, queen, and chiefs of that district.

You are empowered to offer the same terms to the kings and chiefs of Western Akim that have been promised to the other kings.

You will take with you 100l. for your own expenses.

Copies of the proclamation lately issued are enclosed for distribution by you to the kings and chiefs, and you will use your best endeavours to raise the whole of the fighting men in Western Akim for the purpose of closing in upon Amonquatier's army, as it is endeavouring to recross the river Prah into Ashanti.

You are fully aware of the position of affairs here at present, and you will not fail to keep the Major-General well informed every two or three days—through Mansu—of your movements, and how you succeed in your mission.

Your messengers will be paid at Mansu, on an authority from you, whatever sums you may consider necessary for carrying your despatches.

It is impossible to give you more precise instructions; accordingly, there is nothing to add further than that the Major-General relies upon your zeal and discretion, and on your knowledge of barbarous people, to carry out quickly the objects of this most important mission which has been confided to you.

By command,

J. S. BAKER, Major,

Acting Chief of the Staff.

No. 2.

ACCRA, 5th Nov., 1873.

SIR,—Upon landing here yesterday morning, at 6.30, I found that Captain Glover had not yet started for his camp at Addah.

The town was almost denuded of workmen; all the male inhabitants being either *en route* to the camp, or engaged in making "custom" with rum and gunpowder for their approaching war.

I have succeeded, however, in obtaining the necessary number of bearers and carriers, and everything looks fair for a start in one hour's time.

King Quabina Fuah has disregarded the injunction to remain at his capital, and he is reported to be within two days' march of this place. Upon my arrival yesterday, I despatched a messenger to him, announcing my coming, and requesting him to remain at his camp until I should join him at the earliest moment. The kings of Croboe, Eastern Akim, and Aquapim have already moved towards Captain Glover's camp at Addah.

I have the honour to be, sir,
Your most obedient servant,
W. F. BUTLER, Captain.

The Chief of the Staff,
    Cape Coast Castle.

No. 3.

ACCRA, 4th Nov., 1873.

To his Majesty King Quabina Fuah, of Western Akim.

This is to inform your Majesty that I have reached the port of Accra on my way to your capital city, as the Envoy and Commissioner from his Excellency Sir Garnet Wolseley, the great General of the English army at Cape Coast Castle.

I will join you at the earliest moment, and deliver to you the special message from the General.

I will stay with you through this war. We will march together against the enemy; we will fall upon the Ashantis as they fly across the Prah, driven off before the victorious English General.

Let your chiefs and head-men assemble; let all your fighting men come together; let only the cowards and the women stay at home.

Then it will be said of your Majesty, "The King of Akim's name is a terror in Coomassie."

W. F. BUTLER, Captain.

No. 4.

IS SABAN, 8th Nov., 1873.

SIR,—On the 5th instant, an hour before sunset, I got away from Accra with a very motley group of carriers and

bearers—the only people that could be procured in the confused state of that city.

On the evening of the 5th I reached the village of
Obootoo, and there found messengers from King Quabina
Fuah on their way to Accra.   They reported their master to
be only half a day's journey distant, and they begged I
would await his coming at Obootoo.

I replied that the Governor had already written to King
Quabina Fuah, requesting him not to go to Accra; that I had
also written from Accra to tell him of my approach, and that
if he were only 100 yards distant I must still go on to meet
him, as Accra was only occupied by the lame, the blind, the
women, and the children; while at Akim and along the Prah
the enemy was to be found ; that there all brave men, kings or
soldiers, should turn their steps.

I sent the messengers back to the king, and early next
morning started forward to meet him.

I soon fell in with his advanced parties.   At mid-day I
reached the village of Edooefoo, and found the king was
close at hand.

We met in an open space at the entrance of the village.
He was surrounded by his chiefs and soldiers, and preceded by drums adorned with many skulls.   Two mace-
bearers stood on either side, bearing maces made of human jaw-
bones, the teeth of which formed the outer surface of the
bludgeons.

I received him with all the ceremony possible—the Union
Jack unfolded.   I read and explained to him the letter of his
Excellency, and the proclamations relative to the recent movements against the Ashantis, and then I urged upon him the
necessity of taking immediate steps to intercept the enemy at
the Prah.   All was of no use.   " He humbly begged my
pardon and the pardon of his Excellency, and the pardon of the
Queen ; but he must first go to Accra to do ' fetish.' "

During nearly two hours I made use of all the arguments

which are supposed to sway the savage mind. I told him that his name and fame had gone before him to the ears of the Governor at Cape Coast Castle; that people said of him that he was ever forward against the enemy, and that now Accra was held by women, and the enemy was seven days' journey behind him. All was of no avail. "He most humbly begged pardon! but he must go to Accra."

He appeared sorely puzzled and distressed, and seemed to labour under a belief of the imperative necessity of his going first to Accra. Then I told him that I would go on alone to Akim and rouse his people.

He said that he would only stay one day in Accra, and would follow me quickly to Akim; that his generals and his army were still at home, and that they would do all I wished if I should arrive before him. So we parted.

This evening (the 8th) I reached Is Saban, and was received by the King of Agoonah—a very old man, almost in his dotage.

I am still confident that I will arouse in these people a certain fighting ardour.

It is my intention, after seeing King Coffee Ahencora, who is reported to be within a few miles of this place, on his way to Accra, to proceed with all rapidity to Akim, and at once hold palaver with the chiefs who, in the king's absence, command there.

I am now four days' journey from Insuaim (the king's capital) and seven from Prahsu in Akim. I reckon my distance from Accra by track to be about forty-seven miles. From the north of the Seccoom river my course has been N.W. and N.N.W., with many windings. Hammock travel is impossible, and the path is hilly and much obstructed by fallen timber.

On the evening of the 7th I crossed the Ayeshu river (which enters the sea at Winnebah) near the town of Koniako. The country continues to ascend as I proceed ; the elevation of this place being by Aneroid 400 feet above the sea. The villages are prosperous, and the country well stocked with supplies.

The road from here to Mansu runs *viâ* Esse Comah, and is three days' journey. Agona-Swaidroo is a day's journey to the south, and Esse Comah a day to the W.S.W.

The river Ayeshu is about thirty-five feet wide, seven feet deep, and has a strong current. It is useless for canoes, owing to its rapids. The country from the mouth of the Seccoom river is free from forest. Scattered clumps are met as we proceed inland, and the bush is reached at some seven miles from the sea. As we proceed further inland the forest becomes denser, the hills are steep, and the trees are of enormous growth. In the hollows much mud and water lies upon the track.

The obstinate reluctance of King Quabina Fuah to abandon his visit to Accra is the natural result of the formation of a base of operations at Accra at a period prior to the arrival of his Excellency at Cape Coast. Summoned first to Accra, and afterwards to Dunquah—hearing of presents being made at Accra, and of the arrival of a governor there—the chiefs of Akim and Akim-Swaidroo have already become sorely puzzled as to the point at which their true interests lay.

Finally they have decided that Accra was their real base, and every effort to convince them to the contrary has but tended to confirm that impression, and to foster the natural suspicions of a barbarous people.

I have no doubt that I shall be able to eradicate that impression, and to prove to them that at Cape Coast lies their best interest; but much valuable time will be lost, and the long start which Accra has had cannot be overtaken at once.

For many reasons I deemed it wiser to leave King Quabina Fuah, and push on alone to Akim. Already he is much perplexed as to the state of affairs, and my warning that he was turning away from his interests, as a king and a soldier, will have greater force when he finds that I am pushing on towards his country.

9th Nov.

I have just finished a long palaver with King Yowdowdoo, of Agoonah. He is a very old man, but his chiefs promise in his name a fighting force, which they estimate at 2000 (probably 500) men. I have directed them to assemble at Akim-Swaidroo, on the Birrum river, with all possible despatch; but that phrase applied to African warfare is a burlesque.

I have promised that arms and ammunition for a portion of them will be procured as soon as possible viá Mansu; but I have said that their own weapons must be taken to the field, pending the reception of the new ones.

If I am rightly informed, Akim-Swaidroo is equi-distant from Mansu and Prahsu.

ENI-A-CROOM, 9th Nov., Evening.

To-day I came on here, three and a half miles W.S.W. from Is-Saban, and found King Coffee Ahencora with a considerable retinue awaiting me. He is bound also for Accra. I held two palavers with him, and soon discovered the drift of his grievance. "The arms and ammunition sent from Accra on the 9th of October had all gone to his rival, King Quabina Fuah; nothing had come to him, King Coffee Ahencora. He had done much fighting against the Ashantis in the summer, more than King Quabina had; how was it that he was forgotten?"

I explained to him the difficulty of communicating with him through Accra, but that now all would be made right. There was a wide road to Mansu. We would send there and get arms and ammunition for him, the same as that already sent to King Quabina.

Again and again he returned to this grievance; and again and again I assured him all would be right. I gave him four of my own rifles and three sovereigns as a present, and told him that if his carriers were ready, they could start for Mansu at once. He is an intelligent man, and evidently has a good deal

s 2

of authority with his people. He wishes me to wait here for the return of his messengers from Mansu; but I combat this wish with all my power.

I tell him that his interest is my interest; that we are not as palm-oil traders, wishing to outwit him, but that if he will join us, our interests will be the same, and he will be well cared for.

ENI-A-CROOM, 10*th Nov.*, 1873.

Another long palaver this morning. It is slow, slow work, but I tell a little each time upon these suspicious natives. Captain Glover's "dashes," and the unlimited distribution of rum at Accra, have long since reached here, and at present I have only my oft-repeated word against this powerful impression.

I must urgently request that supplies of arms, ammunition, and rum be sent to me at the earliest moment, and a letter written by his Excellency to King Coffee Ahencora will have a good effect.

I feel sure that I can make something of him. There is a considerable rivalry between him and King Quabina, which I must turn to advantage. I expect his final answer in a few moments, and meantime I will close this already long letter, written under no little inconvenience, with the assurance that nothing shall be left undone to assemble on the Birrum river a force which shall make itself felt either at Assin-Prahsu, or at Akim-Prahsu, as his Excellency may desire.

I have the honour to be, sir,

Your obedient servant,

W. F. BUTLER, Captain.

King Coffee has just consented to return with me to Akim-Swaidroo, and to proceed at once with the calling in of his men to Akim, his capital.

No. 5.

LIST OF ARMS, AMMUNITION, &c., required for use of King Coffee Ahencora at Akim-Swaidroo. To be forwarded from Mansu as soon as possible.

500 Guns (a certain proportion Enfields).
125 Kegs of Powder.
  5 Bags of Lead.
100 Bars of Iron.
100 Cutlasses.
    Flints.
    Ammunition for Enfields.
    Gun Caps.
£100 (half in silver), for disbursement to chiefs, soldiers, &c., as pay from the date of enrolment.

All to be addressed to me at Akim-Swaidroo, and a responsible person sent to see that they are brought direct to me from Mansu.

In addition to the above,

    20 Gallons of Rum, and a share of Tobacco will be required.

W. F. BUTLER, Captain.

ENI-A-CROOM,
  10th Nov., 1873.

No. 6.

BRANQUA, Nov. 15th, 1873.

MY DEAR MAJOR,—I fear I am not up to official form, so please excuse this pencil note. On the evening of the 11th I reached Dobbin, and half an hour after arrival was down with fever.

For three nights it held me hard, but yesterday morning I was able to make a start, and got to this place last evening.

Both places are wrongly placed on all the maps—Dobbin too much to north and east, and Branqua to south and west.

I need scarcely say what a blow this delay has been to me ; but the cause of it is easy enough to see now. I had such a set of rascals as bearers and carriers from Accra, that I had to urge them unceasingly, and so overtasked myself.

Then these wretched kings, all bent on going to Accra the very moment they should have been at home. This morning I am better. I will try and get to Akim-Swaidroo this evening, or at latest to-morrow noon. King Coffee Ahencora is with me, and of course will not move without me, though I have asked him to go on, and make all arrangements ; but all these people are like children.

Quabina Fuah's city is a short distance from Akim-Swaidroo, higher up the Birrum river. From Akim-Swaidroo to Prahsu (Akim) about the same distance.

The chief of this place promises 150 men. If the fever gives me a chance, I may yet get together a respectable number. As well as I can ascertain, some part of the road between Mansu and Prahsu must be only a day's journey from Swaidroo ; a direct road to it could be easily cut.

A rumour has reached us of a fight near Abracrampa, and defeat of the Ashantis.

I send for some things to Cape Coast Castle. I came away in such haste, that the little things one can eat when one isn't hungry were forgotten. From Akim-Swaidroo I will write at length. If possible, I would like to get eight good bearers from Cape Coast ; the people here don't know how to manage a hammock, and I must send back the Accra men. I keep my hammock.

Very truly yours,

W. F. BUTLER, Captain,

No. 7.

AKIM-SWAIDROO,
17th Nov., 1873.

SIR,—I arrived here yesterday afternoon from Boonsu, a small village where I was obliged to halt after leaving Branqua. The journey was of necessity very slow, as I was quite unable to assist the bearers by alighting from the hammock, and the path was tortuous and muddy.

At Accassie, a good-sized town six miles north from here, I saw the chiefs and leading men; and this morning I visited Queen Amaquon (mother of King Coffee Ahencora). In all these interviews I have not failed to press upon my hearers the objects set forth in the Major-General's instructions; but, although I meet a ready verbal acquiescence in my views, I cannot say that any desire is manifested to carry them into immediate execution.

The fact is patent that these people, whether they be called Fantis or Assins or Akims, are all alike in their total want of anything approaching to soldierlike qualities. If they cannot possibly avoid fighting they will fight; but I doubt much if it be found possible to retain them for any length of time in the field.

In Captain Glover's case, as long as his operations are confined to the left bank of the Volta, he will have no reason to fear the abandonment of his native allies, because his boats on the river can prevent them re-crossing to their own shore.

In dealing with the various kings and chiefs here, I have made frequent mention of the bravery and readiness with which some other king or tribe has come forward in this struggle. This pardonable, but somewhat false, statement has usually met with the same reply, " that the king or chief present is also a very brave man, and ever ready to fight." But the only readiness I have noticed is one to profit by the necessities of the occasion, and to obtain arms and ammunition as soon as possible.

With regard to the situation of this place, I find that the Birrum river is about four miles to the north, and that the two Prahsus are about three days' journey distant.

18th Nov., 1873.

I am now in receipt of your letter of the 15th inst., delivered this morning at eight o'clock.

Two hundred carriers leave here to-morrow for Dunquah, where they should arrive on the 22nd, or early on the 23rd.

I have again urged on King Coffee Ahencora the immediate assembling of his men. I have also sent messengers to King Amoorkoo-Attah, of Kabil (four days N.E. of this place), urging his presence, with all the men he can get together. I am anxiously expecting the return of Quabina Fuah from Accra; and if he acts according to his promise, and makes but a short delay at the sea-coast, I may be able to get together a few hundred, or perhaps a thousand, fighting men in a reasonably short space of time.

I will ask you to keep me well informed as to the Ashanti line of retreat. If I am able to command sufficient men, I propose to move upon some point between Faissowah and Prahsu.

I forward a rough sketch map of my route from Accra.

The détour to the west was made in consequence of the presence of King Coffee Ahencora at Eni-a-Croom. By this flank march I secured the return of that king to Akim, as I deemed that literally, as well as figuratively, "one king in the hand was better than two in the bush."

I have the honour to be, sir,

Your obedient servant,

W. F. BUTLER, Captain.

To the Chief of the Staff.

No. 8.

ESSECOMAH, 21*st Nov.*, 1873.

SIR,—I arrived here from Akim-Swaidroo this evening, having left that place at mid-day on the 20th.

I made this move for the following reasons:—On the 19th I held many interviews with King Coffee Ahencora and his chiefs, in which I again and again urged upon him a movement against Prahsu.

He declared, in answer to my repeated arguments, that even the assembly of his men would be impossible until *after* his arms and ammunition had arrived from Mansu; this, at the earliest, could not take place for nine days. He declined to state what time should elapse between the arrival of the arms and his being ready to take the field.

I had been confined to my hut for three days, and these interviews had taken place at my bedside; and I now saw that the king was taking advantage of my state of health to procrastinate, while fresh demands were constantly being made for money. Seeing that there was not the slightest chance of a rapid movement, and feeling very doubtful that I could continue for ten days in the condition I was in, I determined to set out for Mansu. By doing so I would hasten the movements of the party of carriers despatched for the arms, &c.; I would also put myself in closer communication with you, while I might derive some benefit from change of scene and sense of motion.

I sent for the king, and told him I had resolved to go to Mansu; that I would hurry on his people; that I hoped he would now see the importance of bringing his men together; and that if he was ready when I returned, strong and well, I would still say to the General that he (Coffee Ahencora) was a brave man.

He seemed a good deal put out by this resolve, and endeavoured to throw many obstacles in the way of it.

On the morning of my departure I again said to him that, if now he would give me three or four hundred men, I would go to Prahsu, and not to Mansu; but he either would not or could not do it: so I started.

I cannot express to you what a bitter disappointment this delay has been to me. I pushed on from Accra under many difficulties; I reached Swaidroo weak with fever; but through it all the hope of a rapid movement on the Prah sustained and strengthened me.

After four days of utter inactivity, I found myself condemned to an indefinite delay in the same miserable surroundings.

Already I have overtaken the body of carriers at this place, although they are light, and have had a day's start of me.

I am writing to Quabina Fuah (towards Accra), to Coffee Ahencora, and to King Yowdowdoo, asking them to send as many men as they can get together to Accassie to meet me on the 30th. The arms will then be back. I am offering them 2l. for every hundred armed men there that day.

With these men I hope to move on Amponsie Quantah, on the main road to Prahsu. If the Ashanti retreat is as slow as Captain Buller reports it to be, they will not be abreast of Amponsie Quantah for ten days. From Accassie to Amponsie Quantah is two days; from here to Accassie is one day. So far as my own movements are concerned I had ample time, but for my soldiers—it is another matter.

On the road to-day your letter of the 18th reached me. You urge haste on the part of the Akims. They do not know what it means—ten days and one are the same to them. I am just twenty days too late; the work I am now engaged in should have been accomplished ten days ago, and even then it would not have been too soon for these wretched people.

22nd Nov., Morning.

I have started the carriers off at daylight, with orders to make all haste. One hundred only have gone—the list furnished by you on the 15th inst. requiring more than seventy. I have sent for another hundred, and they should leave Swaidroo this morning.

To-day I am sending messages to different chiefs to meet me at Accassie on the 30th, with what men they can muster. Already I feel stronger from the move of yesterday. I hope to reach Mansu to-morrow. Referring to the matter of bearers, it is of the utmost importance to me to obtain them. My present bearers were obtained by the native dealer in Accra only for the trip to Swaidroo; they are mutinous to return.

I have the honour to be, sir,

Your obedient servant,

W. F. BUTLER, Captain.

To the Chief of the Staff.

No. 9.

ESSECOMAH, 21st Nov., 1873.

To King Quabina Fuah.

While you have been foolishly wasting your time in Accra, where only old men and women remain, the whole of Fanti and Assin and Wassaw and Tufel have been fighting and driving the Ashantis towards the Prah.

What will men say of Quabina Fuah?

They will say that when all were at war he did not fight— will you let this be said of you? You have a brave name. Come to me at once to Accassie, if you would still make men think you a brave king. I will still be your friend, if you join me at Accassie on the 29th with all the men you can get together. I will pay you well, and write to the General to tell him you are a brave king.

W. F. BUTLER.

No. 10.

MANSU, *27th Nov.*, 1873.

SIR,—I purpose starting from here to-morrow morning for Accassie, once more to induce the Western Akims to make a movement on Prahsu.

Since my departure from Swaidroo, one week ago, no tidings have reached me as to the movements of the Akims; but my former experience of these people makes me hesitate ere I too sanguinely count upon their assistance now.

From Essecomah I sent letters to Quabina Fuah and the King of Agoonah; and if the former king has returned from Accra to his own country, it is possible that he may meet me on the 30th at Accassie.

I have sent a letter to Colonel Wood, advising him of my probable movements, but as he is acting upon a very much shorter line than that *viâ* Essecomah and Accassie to Amponsie Quantah, it is likely he will reach the last-named place before me. With regard to the question of throwing scouts as far as Prahsu, I will do all in my power to induce men to visit Asampanya from the east; and will, of course, forward any information obtained from them at the earliest moment.

The present of arms and ammunition for King Coffee Ahencora should reach Akim-Swaidroo this evening.

The 100*l.* had not arrived at Dunquah yesterday, nor can I trace it in any way. I presume it has not yet left Cape Coast Castle.

I have, &c.,
W. F. BUTLER, Captain.

To the Chief of the Staff,
Cape Coast Castle.

No. 11.

MANSU, *30th Nov.*, 1873.

MY DEAR MAJOR,—When I last wrote to you, I did not expect to be here to-day; but when the news of Wood's "strategic movement" reached Mansu, I started for Sutah with men and ammunition:

I reached Sutah to find the scare had subsided, and a partial recovery of lost property going on. The behaviour of these staunch allies, the Houssas and Kossohs, was simply disgraceful, and the stampede from Faissowah will live long in the recollections of the officers who were borne away, in some instances very much after the manner of a cork on the crest of a Cape Coast roller.

There can be little doubt that the 'Shantis have struck some supplies, their backs are to their friends, and it is possible they may await our coming this side of the Prah. One thing is certain, they are not a disorganized or demoralized crowd, and Huyshe, Hume, and those people who went "a seeking" them through the bush with small parties of native troops may reckon themselves fortunate that they did not find the main body of their game.

It was my intention to strike from Sutah to Kukissu and Accassie, but the Assins assure me there is no road except that from Faissowah; and as Wood could not say when he would be at the latter place, I determined to try again the old route by Essecomah.

I sent a messenger to Accassie telling any chiefs who may be there to wait my coming. To-day I start for the old ground again.

My eight bearers and four carriers have run away, as I told you they would. I have got eight others here, but they are a poor-looking lot.

I hope to reach Accassie on Tuesday, and will open communication with you through Wood.

Have picked up a good deal, and can now do ten miles at a pinch.

Yours very truly,

W. F. BUTLER.

No. 12.

ACCASSIE, *4th Dec.*, 1873, 6.30 a.m.

SIR,—I arrived at this town yesterday from Mansu (estimated distance fifty-four miles). I found King Coffee Ahencora here, but with only a small body of followers in attendance.

Neither the Agoonahs nor King Quabina Fuah's people had arrived, but a letter from the latter reached me *en route* (copies of which, and of the remonstrance from me, to which it is a reply, are subjoined).

By this letter it will be seen that, on Tuesday next, Quabina Fuah reckons upon reaching this country. It is needless for me to add, that no time will be lost in endeavouring to get his men together at this place.

Immediately after arrival yesterday, I saw Coffee Ahencora in presence of his people, and expressed myself in no measured terms regarding their delays. I countermanded the transfer of the remainder of his present of arms, &c., from Dunquah (about seventy loads) until such time as the Akims had given me proof of being soldiers, not cowards who stayed at home when all others went to war.

I declared my intention of at once quitting the country to join some people who were not afraid to fight (a difficult race to discover in these parts). Finally, the king promised to return here, and on Saturday move to Amponsie Quantah with all his people. I told him I would myself start to-morrow (Friday), and demanded a scouting force of even fifty men; these he promised, and he left for Swaidroo (four and a half miles N.) at dusk, to follow me towards the West on Saturday.

I must now refer to information brought in by a scouting

party of Coffee Ahencora's, which reached Acumfudie on Saturday last, the 29th ult.

Acumfudie, on main road, was found unoccupied, camp-fires still smouldering, and a few sick and stragglers on the path. Two were killed and two captured. One of those killed was the bearer of two skulls in a box.

The prisoners' information is to the effect that Amonquartier left Acumfudie for the Prah on Thursday, the 27th ult. ; that 600 men had arrived from Coomassie on the previous Monday with ammunition, &c. ; that news had come at the same time from the King of Ashanti of an invasion of his territory by the people of the kingdom of Gaman, ten days' journey to the N.W., and that, consequently, an urgent call for the return of the 'Shanti army in Fanti-land was made to resist these new invaders.

I received at Essecomah a letter from King Amoorkoo-Attah in reply to a summons which I sent him.

It is needless to remark that this letter furnishes an additional proof of the unfortunate results which have followed the establishment of a dual base of operations at Accra.

Although this king is called " of Eastern Akim," his territory really extends close to the road to Assin-Prahsu, the town of Accassie, in which I now am, being part of his dominion.

I have the honour to be, sir,

Your obedient servant,

W. F. Butler, Captain.

The Chief of the Staff,
Mansu.

No. 13.

(Copy of Letter from King Amoorkoo-Attah.)

Kabil, 26th Nov., 1873.

Sir,—I am in receipt of your letter desiring me, at wish of his Excellency Garnet Wolseley, to render my assistance to the

Ashanti war in the Fanti country. I beg to say I would do so, if I am not positively ordered by John H. Glover, her Majesty's Special Commissioner, to have all the way leading from this to Accra clean, as well as to the Ashanti frontier. I am again sending more men to Accra for the Government loads which are in charge of me and Captain Sartorius, who is expected here in a short time from Croboe. I shall comply with this request as soon as I hear from Mr. John H. Glover as to aid in the Fanti expedition.

I have the honour to be, sir,

Your obedient servant,

KING AMOORKOO-ATTAH,

Kabil.

P.S.—I arrived here from Accra on the 24th inst. with full orders from the Government towards the Ashanti war.

No. 14.

AKRAPON, 8th Dec., 1873.

SIR,—Starting from Accassie on the morning of the 5th, I reached Akrapon on the evening of the 6th (estimated distance thirty-six miles), the path alternating between hill and swamp, and being frequently intersected by watercourses flowing towards the north.

Coffee Ahencora had promised to follow me with all his men and at Apradie, on the evening of the 5th, his messenger came to assure me that he would reach Akrapon on the 8th inst. I dismissed them with a short message, that, if he and his men were not with me by the time stated, I would hand over to Quabina Fuah (now on his way from Accra) not only the reserve of ammunition stored at Dunquah, but also all the rifles, &c., already given to him (Coffee Ahencora).

Three paths lead from here to the main road—one striking it at Faisoowah, the second at Yancoomassie, and the third at Amponsie-Quantah.

If Coffee Ahencora should arrive to-day, I will direct him to move on the last-named place, where I will join him to-morrow after visiting Yancoomassie, and conferring with the officer commanding at that place.

Should the Akims be in any force, I will push on to Prahsu with them.

The return of Quabina Fuah from Accra will do much towards rendering possible the assembly of a considerable body of natives in Akim to threaten the crossing of the Prah in that kingdom. Akim-Prahsu is only two days' journey from Swaidroo, or from Insuaim (Quabina Fuah's capital), and I gather that a movement on it would be more popular with the kings than one at Assin-Prahsu.

Preparatory to returning again to Akim I would request to be allowed the services of a non-commissioned officer, and a few native police or soldiers.

In all intercourse with the natives of this country persuasion loses nothing of its force by having power of coercion behind it; and, absurd though it may appear, three or four armed men *in uniform* are sufficient to convey to kingly or to native mind the idea of that power.

I have the honour to be, sir,
Your most obedient servant,
W. F. BUTLER, Captain.

1.30 p.m.—Coffee Ahencora has just arrived, but it is impossible to find out the number of his men, as they are straggling in. I will parade them to-morrow at Amponsie Quantah.

No. 15.
Dec. 8th, 1873.

MY DEAR MAJOR,—I should have written to you yesterday, but was "down with fever;" however, I am fit to-day. I shall see Wood this evening, if he is at Yancoomassie.

Of course it is all too late to do anything now on the Prah;

T

but if this Gaman news is not all gammon, matters may be made more easy beyond it.

In future, letters, &c., will find me through Colonel Wood.

I now find that a long hard day through swamps, &c., is almost certain to be followed by fever.

With kind regards,

Very truly yours,

W. F. BUTLER.

No. 16.

PRAHSU, 10th Dec., 1873.

SIR,—I have the honour to report my arrival here this morning at 10.30 o'clock.

I estimate the distance from Yancoomassie at twenty-two or twenty-three miles. The track is generally good and level, but there are many swampy places, and in the last six miles there is a great deal of fallen timber.

The village sites are all good ones, but much fouled by Ashanti occupation ; and the neighbourhood of the Prah is one huge deserted camp. A few canoes are visible on the shores ; the river is about eighty yards wide, south bank higher and steeper than north ; current two and a half to three miles an hour, deep and turbid ; the scenery by no means of the impressive character described in works of travel. A few Ashanti huts stand on the north shore, and a stream enters the main river at the same place.

On the south shore the clearing necessary for a large camp can easily be effected. There is another crossing-place about two miles higher up the river ; a track branches from the main road to strike it half a mile from Prahsu. I propose returning to Damsam-su this evening.

I have, &c., sir,

Your obedient servant,

The Chief of the Staff,   W. F. BUTLER, Captain.
Cape Coast Castle.

No. 17.

YANCOOMASSIE, 17*th Dec.*, 1873.

SIR,—I have the honour to acknowledge the receipt of your letter of the 15th inst. (No. 112), having reference to a proposed independent movement of the Western Akims upon Ashanti.

I have now, in reply, to convey to you my opinion on the subject, and to estimate the probable numbers of men we might expect to raise in Akim.

In all calculations upon this subject, I think it would be advisable to exclude the probability of Captain Glover's co-operation, and to count only upon the movement as being connected with the main body which is to cross at Assin-Prahsu.

I am of opinion that, with the time at our disposal, a force of not less than 2000 Akims can be collected for an advance into Ashanti. These I would propose to cross at a point where the trail from Ansah in Ashanti to Gademwaah in Akim crosses the Prah (see Itinerary, page 5); or, taking a path still more to the east, to strike for Gimmahsu (see Guide, page 5), at the foot of the Moinsey Hills.

This line, supposing the Guide to correctly state the existence of the paths from these places to Akim, would possess advantages which it is needless to point out.

Before committing my opinion altogether to this programme, I would deem it better to revisit Akim; and as time will permit of more deliberate work than circumstances have heretofore allowed me, I can have ample opportunity of estimating the chances of a movement across the Prah on the right of the main body. I will therefore set out to-morrow for Damsam-su, so as to reach Akim by the end of the week, and will forward you early information as to the numbers which it is possible to obtain.

Should the information upon this point be of a nature to

justify further movement, I will be glad to receive the assistance of the three officers spoken of in your letter.

I have, &c., sir,

Your obedient servant,

W. F. BUTLER, Captain.

The Chief of the Staff,

    Cape Coast Castle.

No. 18.

Copy of Instructions given to Captain Butler, Commissioner to Western Akim.

The plan of operations is to invade the Ashanti country on the same day, viz. the 15th January, from as many points as possible—the lines by which the different columns are to advance converging on the objective right of the campaign—Coomassie.

On the extreme right Captain Glover's force will cross the Prah at *Ammoonoom*, and move by the Duabin road.

As a connecting link between the main body, which will advance by the Prahsu-Coomassie road, a column composed of Western Akims, under the command of Captain Butler, h. p., late 69th Regiment, will cross at *Prahsu-Akim*, near the place marked on the map as *Gervasse*.

While on the extreme left every effort is being made to collect a force of Wassaws, Denkeras, and Commendah natives to advance by the *Ensuaquesoo-Abatia* road on Coomassie. This latter duty has been assigned to Captains Dalrymple and Moore, 88th Regiment.

Captain Butler, who has been employed for some considerable time as Commissioner to the kings of Western Akim, viz. since the end of October last, having been sent there then with a view of endeavouring to collect a sufficient force of the Akims to allow of his striking the main track south of the Prah, and acting against the enemy's line of retreat. Notwithstanding that every effort was made on the part of Captain Butler to bring this mission to a successful issue, he was unable to induce the Akims to take the field in time.

He has now been directed (with the assistance of Kings Quabina Fuah and Coffee Ahencora of Western Akim) to collect as large a force as possible, and to move as above mentioned by an independent line as a connecting link. He is to cross the Prah at Prahsu-Akim, near the place marked Gervasse on the map, which leads by Sirrasoo Koofoofoom into the main track at *Sirrasoo*, about ten miles south of Coomassie.

Four officers, as named in the margin,[1] have been sent to Captain Butler with the view of assisting him in carrying out the important duty which has been allotted to him.

A large supply of ammunition, as also a rocket-trough and rockets, have been forwarded to him; and Captain Butler reports that he hopes to be able to move as directed on the day named.

His instructions, as also Captain Glover's, are on no account to go into Coomassie, nor to enter into any negotiations with the enemy—all messengers from the King of Ashanti being forwarded to the head-quarters of the Major-General. He is, moreover, to keep up a constant communication with the main body while advancing.

No. 19.

ACCASSIE, AKIM,
23rd Dec., 1873.

SIR,—I have just concluded a long palaver with King Quabina Fuah. It would be needless to recapitulate its details. It will be sufficient to say that, as a preliminary, he swore to do all that I required of him. He fully admitted his former error in going to Accra, and asked forgiveness for it, and he promised to

---

[1] Captain Paget, Coldstream Guards; Captain Brabazon, late Grenadier Guards; Lieutenant Macgregor, 50th Regiment; Surgeon Low.

bring all his men together at Tribee by the 2nd of January, and to march wheresoever I pleased. All this was after I had several times cautioned him against promising anything he could not fully carry out, reminding him that there would be an English general, with a large army in his immediate neighbourhood, ready, on the one hand, to reward the brave and loyal, and to punish the liar and the laggard.

I pointed out to him that now he had an opportunity of winning back from the Ashantis the territories which they had taken from him in successive conflicts, and of making Akim the most powerful state in the confederacy ; and I finally told him the terms he would receive, viz. 6d. per diem for each soldier, 4. per diem to every chief of 100 men, 2s. per diem to two subordinate chiefs for every 100 men, and $\frac{1}{4}d$. per diem to himself for every soldier; thus for 1200 men he would receive 1l. 5s. per diem, and so on in proportion.

I consider this plan best calculated to procure numbers, while, at the same time, it does not exceed the gross amount originally offered, viz. $7\frac{1}{2}d$. per diem to each man.

At a previous interview with Coffee Ahencora I offered the same terms, and received his full promise to collect all his fighting men at Tribee by the 1st of January.

Tribee is one march from Akim-Prahsu, and two marches from Swaidroo and Insuaim.

Upon one point, however, both kings were either unable or unwilling to afford me information ; they could not give an estimate of numbers until their men had been mustered ; but they promised that *all* fighting men should appear at the rendezvous.

I think, however, we may reckon upon from 1500 to 2000 Akims assembling at Tribee by the 3rd or 4th of January, and of these two-thirds will probably belong to Quabina Fuah.

Under the circumstances, I think it will be advisable to proceed with an independent movement from Akim-Prahsu, crossing the river Prah near Amantea on or about the 15th of January—a date which will afford time for further consideration of the subject

after the muster on the 2nd ; as time will then scarcely permit
of sending to Dunquah or Yancoomassie-Assin for additional
arms and ammunition, it would be advisable now to bring from
these places not only the remainder of the former present to Coffee
Ahencora (at Dunquah), but also an additional supply commen-
surate with a prolonged movement.

I would . therefore request that the following arms be sent
to Dunquah :—

> 40 Barrels of Powder, 100lbs. each.
> 200 Enfield Rifles.
> 300 Flint Guns.
> 200 Cutlasses.
> 40,000 rounds Enfield Ammunition.
> 50,000 Percussion Caps.
> A considerable supply of Lead Bars.
> 2000 Flints.
> 20 gallons Rum.
> Some Tobacco.

In addition, I would ask for six Snider rifles and three boxes
of Snider ammunition for special present to Quabina Fuah.
By the 26th inst. I hope to send from here a body of 300 or
400 carriers ; these men, moving by Essecomah, should reach
Dunquah by the 30th. There it will be necessary that the loads
should meet them, and, if they can start by the 1st proximo on
their return march, I think we will be in a position to cross the
Prah by the 15th of January.

I have written to Lieutenant Macgregor at Yancoma to return
to Dunquah, and await the arrival of the carriers at that place ;
but if there should now be stored at any station on the main
road the articles required, information can be sent from Cape
Coast to Lieutenant Macgregor, and a corresponding change made
in the destination of the carriers by special verbal message to
meet the chief at Essecomah in charge of the party on or about
the 28th inst.

It will be seen that I have no time to spare in receiving these supplies, if the movement of the Akims across the Prah is to be made on the 18th of January.

A sum of 200*l.* (in silver) will also be required, and it would be advisable to send a guard or police force, partly drilled, of say twenty to thirty men armed with Snider rifles, and carrying 100 rounds per man.

A rocket-trough and a few rockets might also be a useful addition.

I have to acknowledge the receipt of your letters of the 17th and 19th inst. received yesterday, announcing the appointment of three officers to serve in Akim.

I have communicated with them at Yancoomassie with reference to their route here.

I have, &c., sir,

Your obedient servant,

W. F. BUTLER, Captain.

To the Chief of the Staff,
Head-quarters, Cape Coast Castle.

No. 20.

TRIBEE, *6th Jan.*, 1874.

SIR,—In consequence of delays unforeseen when I last wrote, I only reached this town to-day.

A dispute having arisen between King Quabina Fuah and King Coffee Ahencora regarding their rival claims to the service of a chief of Avissa, it was with no little difficulty that the matter was, for the time at least, arranged without actual violence between the rival parties.

By taking the chief of Avissa personally with me, and leaving the question to be settled at the conclusion of the war by Government authority, I finally succeeded in prevailing upon the kings to quit their towns, each having declared that, unless this chief went with him, no movement would take place on his part.

Yesterday Quabina Fuah left his town of Insuaim, and he is now some ten miles south of this place collecting his men.

I have directed Captain Paget and Lieutenant Macgregor to remain—one at Insuaim, the other at Accassie—until all chiefs have moved, and to use every effort to hasten their departure, as well as to see that all arms and ammunition are forwarded to the front.

Captain Brabazon, I regret to say, was ill with fever at Insuaim. Previous to my departure I placed at his disposal bearers and a hammock to enable him to proceed to Prahsu, as time did not permit of my giving personal attention to him, and, of course, both he and Captain Paget are totally unacquainted with the treatment of African fever.

I am about to despatch a messenger to the east to gather tidings of Captain Glover's force. As soon as the Akims have assembled here, you shall be regularly informed of my movements.

With regard to the situation of this town, it lies about eight miles south of the Prah, and I should judge about the same distance *north* of the parallel of Assin-Prahsu, from which place it would be distant, by direct line, some thirty or thirty-five miles.

I have, &c., sir,
Your obedient servant,
W. F. BUTLER, Captain.

The Chief of the Staff,
Head-quarters, Prahsu.

No. 21.

TRIBEE, *7th Jan.*, 1874.

SIR,—I have the honour to acknowledge the receipt this day of your communication No. 10, dated Prahsu, 2nd instant, enclosing copies of despatches for transmission to Captain Glover on the Volta. I had, a few hours previous to the receipt of those despatches, sent a letter to Captain Glover, or any white officer at or near Kabil, and I immediately forwarded the Major-General's commands with urgent instructions to the bearer to overtake my first messenger, and to transmit to him the later-received document.

The second copy will be forwarded in two days' time, as directed in paragraph 5 of your instructions, and a receipt for delivery will in each instance be asked for.

With reference to my own movement upon Akim-Prahsu, I have to report the arrival here last evening and this morning of Kings Quabina Fuah and Coffee Ahencora. The number of their followers is as yet limited ; but they assure me that, once they have moved, their men will soon follow.

The relations between them are not of the most friendly nature—a circumstance which renders it necessary for me to be cautious in intercourse with them. They, nevertheless, strike me as being in earnest with their preparations, and the tidings which they occasionally receive through their own people, of movements at or near Assin-Prahsu, seem to inspire them with confidence.

The next three or four days will be spent in getting together the men of the outlying villages, and on the 12th I hope to move to Berronassie, near the Prah, to which place Coffee Ahencora proceeds to-morrow.

I have offered liberal rewards to hunters for Ashanti prisoners, with the view of obtaining information regarding tracks on the north side of the Prah.

I regret to have to inform you that Captain Paget, Scots Fusilier Guards, and Lieutenant Macgregor, 50th Regiment, are both ill of fever at Insuaim. Upon receipt of a note from Lieutenant Macgregor to the effect that Captain Paget " was as bad as he could be," and that he himself " was not much better," I immediately sent eight carriers (my last) and my servant, who has some experience in fever, to their assistance, with directions to have them taken to Prahsu at once, by Swaidroo and Damsam-su.

I have to request the immediate return of my men, as I have left myself without carriers under the urgent circumstances of the case.

The bearer of your letter only reached me to-day. He followed a wrong road. I send an Akim with him now to conduct him by Acquirrissoo. It would be perhaps advisable if another policeman should accompany this Akim on his return here, so that in future no mistake may arise as to the direct road.

I have, &c., sir,
Your obedient servant,
W. F. BUTLER, Captain.

To the Chief of the Staff, Prahsu.

No. 22.

TRIBEE, 10th Jan., 1874.

SIR,—I have the honour to acknowledge the receipt, yesterday evening, of your communication of the 8th instant (No. 42—74), enclosing letter for transmission to Captain Glover, which letter has already been forwarded to that officer.

With reference to my crossing the Prah at a date earlier than that heretofore specified, I do not think it will be possible to do so.

From the tone of my previous letters you will have gathered the general difficulties I have had to contend against ; and, if I did not too particularly dwell upon their unceasing presence, it was with a view of not unnecessarily adding to the graver difficulties which beset the Major-General, and from a knowledge that his experience of the untrustworthy nature of native assistance had already made him acquainted with these difficulties.

I looked upon the opportunity afforded by a movement from Akim-Prahsu to be so good that I determined to stretch to the last limit of patience the endeavour to carry it into effect. That limit has not yet been reached; and, notwithstanding many discouraging features, it is still my hope to realize, in some form or other, the original conception.

My situation is simply this: Coffee Ahencora, with several chiefs and some 200 followers, is at Beronassie, close to the Prah; Quabina Fuah is in the town with only a few followers.

To repeated and urgent calls for haste he replies that his men were on the road; that they will be here in a day or two; that he has sent fresh messengers to call them, &c., &c.

I have told him that our days are as fixed as the sun ;that, when we name a date, it is kept to the moment; that the main advance is already across the Prah; that he was losing money and good name by this delay: but of what use are the arguments and impulses which actuate human nature, when the groundwork of that nature in this case is so utterly animal as to be capable of acting only under one motive—that of fear ?

This motive I cannot work on; alone it is not in my power to coerce these people.

Since I begun this letter a good many men have come in. The chief of Accassie has come, announcing his followers to be here to-morrow.

Quabina Fuah has now named Monday (12th) as the day for all his people to arrive.

I have still four days before me. On the 15th instant I will cross the Prah, but whether it shall be with 2000 men, or only a few hundreds, I cannot now possibly determine.

The accounts received yesterday from Insuaim announce Captain Paget as having been sent in to Prahsu, very ill, and Captain Brabazon and Lieutenant Macgregor as better.

I have just now received a note from Captain Sartorius, a copy of which I enclose.

The chief named by him as belonging to *East* Akim actually

commands those villages lying *West* of where I now write from, one of which is not a day's march from Assin-Prahsu.

I move to Beronassie on Monday the 12th instant.

I have, &c., sir,

Your obedient servant,

W. F. BUTLER, Captain.

The Chief of the Staff,
Head-quarters, Prahsu.

No. 23.

(Copy of Letter from Captain Sartorius.)

KEBI, 4/1/74.

MY DEAR SIR,—Yours of 24th December met me on my way in here yesterday.

I am sorry to say that, as I had not finished with the Awoonahs and Aquambos when we got the General's order to move upon Zuabin by the 15th ult. with all the men we could get, the Aquapims, Croboes, Kreppees, Crookoos (?), &c., refused to leave till such time as they had finished with Trans-Volta tribes, and so leave us with a force of eight hundred Houssas and Yourabas, one thousand Croboes, and the Akims.

Amoaco-Attah, King of Akim, leaves this with me *en route* to Ashanti, on the 6th. You have one of his chief captains, "Darco" by name. Please send him down at once, for I shall want all the men I can get to advance on Guahoo (Ashantis are very numerous). Captain Glover sent up a large number of guns and ammunition to your men, so anything that you may have given "Darco" he had better keep.

(Signed) R. SARTORIUS.

No. 24.

BERONASSIE, *14th Jan.,* 1874.

SIR,—I have the honour to forward the enclosed letter received this morning from Captain Glover by the return messenger who was sent with the first copy of your despatch to Kebi on the 7th inst.

I have to report my arrival here yesterday. About 250 Akims are assembled here. The King of West Akim is at Tribee with about the same number of men.

Many small parties are reported as "coming in," but it is impossible to state what their numbers may amount to.

The King of Akim has promised to be on the Prah with all his men by Saturday, the 17th inst.

I hope to cross the river to-morrow with the Akims now here, and to occupy Amantea.

Scouts have already crossed the Prah, and found that place deserted.

I have, &c., sir,
Your obedient servant,
W. F. BUTLER, Captain.

The Chief of the Staff,
Prahsu.

No. 25.

NORTH BANK OF THE PRAH,
15th Jan., 1874.

SIR,—I have the honour to report, for the information of the Major-General Commanding, my arrival here this day.

No amount of persuasion, or pressure of threat, or promise, could induce the Akims at Beronassie to cross the river. They advanced twenty different excuses, all of which had been anticipated by me in palavers during the last month, over and over again.

The chief reason now put forward for extra delay is the non-arrival of the bulk of the men. Saturday, the 17th inst., is now named as the final day by which the chiefs and their followers are to be here. Until that day I shall remain here, and then—having stretched endurance of these miserable beings to a limit difficult to comprehend by any person not similarly situated—I will, if delay is again demanded, move to Assin-Prahsu.

I cannot say that I entertain hopeful anticipations that the conduct of these people will, no matter what may be their numbers, differ materially from that which I have frequently reported during a long correspondence.

I have, &c., sir,

Your obedient servant,

W. F. BUTLER, Captain.

The Chief of the Staff.

Head-quarters, Prahsu.

16/1/74.

I forward two letters from Captain Glover—one received yesterday, the other his despatch to me, dated 14th inst., just come to hand this morning.

No. 26.

NORTH BANK OF RIVER PRAH,
Sunday, 18th Jan., 1874.

SIR,—This morning I sent an order to the kings and chiefs to cross the Prah, and hear my final message.

They had assembled on the south bank yesterday, but would give me no estimate of their numbers, and, from their halting operations, were evidently prepared to make a long stay.

They came across the river, and I immediately told them what I wanted, viz. a march on Moinsey, *viâ* Yancoma, to be made in six days from to-day. They said they could not do so, and advanced many absurd reasons against their moving at all; begged for white soldiers to assist them, and finally went so far as to ask for immediate payment before they would consent to move in any direction.

I then told them my final resolution, viz. to leave them to-morrow, return to Prahsu, and report their conduct to the Major-General—threatening them with the future consequences of their disobedience.

Matters having now reached a point which renders it impossible to entertain a future hope that these people can be made in any way to conform to the usages of soldiers, so as to render them of the slightest service to the Expedition.

It therefore becomes necessary to abandon the mission entrusted to me by the Major-General—a result not unforeseen for some time past, but which has been delayed until the latest moment at which success remained a possible contingency.

I have, &c., sir,
Your obedient servant,
W. F. BUTLER, Captain.

It is still possible that these people will make a move against an Ashanti village; but it will only be done in their own time, and according to the direction which may best suit their particular wish.

Since morning they have been busily engaged cutting lead, &c.; but time has now become so precious, and delays are still so certain to occur, that their movement can have no influence on the efforts of the enemy against the main attack.

Should the Major-General still wish me to remain, a very fast runner will catch me at Acquirrissoo on my way in.

W. F. BUTLER, Captain.

The Chief of the Staff,
    Prahsu.

No. 27.

RIVER PRAH, 19/1/74.

SIR,—This morning the Akim kings and chiefs, finding that I was about to start for Prahsu (Assin) made an unconditional surrender.

They now agree to go as I may direct—to lose no time—and to ask no delay.

I therefore proceed with the original movement, and expect to be at Gademwaah on the 21st inst.

From thence I will endeavour to move west towards the main line at Moinsey.

I have to report the arrival of Dr. Lowe on the 16th inst.

I have, &c., sir,

Your obedient servant,

W. F. BUTLER, Captain.

The Chief of the Staff,
Head-quarters, Prahsu.

No. 28.

EMBRONEM,
20th Jan., 1874, 5.30 P.M.

SIR,—I have the honour to report my arrival here this evening with 400 Akims.

It would be impossible to give you an adequate idea of the toil and labour necessary, before these people could be induced to move.

I had left them, and got as far as Beronassie on my journey to head-quarters, when their urgent messages reached me, asking for my return, and promising better conduct.

Now that they have moved I hope to continue the march to-morrow, and to reach Gademwaah early on the 22nd.

From thence I will strike towards the main road due West,

U

cutting a track if none should be found to exist in that direction.

Many stragglers are still south of the Prah; but the two kings and the chief "Darco," of Accassie, are with me.

All the officers are in good health, and Dr. Lowe has been of the greatest assistance to me.

I will communicate with you again from the halting-place of to-morrow.

I have, &c., sir,

Your obedient servant,

W. F. BUTLER, Captain.

No. 29.

BRANQUA, 22nd Jan., 1874.

SIR,—I have the honour to report my arrival here with about 500 Akims last evening. The advanced guard under Lieutenant Macgregor found the place deserted and in ruins, and no trace of occupation for a long period.

We move to Yancoma to-day.

As the great object of the kings is to delay my advance in every possible way, I find it most difficult to obtain information as to roads, distances, &c.

From Yancoma the news of our advance must soon reach Coomassie, as the place is not more than twenty miles from the Prah at Amantea.

The road followed yesterday was good, but evidently had not been used for some time.

Your letter of the 19th inst. was received here last evening, and its enclosure forwarded *at once* to Captain Glover; but until that officer opens direct communication with me, letters from head-quarters to him will save a day or two by direct transmission.

The letters sent by his Excellency to the kings of West

Akim were delivered to them immediately and fully explained to them, at their own request, later in the evening.

Straggling parties continue to arrive.

The officers are in excellent health.

I have, &c., sir,

Your obedient servant,

W. F. BUTLER, Captain

The Chief of the Staff,

Head-quarters, Moinsey.

No. 30.

CAMP PRAHSU, *Jan.* 19*th*, 1874.

KING,—I have made you large presents of arms and ammunition. I have given you white officers to help you. My troops have cleared the way into Ashanti for you. In return you have done nothing. This is the conduct of a traitor, and as a traitor you shall be dealt with. I am now writing to order Captain Butler to arrest you, and to bring you in here to answer to me, if you delay for one more day to obey his order to advance.

You are too late now to give me any real help. My troops hold in force the Adansi hills; they are within ten hours march of Coomassie. But you can still show whether you intend to behave better in future or not. For your own sake I advise you not only to advance at once, but to act quickly afterwards. The King of Ashanti has twice sent me messengers, and is begging for peace. In a few days I shall dictate terms to him in Coomassie.

If you leave all the work to be done by my men, while your people do nothing in the meanwhile, you will answer for it to me.

I am, King,

According to your conduct,

Your friend or otherwise,

G. J. WOLSELEY, Major-General.

U 2

No. 31.

YANCOMA, 6 A.M., *23rd Jan.,* 1874.

SIR,—I have the honour to forward a letter received here yesterday evening from Captain Glover. The messenger refused to proceed further with it.

I have to report my arrival here yesterday from Branqua, distance seven or eight miles.

The enemy has not been seen, but recent traces of his scouts were met with close by this place. Two paths lead from here, one across the river Ennoom towards Dadiasoo, the other to lake Boosoomaque.

I find it almost impossible to collect information as to distances in advance, as the kings and men throw every obstacle in my way. To-day both roads will be examined, and a strong party left some miles along the one leading towards Dadiasoo and the West-Nor'-West.

I have, &c., sir,

Your obedient servant,

W. F. BUTLER, Captain.

The Dadiasoo road I propose to follow on to-morrow with the entire force.

The Chief of the Staff,

Head-quarters.

No. 32.

YANCOMA, *24th Jan.,* 1874.

SIR,—I have the honour to report that the scouts sent from here yesterday entered the village of Ennoon-su this morning— the inhabitants having escaped into the bush without offering any resistance.

It is difficult to ascertain whether the alarm was conveyed to the people of the village by the scouts themselves, or by another party of Akims sent along the Dadiasoo road towards Akonwherry. In any case no prisoners were taken, although a large reward has been offered for their capture by me.

The village was looted and burned, and the scouts returned here this morning.

I have to-day succeeded in starting a party of 150 Akims, with two officers, to re-occupy the village, and to remain there until I join them to-morrow with the rest of the force.

I can scarcely convey to you a true conception of the position in which I find myself. All information is studiously withheld from me; carriers are constantly refused; distances are grossly exaggerated; the most vexatious and trifling pretexts are put forward; anything and everything is done to effect the one great object—delay.

Were it not that I fully understand the object of the movement entrusted to my command, namely, "to make the Ashantis believe that an army was marching along this line," I must long since have abandoned as hopeless the task assigned to me.

Alternately by bribes, threats, promises, and reproaches, I have succeeded in getting these savages so far. To the officers under my command I am deeply indebted for their unwearied exertions. Yesterday nothing could induce the kings to move; to-day a fresh struggle has resulted in a partial movement, and to-morrow I hope to get the whole force in motion.

They (the kings) were so adverse to the west, or Dadiasoo road, that I was forced to abandon the idea of following it.

If Captain Glover has taken the route marked (2) from Obogoo, he should be close to me at Aprasoo, or, as he has written it, Apassa; but I cannot venture to state now what may be my probable movements.

I have, &c., sir,

Your obedient servant,

W. F. BUTLER, Captain.

Dr. Lowe is ill with fever to-day. Captain Brabazon and Lieutenant Macgregor have gone with the advanced party to Ennoon-su.

The Chief of the Staff,
Head-quarters.

No. 33.

ENNOON-SU, *25th Jan.*, 1874.

SIR,—I have the honour to report, for the information of his Excellency, the occupation of this place yesterday evening by a force of 100 Akims under Captain Brabazon and Lieutenant Macgregor.

In consequence of reports brought ·by scouts, I determined upon this movement, feeling certain that the Ashantis (who had been alarmed at two or three points) would endeavour to reoccupy the place which, according to report, they had hastily abandoned.

After some difficulty I finally persuaded the kings to furnish the required number, and the whole party reached Ennoon-su shortly before dark on the 24th inst.

During the night there was an alarm of approaching Ashantis, and considerable confusion appears to have resulted from it; but no enemy appeared, and in the morning all was quiet.

About 9 o'clock a.m. a body of Ashantis suddenly appeared along the road leading north from the village. They seem to have held some parley with the Akim guard stationed there, saying that they "had heard there were white men on the main line, and that they had come to see if there were white men on this road also." This parley was followed by two Ashanti shots. The Akims in the vicinity, about twenty-five, fired a couple of rounds each, and three of the enemy dropped dead in the bush, their heads being immediately taken.

Lieutenant Macgregor reports that, upon his reaching the cene, some eighty yards from the skirts of the little village, he ound the Akims dragging in the dead bodies. They (the Akims) showed every disposition to rally to the front again; but the enemy had vanished.

No prisoners were taken, and no wounded seen; but from the fact of three having been killed, many more must have been wounded. On our side there were no casualties.

I had started from Yancoma at 7 a.m. this morning, and was soon followed by the whole force; but I did not reach Ennoon-su until 10.15 a.m., fully an hour after the skirmish. The distance is between ten and eleven miles.

In consequence of Dr. Lowe's illness, carriage had to be found for him.

I feel satisfied with the result of this skirmish, which, though insignificant in itself, will still tend to give confidence to the Akims, by whom confidence is so much needed.

I have not failed to point out to them that, by the occupation of the village yesterday, they have been able to meet their enemies at an advantage; whereas delay would have allowed the Ashantis to reoccupy it; and, from its strong position on the right bank of the Ennoon river, which is here forty yards wide, to inflict loss upon us as we crossed the water.

I hope to push a strong party along the Mansu road, that which leads to lake Boosoomaque, to-morrow, and will, if possible, attack the village of Accassiewa, which lies next before me. From here to Obogoo cannot be more than eighteen miles. At Accassiewa I shall still be nearer to Captain Glover's line, and will endeavour to communicate with him direct.

Your letter, dated 17th inst., was received here only to-day. I deem it better to retain the enclosure for Captain Glover, in the hope of communicating directly with him, as it is seven days to Obogoo *viâ* Beronassi.

I have, &c., sir,

Your obedient servant,

W. F. BUTLER, Captain.

The Chief of the Staff,

Head-quarters.

No. 34.

AKINA, 28/1/74.

SIR,—I have the honour to report my advance to this place from Ennoon-su yesterday.

Our advance under Captain Brabazon fell in with the Ashanti scouts four miles from Ennoon-su, the enemy retreating before us without firing. At 10.30 a.m. the village of Akina was reached, the advance leading well into it; the place had been hastily abandoned, but the enemy lined the further edge of the bush, where the ground dipped suddenly downwards.

A scattering fire was opened from this position on the Akims in the village, and kept up for about ten minutes.

Our men replied vigorously, and the enemy fled along the path leading west and north, and the remainder of our column was soon in occupation of the place.

Our loss was two Akims killed; that of the enemy is unknown; but his position on the inner slope of the ridge rendered him comparatively secure from our fire.

Captain Brabazon reports that the men under his orders fought well.

This morning at one o'clock one of the Akim camps was fired into by a party of Ashantis, and two of our men were wounded, one slightly. Beyond some eight or ten shots at the point in question, there was no confusion at the other Akim camps.

I have now about 1400 men present.

I will endeavour to move to Mansuah, near lake Boosoomaque, to-day, but fear another cause for delay on the part of the kings. I reckon Mansuah to be four or five miles distant.

The country is rugged, broken into steep valleys, the general elevation being about 1000 feet above sea level.

It would appear that there is a road from Mansuah to Amoaful on main line.

Two of my officers have been ill with fever, Dr. Lowe seriously; he is still in a very weak state. Captain Paget reached here last evening.

Your letter, dated Moinsey, 23rd inst., was received this morning. I have forwarded the enclosures to Captain Glover, but many days must elapse ere they can reach him, as he would appear to have taken the most eastern route from Obogoo.

I have, &c., sir,

Your obedient servant,

W. F. Butler, Captain.

The Chief of the Staff,
Head-quarters.

No. 35.

Akina, 29/1/74.

Sir,—Your second despatch, dated Moinsey, 23rd inst., reached me here to-day.

As I had anticipated in my last letter, the kings made another demand for delay, until the position of the main attack could be ascertained by them. My position is as follows: I reckon the main road to be distant from here due west about twelve miles, its nearest part being at or close to Koroman. This reckoning is not, however, derived from information, but by dead reckoning from Tribee. Dadiasoo lies nearly west, seven or eight miles distant; the road from that place to Amoaful would appear to be about five miles.

There are many villages between here and Dadiasoo, but they are probably deserted, or nearly so. Mansuah was reported abandoned yesterday by my scouts.

My movement on this place from Ennoon-su was prompted by later information than that received at the moment of writing my letter of the 25th inst.

By inclining to the left, after crossing the Ennoon river, I endeavoured to join the line I had before urged upon the chiefs and kings at Yancoma with the object of striking the main road at Amoaful.

I am now within a very short distance of that place, and yet

these kings refuse again to go on. I have offered liberal rewards to any person who will carry a letter direct to the main
line, and may yet succeed in getting some one to do so.

I am forwarding to Captain Glover the information received
from you.

A messenger from King Attah arrived yesterday with a report
that Captain Glover was at Conomo eight days ago.

My last messenger but one returned from Assoom, after an
absence of five days, without having delivered his letter,
declaring he had been afraid to proceed further. I procured another messenger, and again forwarded the despatch to
Obogoo.

If I can finally persuade or force the kings to move to
Dadiasoo, I will endeavour to communicate with the main line
by a party with a bugler.

> I have, &c., sir,
>> Your most obedient servant,
>>> W. F. BUTLER, Captain.

P.S. 2.45 P.M.—A complete panic has just taken place, owing
to causes I cannot divine. The entire force is now in full retreat on Yancoma, from which place I will try to gain main
road at Quisah or elsewhere. There has been no attack of any
kind, but the desertion of an Ashanti long domiciled in Akim
seems to have inspired this most dastardly conduct.

> W. F. B.

The Chief of the Staff,
> Head-quarters.

No. 36.

> TRIBU, 2/2/74.

SIR,—After the despatch of my letter of the 29th and 30th
ult., a rapid retreat commenced in the whole Akim force; so
universal was the panic that, during the greater portion of the

night, bodies of men continued to move south, and early on the morning of the 31st Yancoma was reached and left behind.

No attempt was made on the part of the kings to excuse or explain their gross treachery, and I could elicit nothing more tangible than that they were too far advanced into the Ashanti territory, and that they must be cut off before assistance could reach them.

My belief is that the statements of a blind Ashanti prisoner, taken at Mansuah, coupled with a verbal message from King Attah of East Akim, the purport of which I was not made aware of, did much to induce this disgraceful flight.

In the hasty postscript to my letter of the 30th ult. I had only time to make you acquainted with the fact of the retreat.

No previous warning, no intimation whatever, had been given to me that it was the intention of the kings and chiefs to abandon Akina; indeed, up to the very moment that the retreat began I was moving through the camp endeavouring to get the Akims to move to Dadiasoo *en route* to Amoaful; and I had actually to engage a party of hunters to proceed through the bush to the main line near the latter place; yet so complete was the flight that within two hours not a man was left in Akina, and long before midnight every Akim was behind the Ennoon river, ten miles distant; and all this without a reverse having taken place, and after a loss of only two killed and two wounded in the entire force.

I cannot express to you the feelings with which I beheld this total break-up of the movement. Little by little, step by step, I had succeeded in leading these savages to within a very trifling distance of the point aimed at. It is true that there were many indications of how utterly untrustworthy was the composition of the force under my command; but, nevertheless, at Akina I naturally looked at the task as all but accomplished, and my junction with the main body at Amoaful, within a few miles of Coomassie, as only a question of some hours.

Encumbered with baggage; without carriers, save those given

me by the kings, and with three of my officers sick from actual fever or its recent presence, I dared not await at Akina the chances of communication with the main body. I had to abandon the fruits of no little labour at the moment success seemed most assured.

The kings, with about a quarter of the original force, are now encamped close to the Prah at Embronem; they have refused to move to Prahsu. The remainder of the men are scattered or dispersed to their homes.

I will proceed to head-quarters with all speed, and afterwards shall be ready to undertake such punishment as the Major-General may determine to inflict upon the Akim chiefs.

I have, &c., sir,

Your obedient servant,

W. F. BUTLER, Captain.

Captain Paget has had a relapse of fever; he proceeds with carriers to Prahsu.

The Chief of the Staff,

Head-quarters.

Printed and bound by Antony Rowe Ltd, Eastbourne

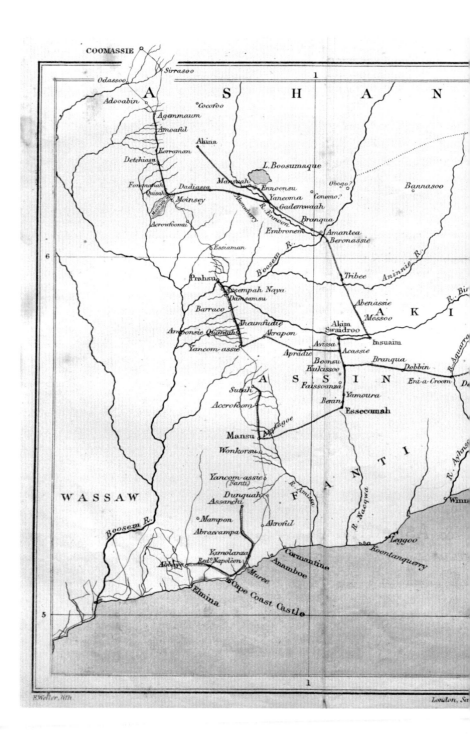

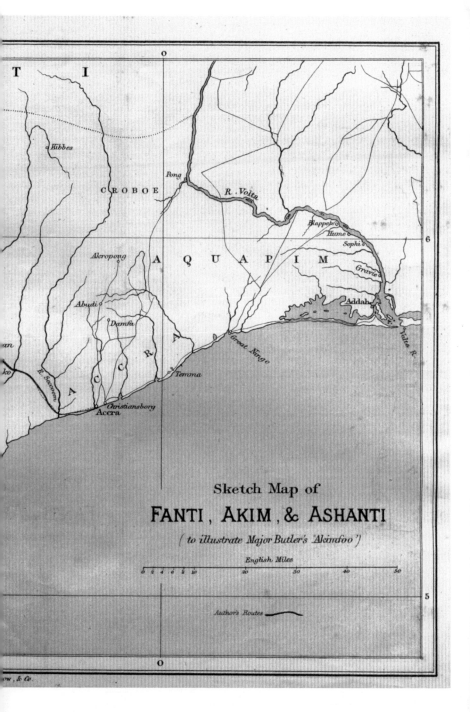

Sketch Map of

FANTI, AKIM, & ASHANTI

(to illustrate Major Butler's 'Akimfoo')

English Miles

Author's Routes